Unlike his contemporaries Virginia Woolf and Henry James, Kipling always denied he was a critic. But his letters, speeches, poems and stories are full of comments on writing and writers. This collection, including many previously unpublished private letters and papers, details Kipling's response to the commercialisation of literature and the emerging role of the writer as celebrity in the turbulent literary world of the 1890s and beyond. They reveal a mind intensely concerned with questions of literary value, with language and imagination, with truth, realism and romanticism. Kipling's fame made him a significant spokesperson for important segments of the reading public – the soldiers, engineers and functionaries central to Britain's imperial expansion. He profoundly influenced English literary language and our perception of English national character. This book offers new access to the private and public history of a writer whose continuing influence is still a matter of fierce controversy.

Writings on writing

Writings on writing

BY RUDYARD KIPLING

*

edited by
Sandra Kemp
Quintin Hogg Research Fellow
University of Westminster
and
Lisa Lewis
Former Chairman of
The Kipling Society

CAMBRIDGE
UNIVERSITY PRESS

Published by the Press Syndicate of the University of Cambridge
The Pitt Building, Trumpington Street, Cambridge CB2 1RP
40 West 20th Street, New York, NY 10011–4211, USA
10 Stamford Road, Oakleigh, Melbourne 3166, Australia

First published 1996

Printed in Great Britain at the University Press, Cambridge

A catalogue record for this book is available from the British Library

Library of Congress cataloguing in information data

Kipling, Rudyard, 1865–1936.
[Selections. 1995]
Writings on writing / edited by Sandra Kemp
and Lisa Lewis.
p. cm.
Includes index
ISBN 0 521 44527 2 (hardback)
1. Kipling, Rudyard, 1865–1936 – Quotations. 2. Literature – History and criticism – Theory, etc. 3. Literature – Quotations, maxims, etc. 4. Criticism – Quotations, maxims, etc. I. Kemp, Sandra. II. Lewis, Lisa. III. Title.
PR4852.K45 1995
828′.802 – dc20 95-35332 CIP

ISBN 0 521 44527 2 (hardback)

SE

Contents

*

Contents

Illustrations

Note on the text

Where texts from the collected works have been used, they are as first published in book form. The sole exception is 'The Last of the Stories', which was pirated in *Abaft the Funnel* and immediately reprinted by Kipling's official American publisher: the present text of this story is that of the Sussex and Burwash editions, where Kipling first had the chance to revise it. Included are a number of Kipling's (unpublished) sketches and drawings, which have an intertextual relationship to the texts beside which they are placed. For ease of reading, spelling and punctuation have been standardised throughout and missing punctuation inserted, except in those unpublished texts where Kipling's idiosyncrasies are particularly characteristic or used for ironic effect (for example in the letter to Stanley Baldwin (128)). 'Buried Treasure', Kipling's working notes for his last story, is given as closely as is practicable to the holograph text. The editors' critical notes to the texts are given below on pages 160–203, numbered according to page.

'Buried Treasure' is published here by special permission of Durham University Library and the National Trust for the Preservation of Places of Historic Interest. So too, by special permission of Mrs Mary Clapinson, Keeper of Western Manuscripts, Bodleian Library and of the National Trust, is the author's note on the metre of one of his most innovative poems. Other unpublished texts are by permission of the National Trust. Grateful thanks are extended to these bodies.

The editors would also like to thank warmly Thomas Pinney and David Trotter for their help and support; Philip Mason, who advised on 'Home'; Fiona Campbell, Sara Johnson and Margaret Newsom who helped with the research. The location of unpublished material is indicated in brackets at the beginning of the first relevant note. The editors would like to thank the librarians concerned for making these texts available: Rare and Manuscript Collections, Cornell University Library; Kipling Collection, Dalhousie University Libraries; Houghton Library, Harvard University; House of Lords Record Office; Warden and Fellows, New College, Oxford; Henry W. and Albert A. Berg Collection, New York Public Library; the Pierpont Morgan Library; Manuscripts Division, Department of Rare Books and Special Collections, Princeton University Libraries; Special Collections, Sussex University Library; Department of Special Collections, Syracuse University Library; Harry Ransom Humanities Research Center, University of Texas at Austin; Beinecke Rare Book and Manuscript Library, Yale University.

Abbreviations

AF	*Abaft the Funnel*: unauthorised edn, New York, B.W. Dodge and Co., 1909; authorised edn, New York, Doubleday, Page & Co., 1909. Uncollected articles and stories from *C&MG*, *The Pioneer* and *WN*, 1888–1890.
AR	*Actions and Reactions*, London, Macmillan, 1909.
AW	Angus Wilson, *The Strange Ride of Rudyard Kipling*, London, Secker & Warburg, 1977.
BRB	*Barrack-Room Ballads and other Verses*, London, Methuen, 1892.
BW	*A Book of Words: Selections from Speeches and Addresses delivered between 1906 and 1927*, New York, Doubleday Page, 1928.
CC	*Captains Courageous*, London, Macmillan, 1897.
CK	C.E. Carrington's notes from Caroline Kipling's diaries.
C&MG	*Civil and Military Gazette*, Lahore.
D&C	*Debits and Credits*, London, Macmillan, 1926.
DD	*Departmental Ditties and other Verses*, London, W. Thacker, 1890.
DOC	*A Diversity of Creatures*, London, Macmillan, 1917.
DV	*The Definitive Edition of Rudyard Kipling's Verse*, London, Hodder & Stoughton, 1940.
DW	*The Day's Work*, London, Macmillan, 1898.
EV	Andrew Rutherford (ed.), *Early Verse by Rudyard Kipling 1879–1889: Unpublished, Uncollected and Rarely Collected Poems*, Oxford, Clarendon Press, 1986. (Not to be confused with *Early Verse* in OB and SB.)
FN	*The Five Nations*, London, Methuen, 1903.
FSS	*From Sea to Sea*, 2 vols., London, Macmillan, 1899–1900.
JB	*The Jungle Book*, London, Macmillan, 1894. Not to be confused with *The Jungle Book* in OB.
JB2	*The Second Jungle Book*, London, Macmillan, 1895. Not to be confused with *The Second Jungle Book* in OB.
JSS	*Just So Stories for Little Children*, London, Macmillan, 1902.
KI	Pinney (ed.), *Kipling's India: Uncollected Sketches 1884–88*, London, Macmillan, 1986.

KJ	*The Kipling Journal*, published by the Kipling Society, 1927–.
KP	Kipling Papers, Sussex University Library.
Letters	Thomas Pinney (ed.), *The Letters of Rudyard Kipling*, 2 vols. published, London, Macmillan, 1990 [3 further vols. projected].
LF	*The Light that Failed*, London, Macmillan, 1891.
LH	*Life's Handicap*, London, Macmillan, 1891.
LR	*Limits and Renewals*, London, Macmillan, 1932.
LST	*Land and Sea Tales for Scouts and Guides*, London, Macmillan, 1923.
MI	*Many Inventions*, London, Macmillan, 1893.
NTInv	Inventory of the books in Kipling's study, compiled by the National Trust and kept on card-index at Bateman's, Burwash, Sussex.
OB	The Outward Bound edition: *The Writings in Prose and Verse of Rudyard Kipling*, New York, Charles Scribner's Sons, first 11 vols. 1897, the remaining 25 vols. 1898–1937. Some titles in this edition have different contents from the same titles in other editions. In notes, the vol. nos. are given as OB[number].
PPH	*Puck of Pook's Hill*, London, Macmillan, 1906.
PT	*Plain Tales from the Hills*, Calcutta, Thacker, Spink, 1888.
RF	*Rewards and Fairies*, London, Macmillan, 1910.
RG	Harbord (ed.), *The Readers' Guide to Rudyard Kipling's Work*, 9 vols., privately printed by the Kipling Society, 1961–72.
RK	Rudyard Kipling.
S&Co.	*Stalky & Co.*, London, Macmillan, 1899.
S3	*Soldiers Three and other Stories* (including 'The Story of the Gadsbys' and 'In Black and White'), London, Macmillan, 1892.
SB	*The Sussex Edition of the Complete Works in Prose and Verse of Rudyard Kipling*, in 35 vols., London, Macmillan, 1937–9. *The Burwash Edition of the Complete Works in Prose and Verse of Rudyard Kipling*, in 28 vols., New York, Doubleday, 1941 (text as in Sussex but some volumes include two Sussex titles).
SOM	Thomas Pinney (ed.), *Something of Myself and Autobiographical Writings*, Cambridge University Press, 1990.
SS	*The Seven Seas*, London, Methuen, 1896.
TD	*Traffics and Discoveries*, London, Macmillan, 1904.
Unpubl.	Text hitherto unpublished.
UP	*Uncollected Prose*, vols. XXIX and XXX of Sussex edn; vol. XXIII of Burwash edn (see *SB* above).
WN	*The Week's News*, supplement to *The Pioneer* edited by RK, 1888–9.
WWW	*Wee Willie Winkie and other Stories*, London, Macmillan, 1892, including 'Under the Deodars' and 'The Phantom Rickshaw'.
YB	*The Years Between*, London, Methuen, 1919.

Chronology of Kipling's life and work

1865 30 December, Joseph Rudyard Kipling born in Bombay, son of John Lockwood Kipling (Head of Department of Architectural Sculpture at the government School of Art) and of Alice Kipling, née Macdonald. Both grandfathers were Methodist ministers.

1868 First visit to England; his sister Alice ('Trix') Kipling born there.

1871 RK and Trix again taken to England and left there for six years, boarding with Captain and Mrs Holloway of Lorne Lodge, Southsea; their parents returned to India. Captain Holloway died, Mrs Sara Holloway disliked RK, who was also bullied by her son. RK became deeply unhappy. He would describe occasional holidays spent in London with his mother's sister Georgiana Burne-Jones and her husband, the artist Edward Burne-Jones, as 'a Paradise that I verily believe saved me'.

1877 Alice Kipling arrived from India and took her son away from Southsea, though Trix returned there for a time.

1878 RK became a pupil at the United Services College, Westward Ho!, Devon, a cheap boarding-school for the sons of army officers and Indian officials, where conditions were spartan but the teaching good.

1880 Returning to Southsea to fetch his sister, RK met her fellow-boarder Florence Garrard, with whom he fell in love. The relationship, more important to him than to Flo, would be broken off and resumed several times.

1881 RK made editor of the school magazine. *Schoolboy Lyrics* privately printed by his parents without his knowledge.

1882 Left school and returned to India in October and travelled to join his parents, now at Lahore. Began work there as assistant editor on the *Civil and Military Gazette.*

1883 Verses published in *The Englishman* and *C&MG.*

1884 *Echoes by two Writers,* RK and Trix.

1885 *Quartette,* a Christmas Annual by all four Kiplings.

1886 RK spent a month at Simla as correspondent of *The Pioneer*, sister paper to the *C&MG*. *Departmental Ditties* privately printed and immediately sold out. Second edition by Thacker, Spink & Co. of Calcutta.

1887 RK transferred to *The Pioneer* at Allahabad. Made friends with Professor and Mrs Hill (Alec and Edmonia). Sent to Rajputana as special correspondent, writing articles afterwards collected as *Letters of Marque* (1891) (*From Sea to Sea*, vol. 1).

1888 Went to board with the Hills at their house in Allahabad. Made editor of a weekly supplement, *The Week's News*. *Plain Tales from the Hills* published by Thacker, Spink & Co. His Railway Library series published: *Soldiers Three, The Story of the Gadsbys, In Black and White, Under the Deodars, The Phantom Rickshaw, Wee Willie Winkie.*

1889 Left India to become *The Pioneer*'s roving correspondent. Travelled with the Hills to Burma, Singapore, Japan, San Francisco. Crossed America, visiting Mrs Hill at her family's home in Beaver, PA, where he met her sister Caroline Taylor, with whom he 'formed an understanding'. Arrived in London in September and took rooms in Villiers St, off the Strand. Retained A.P. Watt as literary agent.

1890 His work was the subject of a leading article in *The Times*, 25 March. All his earlier books published in English and American editions. Engagement to Caroline Taylor broken off. Had a nervous breakdown. Met Florence Garrard in the street and tried unsuccessfully to resume the relationship. Made a new friend, American writer and publisher Wolcott Balestier, and met his mother and sisters. Wrote *The Light that Failed*. *The City of Dreadful Night*, a collection of articles from *The Pioneer*, published in Allahabad without his permission.

1891 RK had further breakdown from overwork. Set off on voyage to South Africa, Australia and New Zealand. Returned to India to spend Christmas with his family, but hearing of the death of Balestier he rushed back to London.
Life's Handicap published.

1892 18th January, married Balestier's sister Caroline. They left for a voyage round the world, stopping in Brattleboro, Vermont, to visit her family, where her brother Beatty sold them a plot of land for a nominal sum. They continued to Japan. RK's bank failed. They returned to live in Brattleboro. Daughter Josephine born in December. RK began writing for children.
The Naulahka, written in collaboration with Wolcott Balestier, and *Barrack-Room Ballads and other Verses* published.

1893 *Many Inventions* published.

1894 *The Jungle Book* published.

1895 *The Second Jungle Book* published. *The Pioneer*'s files were sold and some of RK's 1887–8 travel articles published in America, without his permission, as *Out of India*.

1896 Second daughter Elsie born. The Kiplings quarrelled with Beatty

Balestier and it ended in court. They left Brattleboro and moved to Torquay, in England.
The Seven Seas published.

1897 Settled in Rottingdean, Sussex, near the Burne-Joneses and other connections. Their son John born.
Captains Courageous published.

1898 The first of many winter holidays in South Africa. RK travelled to Rhodesia. Friendship with Cecil Rhodes.
The Day's Work and *A Fleet in Being* published.

1899 The family paid their last visit to America. All the children became ill; RK and Josephine developed pneumonia, from which Josephine died and RK almost did. On outbreak of Boer War, RK became involved in campaign for service charities: 'The Absent-Minded Beggar Fund'. Published *From Sea to Sea*, the authorised version of travel articles from *The Pioneer*, in two volumes. *Stalky & Co.* published.

1900 Continued war work and writings, including two weeks on newspaper *The Friend* of Bloemsfontein. Also working on long-running imaginative projects, *Kim* and *Just So Stories*.

1901 *Kim* published.

1902 The Kiplings' final move to Bateman's, Burwash, Sussex.
Just So Stories for Little Children published.

1903 *The Five Nations* published.

1904 *Traffics and Discoveries* published.

1906 *Puck of Pook's Hill* published.

1907 RK awarded the Nobel Prize for Literature. Visit to Canada.

1909 *Actions and Reactions* and *Abaft the Funnel* published.

1910 *Rewards and Fairies* published.

1911 Collaborated in *A School History of England*, with C.R.L. Fletcher.

1913 Visit to Egypt. *Songs from Books* published and *The Harbour Watch* (a play) performed.

1915 John Kipling reported missing, believed killed, in his first battle on the Western Front. From this time Kipling was constantly in pain from a gastric ulcer. War journalism: *The New Army in Training* and *France at War*.

1916 *Sea Warfare* and *The Eyes of Asia* published.

1917 RK joined War Graves Commission.
A Diversity of Creatures and *The War in the Mountains* published.

1919 *The Years Between* published.

1920 *Letters of Travel 1892–1913*, a collection of old articles published.

1923 Published *The Irish Guards in the Great War*, 2 vols; and *Land and Sea Tales for Scouts and Guides*, a collection of old stories with two new additions and extra verse.

1924 Daughter Elsie married Captain George Bambridge, MC, ex-Irish Guards.

1926 *Debits and Credits* published.

1927 Voyage to Brazil.

1928	Published *A Book of Words*, collected speeches.
1930	Published *Thy Servant a Dog*. Visit to the West Indies.
1932	*Limits and Renewals* published.
1933	RK's ulcer finally diagnosed. *Souvenirs of France* published.
1936	Following a haemorrhage, Kipling died 18 January.
1937	*Something of Myself for my Friends Known and Unknown* was published, written in the last year of his life and edited by his widow with the help of Lord Webb-Johnson, his surgeon and friend.
1937–9	The Sussex edition of RK's works.
1940	*The Definitive Edition of Rudyard Kipling's Verse*, Hodder and Stoughton. Does not include some poems collected in Sussex edition.

Introduction

Writing to Edmund Gosse in 1910, Kipling says:

> I am not a critic and to the best of my recollection have never directly or indirectly criticised the work of any man in my profession, or associated myself with any body that has done so. This is of course a question of temperament and training, and I could not take it upon myself – even to the extent of one in forty – to pass judgement upon another man's claim to praise or blame.[1]

Unlike so many of his contemporaries (for example, Henry James, T. S. Eliot or Virginia Woolf), Kipling was not just reluctant, but averse to making critical pronouncements on other writers.

Inevitably, though, his critical views, and his own private 'canon' emerge both in letters and in his work; in speeches to various institutions, clubs and societies, in his autobiography, in his forewords, but also in his fiction and poems. He was always deeply concerned with the writer's craft. Angus Wilson comments: 'Although he wrote no literary criticism, few authors have said more of value about the creative process in many of his stories and some of his speeches.'[2]

Kipling was a man dedicated from his schooldays to the profession of letters. At fifteen he is writing that poetry 'is never to be treated lightly under any circumstances', and his own first volume of verse was printed that same year. In *Something of Myself* (1937), his posthumous autobiography, he writes of his early fiction: 'I made my own experiments in the weights, colours, perfumes and attributes of words in relation to other words, either as read aloud so that they may hold the ear, or scattered over the page, draw the eye' (pp. 43–4). *Something of Myself* shows how preoccupied he was with questions of literary art. It deals with his life entirely from the point of view of writing, often using metaphors of craftsmanship that recall his family connection with William Morris's Arts and Crafts Movement:[3] carpentry, inlays or goldsmiths' work.

The purpose of the present volume is to offer a selection of Kipling's *covert* criticism. What is revealed is that Kipling did have his own distinct literary preferences, and very definite views on style. He describes his almost spiritual sense of the power of words to the Canadian Authors' Association: 'after all the men who do things have done them, and the men who say things about their doings have said them, it is only words – nothing but words – that live to show the present how, and in what moods, men lived and worked in the past' (see below, p. 130). As a writer and critic, Kipling is preoccupied with the problematics of knowing, and with how and what to tell. As he explains to the Royal Society of Literature:

> Most of the Arts admit the truth that it is not expedient to tell everyone everything. Fiction recognises no such bar. There is no human emotion or mood which it is forbidden to assault – there is no canon of reserve or pity that need be respected – in fiction. Why should there be? The man, after all, is not telling the truth. He is only writing fiction. While he writes it, his world will extract from it just so much of truth or pleasure as it requires for the moment. In time a little more, or much less, of the residue may be carried forward to the general account, and there, perhaps, diverted to ends of which the writer never dreamed.
>
> (See below, p. 81.)

Kipling started to write at a time when questions were being raised about what it meant to be a writer. Earlier in the nineteenth century, arguments had raged between 'naturalists' and romantics: those who felt literature should describe real life in the service of a cause, and those like Shelley who privileged the imagination, hating 'didactic poetry'.[4] Kipling's formative years as a writer were spent in a society where law and order were vital issues. Literally so: for he and his fellow-British in India lived always with the fear of a new Sepoy Rebellion. In a letter of December 1897 he is still unable to write on this topic: ''57 is the year we don't talk about'. He remained a life-long imperialist, which also meant he was a Tory. It is easy to find in any period of his work the comments of a late Victorian clubman: racist, sexist, homophobic and snobbish; a man with a strong (if vicarious) interest in blood sports and all things military. Often these remarks are subverted by their context, but many of them seem sincere.

Kipling regarded himself squarely as a professional writer, and did not fit into any of the turn of the century literary camps, whether the issues were defined (as in Gissing's *New Grub Street*) in terms of the conflict between literary and commercial institutions, or (as by Henry James) as reflecting the contradictory demands of literary form and the literary market, or by reference to the distinction within that market itself between the 'high' and the 'low', the cultured and the popular. Kipling saw himself as a craftsman who was equally interested in the necessities of literary form and the needs of his readers, whom he refused to categorise in high/low terms. His dominant concern was not the status or freedom of the author, nor the status or self-consciousness of the reader, but the mysteries and pleasures of the *processes* of reading and writing themselves.

Kipling had, he says, 'two / Separate sides to my head'. While one side preached conformity, the other played variations on folklore and obsessively polished his craftsmanship, using and experimenting with every trick that language could provide. Could a poem's metre echo the beat of a ship's engine, he wonders: 'Where does legitimate Art end and sheer trick work begin?' He calls his creative self his Daemon, and claims that it comes 'from without', a force beyond his control.

It is not just Kipling's ability (in his own words) 'to think in another man's skin' that is at issue, but what John Bayley describes as 'a compartmented mind'.[5] This would account for the peculiar divisions of voice and vocabulary that haunt Kipling's writings: victim *and* persecutor; the language of trades, professions and the gentleman's club *and* the discourse of dream, drugs and insanity. Popular – even clichéd – themes in Kipling are treated in a highly wrought and intricately textured manner. But there is no way of resolving the conflict of voices by reference to authorial intention. Like Browning's Fra Lippo Lippi, whom he considered a 'not too remote ancestor', Kipling gets 'caught up' in his own art 'by mistake'. He is at once outside and inside, safely distanced by an encircling frame and suitably anonymous narrator, yet imprisoned within and endangered by the text at the same time. This is perhaps what W. H. Auden means when he speaks of 'the anxiety of encirclement from both within and without'[6] in Kipling's writing. It is this aspect of literature, the mythic and the magical, that Kipling most often discusses in speeches to a literary audience.

With the political establishment Kipling had a love–hate relationship. He refused a knighthood on several occasions, and at least twice refused to be considered for the position of Poet Laureate,[7] partly because he would not (could not) write to order, but partly also for the reason he explains in 'The Last Rhyme of True Thomas' – a poet's reward is the emotion of his hearers. When, following World War I, his cousin Stanley Baldwin became a junior minister at the Treasury, Kipling sent him a letter refusing (in comic dialect) to write a poem appealing for money to repay the War Loan: 'when I want to be brod-cast and pressed I bless God can do it on my own...'

Kipling also had a love–hate relationship with the press, whose power had grown hugely in the 1880s and 90s. After he died, Desmond McCarthy wrote:

> ... my mind went back to 1898, when he was lying so gravely ill in New York that there seemed small chance of his recovery: to the public anxiety, and the bulletins, posted up two or three times a day, so urgent was the demand for news. 1898 marked the highest point of his popular renown in England and America. To English-speaking peoples, he then seemed to represent in literature deep instincts of their race. How young he was and yet how much he had achieved![8]

Kipling never courted publicity, flatly refusing to give interviews. This undoubtedly fed the reporters' appetite for writing about him. The 1890s, the decade of his triumph, was a period when literary celebrities were treated as popular stars, their private lives as public property; and when the chance came, the press took revenge on Kipling for snubbing them.

While Kipling claims to have been unmoved by press criticism of his work,[9] this is not borne out by his comments in letters. In 'Home', he maintains that writers who had queried his dialogue and his descriptions did not know what they were talking about: 'But who can show a blind man colour?' At the height of his fame he writes fretfully to C. E. Norton, smarting at an adverse review of *Captains Courageous* 'which has made me lie down and cry salt tears' because, he feels, the reviewer has misunderstood him.

By the 1880s the debate about what it meant to be a writer was fuelled by increasing concern for literary standards: writing for posterity versus writing for the immediate, hungry public who were prepared to pay for what they enjoyed. Kipling believed, with Besant, that the commercialisation of literature was an exciting challenge and one that he was proud to accept. He writes to S. S. McClure, whose Fiction Supply Syndicate he had refused to join, offering a synopsis of a proposed book, and adds: 'the story could be compressed or pulled out to suit' (see below, p. 137). This book was never (so far as is known) written, but Kipling continued to publish in the periodicals of the time, and to accept at least some of their prohibitions. A boil in 'The Brushwood Boy' was changed to a cut finger at the request of *Century Magazine*; but when the *Ladies' Home Journal* demanded at the proof stage that a reference to alcohol be removed from 'William the Conqueror', Kipling rebelled; they had accepted the tale, he wrote, and now they must print it.[10] He could add even more controversial matter when the stories were collected in book form: *Many Inventions* includes 'Love-o'Women', the protagonist of which is a soldier with venereal disease. While this could never have been accepted by the magazines, it rounds out the series of soldier stories he had already published there. Again, in 'Mrs Bathurst', the version in *Traffics and Discoveries* includes a reference to foetuses that would not have been allowed in *Windsor Magazine*, where the tale originally appeared.

For Kipling the business side of writing is inseparable from the creative preoccupations. Early letters to the publishers Thacker, Spink & Co. of Calcutta show a first-hand knowledge acquired by being in the trade himself. He is hard-hitting, level-headed and knowledgeable: their attempts to bargain meet with a firm reply: 'I am also in a fairly large printing office where we do a good deal of publishing.' It is no use talking to him about warehousing, bad debts and trade commissions: 'in these matters [I] am more or less behind the scenes'. In the preface to one of his Railway Library series, published under his eye in Allahabad, he stresses that these are disposable books 'meant to be read in railway trains'. He urges his Calcutta publisher not to make *Plain Tales from the Hills* '... too good to be dirtied. I have noticed that a book one can eat buttered toast over without any special pangs of conscience, gets on well in the world and has a ready sale.'

Later, despite his own quarrels with American publishers who (after he grew popular) had pirated his texts, he worries about what the new American copyright law, beneficial to him, will mean for less famous British writers. In 'Some Notes on a Bill', his facetiousness conceals a serious comment on their lack of future in this increasingly important market.

In 1890 Gissing wrote *New Grub Street*, in which, of a group of authors, only those who are prepared to be exploited will be published, while the only one to make money is the one who prostitutes his art. Soon afterwards Gissing writes:[11]

> Three 'enormous reputations' have been made in England during the past year or so; Rudyard Kipling, Hall Caine, and J. M. Barrie. These are fortunate men; I wish my receipts from literature were one quarter of what each of them earns.[12]

The Society of Authors was founded in 1884, while the spread of the royalty system (imported from America) meant that writers had an interest in the continuing sale of their works. Writers were no longer willing to work for low rewards and the newly founded literary agencies met a ready clientele. Kipling's income doubled in three months after he signed up with the agent A. P. Watt, on Walter Besant's recommendation. Besant also recruited Kipling to the Society of Authors, but advised him not to join in purely literary quarrels; his voice was not heard in the debates on literature that raged in the 1890s.

If silent in the aesthetic debate, British life and character bear the indelible imprint of Kipling. The Edwardian essayist David Murray goes so far as to say that Kipling helped to shape the national character, to '*make* his tribe'.[13] Leonard Woolf, recalling his days as political officer in Ceylon, feels that the British in India, at least, could have been shaped by Kipling:

> The white people were also in many ways astoundingly like characters in a Kipling story. I could never make up my mind whether Kipling had moulded his characters accurately in the image of Anglo-Indian society or whether we were moulding our characters accurately in the image of a Kipling story.[14]

In the 1890s Kipling was seen above all as a young man's writer. Kipling Clubs were formed at Cornell[15] and Yale.[16] When he visited Oxford, Balliol students cheered him so loudly that the Master's voice was drowned.[17] This popularity among the young meant that his works were read in their formative years by many influential writers of the twentieth century. The effect on their writings has been patchily recognised: among names that come immediately to mind are Ernest Hemingway, Bertholt Brecht, W. H. Auden and T. S. Eliot.[18] Jorge Luis Borges, himself a keen and perceptive Kipling reader, sees the influence of *Kim* in his compatriot Guiraldes's nationalist novel *Don Segundo Sombra*.[19] It has also been suggested that

J. R. R. Tolkien was influenced by the Puck books.[20] 'I cannot believe that James Joyce... would ever have written the Cyclops chapter of *Ulysses*, if he had never read Kipling', says Edmund Wilson in a review of Kipling's penultimate collection of stories, *Debits and Credits*.[21]

Around 1900, however, many younger readers turned against Kipling: Leonard Woolf and Lytton Strachey at Cambridge played a literary game in which they awarded 'Tripos' marks to famous authors, placing him with Marie Corelli jointly at the bottom under 'ploughed'.[22] From 1900 on, the tide of critical approval withdrew, even as the only honours Kipling would accept (honorary doctorates and the Nobel Prize for Literature) flooded upon him.

In his rise to fame Kipling had become a spokesman for important segments of the reading public – soldiers, engineers, functionaries, and, in the later stories, doctors. From such people was formed the Kipling Society, founded in 1927, while he was still alive. He also spoke for social misfits and outcasts, male and female, and for children. Some of his subjects were given an idiom and a voice in the English literary canon for the first time: Indian natives, the army's lower ranks (to whom he was '*our* partic'lar author').[23] In opening up this literary ground, Kipling is sometimes guilty of racism and snobbery, but reveals himself as a superb chronicler of human emotions in stories like 'Lispeth' and 'The Story of Mohammed Din' (*Plain Tales from the Hills*), and in poems like 'Danny Deever' (which may have influenced Oscar Wilde's 'The Ballad of Reading Gaol').

George Moore, in an otherwise hostile review of 1904, writes: 'who else, except Whitman, has written with the whole of the language since the Elizabethans?'[24] Kipling has contributed far more expressions, maxims and sayings to everyday language than any of his contemporaries. The third edition of the *Oxford Dictionary of Quotations* includes more than 200 Kiplingisms: a higher number than there are from any other writer except Shakespeare, Tennyson, Milton, Johnson and Browning.

Kipling's reading was both wide and idiosyncratic. Having no formal education after the age of 16, his is an autodidact's library: unexpectedly erudite here and merely populist there. Besides standard literary classics (British, American, French, Latin and Greek), there are obscure poets, collections of folklore from many lands, books on art, architecture and design; histories of the different places he had lived; also practical manuals on matters like farming, bee-keeping and drains. Of critical works, he had

Johnson's *Lives of the Poets*; a number of commentaries on Shakespeare and Horace; and a complete set of Henry James (presumably including the prefaces). Other contemporary critics represented are Brander Matthews and George Saintsbury, with both of whom Kipling corresponded; also Walter Raleigh and Quiller-Couch.[25]

A complete edition of Kipling's critical and metacritical writings would require, from the published work alone, a significant percentage of the 35 volumes of the Sussex Edition. It would need to include (for instance) the whole of *Something of Myself*, his own account of his working life; his novel of art and artists, *The Light that Failed*; and also – arguably – of *Just So Stories for Little Children*, where he plays games with the relationships between thought, speech and the written word. Besides these it would need many complete individual stories and poems. Further relevant passages, ranging in length from a sentence to several paragraphs, can be found scattered throughout his work. The present volume can only offer a selection from all this material. Rather than issue yet another anthology of well-known texts, the editors have concentrated on less accessible pieces, including some that are unpublished, and a selection of unpublished drawings. Some famous passages are represented by short extracts.

This collection opens with a section that illustrates Kipling's opinions, ambitions and dreams in the 1880s, the decade that turned him from precocious schoolboy to famous author. The extract from 'Cold Iron' is his recollection of that lost world in middle age. The next section, 'Aesthetics', selects from Kipling's many reflections on the magic and power of words; on the nature of inspiration; on the human imagination and its workings, whether 'civilised', primitive or mythic; on truth in fiction, or its absence; on the difficulties that beset a writer, and his need for independence and integrity. In part III, 'How to Write: Ingredients and Methods', Kipling is advising would-be writers, discussing his own sources and the use he makes of them, reflecting on questions of metre and style. 'History and Contemporary Culture' opens with a rare example of a published review, then goes on to demonstrate his privately expressed opinions of other writers and his view of art as social force. There follows a section on the commerce of literature, then one on Kipling's response to his critics. Finally, in 'Afterwords' there are extracts from his last story, '"Teem" – a Treasure-Hunter', published in the month of his death, and from his posthumous autobiography. Within these categories items are set out in chronological order.

Many items in this book are relevant to more than one of the categories in which we have placed them. If the themes of 'The Last of the Stories' are the torment of afterthoughts that come too late and the difficulty of making characters live, its plot necessitates a good deal of metacriticism and some ranking of other authors. 'Home', although its chief relevance here is to aesthetics, also has Kipling's replies to two of his early critics. '"Proofs of Holy Writ"', chosen for its discussion of style, also suggests the nature of Shakespeare's (and of Kipling's own) inspiration, and offers a theory about the drafting of the Authorised Version of the Bible. It seemed better to respect the integrity of these pieces than to chop them up into extracts under one or another heading. With letters, such fragmentation would incur duplicated and extended notes. The reader seeking for cross-references is referred to the Index.

The final section offers a unique opportunity to study Kipling's writing methods at first hand. It has long been believed that all his working notes and drafts were destroyed after his death by his widow: but the preliminary notes for his last story '"Teem"' somehow escaped, were identified by one of the present editors and are published here for the first time.

Kipling's approach to writing was far from simple, and his continuing emphasis on craft necessarily made him a critic in the sense defined by T. S. Eliot in his essay 'The Function of Criticism'. Eliot there argues that:

> the larger part of the labour of an author in composing his work is critical labour; the labour of sifting, combining, constructing, expunging, correcting, testing: this frightful toil is as much critical as creative. I maintain even that the criticism employed by a trained and skilled writer on his own work is the most vital, the highest kind of criticism: and (as I think I have said before) that some creative writers are superior to others solely because their critical faculty is superior.[26]

A letter to a young girl, Augusta Tweddell, contains Kipling's own definition of the critical process: 'Read and reread [books] until you pass from mere reading to criticism and begin to see how they are put together and what means the author uses to produce certain effects' (see below, p. 88).

1

PORTRAIT OF THE ARTIST AS A YOUNG MAN

*

Manuscript replies to a printed questionnaire*, undated (1880 or 1881?)

MY NAME IS Joseph Rudyard Kipling **AND I THINK**

1 **That poetry** is never to be treated lightly under any circumstances,
2 **That my favourite poets are** Whittier, Emerson, Browning, Tennyson, Poe.*
3 **That History** [is] a sorry perversion of truth, worth reading if only to find out the extent of human mendacity.
4 **That the greatest historians are** Macaulay, Hume, Gibbons* [sic].
5 **That Fiction** is generally not so surprising as Truth, that it pays well and requires much labour to produce.
6 **That the Novelists I prefer are** E. About, Zola, Ouida, Miss Braddon.*
7 **That a Country Life** is detestable in every state, for me London is the best place in Summer, and the only place in winter.
8 **That a Town Life** has too many advantages to be put down here, that it gives you experience of all sorts.
9 **That the Greatest Living Statesmen are** Bismark [sic], Gladstone.
10 **That my favourite Heroes and Heroines are**, La Dame aux Camélias, John Ridd.*
11 **That Music** varies inversely with the temper of the listener, that street organs and street music are not to be despised.
12 **That the most Delightful Composers are** Rossini, Meyerbeer, Wagner.*

13 **That the Fine Arts are** worth more than the time spent upon them.

14 **That the Finest Painters and Sculptors are** Flaxman, H. Thorneycroft [sic], Leighton.*

15 **That Reading**, taken in large doses is a Stimulant, in small doses it acts as a sedative. N.B. *Never* read French novels.

16 **That my Favourite books are** Lorna Doone, Yeast, Moths, L'amant d'Amanda.*

17 **That Love** is 'A little chill and then a shiver, nice as a tonic but not to be taken in large doses before reaching maturity.'*

18 **That Marriage** – Comes once and is generally a failure, comes a second time and is a mésalliance.

19 **That Dress** is a development of the primal fig leaf, ordained by the creator for the benefit of tailors and dress makers.

20 **That my Favourite Pursuits are** – writing, dissecting, flirting.

21 **That my Favourite Amusements are** fishing, pistol practice, walking.

22 **That my Favourite Flower is** Jasmine.

23 **That my Favourite Fruit is** Peach.

24 **That I would like my Friends to be** just too good to be spoken to.

25 **That the Wittiest Saying I know is** – Few have courage to confess that their vices have left them and not they, their vices.*

26 **That the Finest Passage of Poetry I remember is** –

Every day brings a ship
Every ship brings a word,
Well for him who has no fear,
Looking seaward, well assured
That the word the vessel brings
Is the word that he would hear.*

Introduction to *Schoolboy Lyrics** (1881)

Lo! as a little child
Looks from its window on a mighty town,
And sees the roofs as far as eye can reach
But thinks not, knows not, nay, will not believe,
That there are Fathers, Mothers, Sisters, Homes

All like his own, a thousand homely talks,
Manners and customs – So I saw the world
With millions of my brethren. Then I wrote,
And all my verse sprang fire-new from a brain
That loved it and believed it: but the world
Coldly, in silence passed my numbers by,
Wherefore I sang in fury! When the years
Brought with them coolness, all too late I found
There were ten thousand, thousand thoughts like mine.

From a letter to E. K. Robinson*, 30 April 1886

... For another thing I am deeply interested in the queer ways and works of the people of the land. I hunt and rummage among 'em; knowing Lahore City – that wonderful, dirty, mysterious ant hill – blind fold and wandering through it like Haroun Al-Raschid in search of strange things. 'Section 420 I.P.C.' (originally called 'In the House of Suddhoo')* is the outcome of these researches but the bulk of my notes and references goes to enrich a bruised tin tea box where lies – 350 f[ools]c[a]p pages thick – my 'Mother Maturin'*. The novel that is always being written and yet gets no furrarder.

I'm in love with the country and would sooner write about her than anything else. Wherefore let us depart our several ways in amity? You to Fleet Street* (where I shall come when I die if I'm good) and I to my own place where I find heat and smells of oil and spices, and puffs of temple incense, and sweat, and darkness, and dirt and lust and cruelty, and, above all, things wonderful and fascinating innumerable. Give me time Kay – give me seven years and three added to them and abide the publishment of 'Mother Maturin'. Then you shall sit down in your gas lit, hotwater pipe warmed office, at midnight, and shall indite a review saying that the book ought never to have been written. And perhaps I shall agree with you then...

From a letter to Unidentified Recipient*, 5 March 1890

... It's the amazing selfishness of the White man that ruins your counsel of perfection. 'Money fame and success' are to remain unto me? Surely 'tis just as selfish consciously and deliberately to work for that trinity as to lay siege to a woman or a glass of gin and porter! Where I come from they taught me (with whips of circumstance and the thermometer at 110° in the shade) that the only human being to whom a man is responsible is himself. His business is to do his work and sit still.

No man can be a power for all time or the tenth of it – else would some of my friends who have died at their posts be those powers. Least of all can a man do aught if he thinks about it, and tries to add cubits to his stature mental or physical. It's as bad as waltzing and counting the steps 'one, two, three, one two three' under your breath. Surely the young man does best to pray to be delivered from 'the public demand that walketh in the noonday and the cheque-book that destroyeth in the study.'* For the rest, his business is to think as little about his soul as possible for that breeds self-consciousness and loss of power. The event is in God's hands absolutely and no hawking or clutching for fame or any other skittles is the least use.

Recollect I've tasted power – such power as I shall never get this side of the water – when I knew all the heads of the Indian Government – rulers administrators and kings – and saw how the machinery worked. Sunshine, colour, light, incident and fight I've had poured into my lap: and now the chastened amusements of this black place don't bite. (But, bless you for that hint about debt. It showed you were in earnest. It's all right, though). Wait till you've been shot at* and bossed a hundred and seventy men* and walked 'with Death and morning on the silver horns' in the Himalayas* if you wish to know how far the smoking-room, the club and the music hall, and the cheap ormolu amourettes taste good.

This only do. Pray for me, since I am a lonely man in my life, that I do not take the sickness for which for lack of understanding I should call love. For that will leave me somebody else's servant – instead of my own. My business at present, so far as I can feel, is to get into touch with the common folk here, to find out what they desire, hope or fear and then after the proper time to speak whatever may be given to me. Also to do just enough fairly decent work to keep me going till I have found my calling and my voice. From this ideal I make no doubt I shall most lamentably fall. Then I shall have to walk slowly through a Hell that I have been through once already.* It's an awful thing to think that each soul has to work out its own salvation and more awful to know that if it sits down to think about that salvation it is in deep danger of losing it.

If the success comes* my father's delight will be greater than mine. If

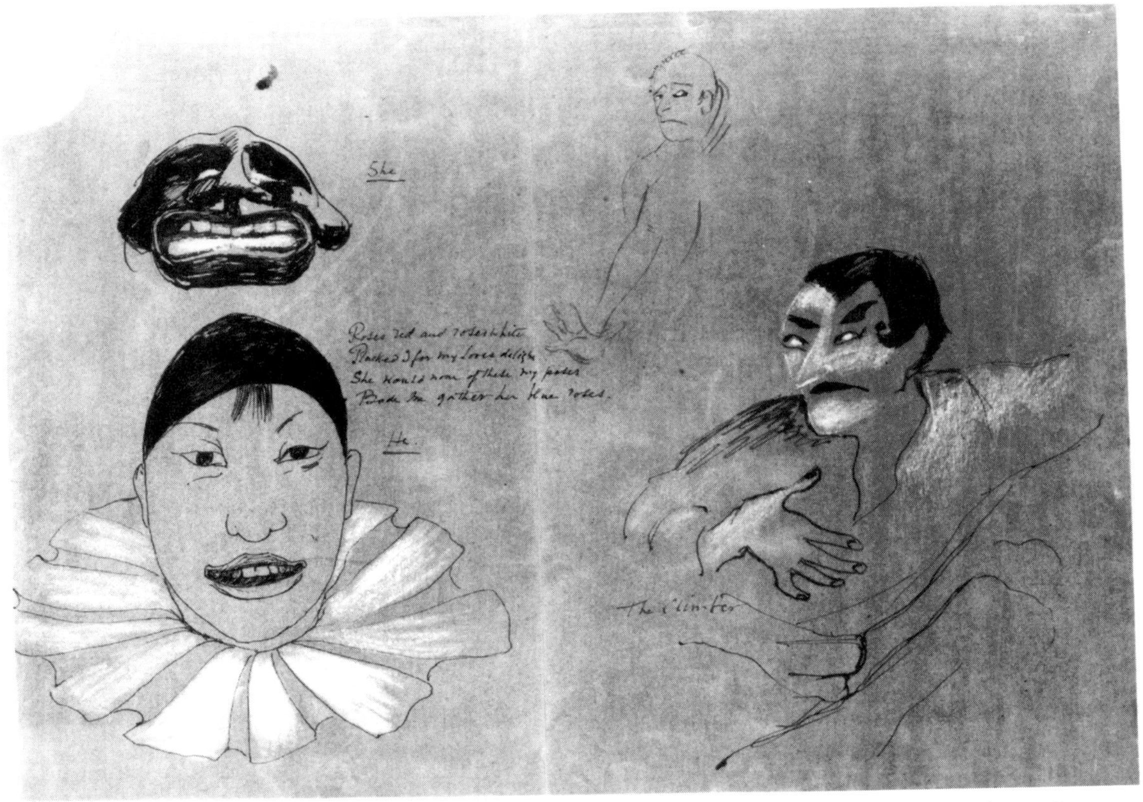

Figure 1 Blue roses: original sketches of four heads. Manuscript captions read 'He', 'She' and 'The Climber'. Verse in centre reads: 'Roses red and roses white / Plucked I for my Love's delight / She would none of these my posies / Bade me gather her blue roses.' (Epigraph from *The Light that Failed*.)

the money comes my Mother will be more pleased than I. The two together may spoil my work and make me think less of waiting than getting more little pieces of newspapers and little cheques. Wherefore, once again, let us pray. You see I've answered at undue length. Here is *my* key-note. Don't believe in me one inch further than you can see. What's the use of pinning faith on things that one uses to write about? Please don't for I must do my own work in my own way and if my notions clashed with yours you'd be hurt for nothing. Look on it as an interesting study and let it go. I'm not going to set the Thames on fire. So I hope I shan't have occasion to get mired in the mud on its banks. Once more, thank you a thousand times.

Sincerely yours
Rudyard Kipling.

P.S. Those commission verses* have found a nest: *Scots Observer*, next Saturday. There will be some little explosion if the other side fight.

From 'Cold Iron'*

'One hot night I saw the Boy roving about here wrapped in his flaming discontents. There was flash on flash against the clouds, and rush on rush of shadows down the valley till the shaws were full of his hounds giving tongue, and the wood-ways were packed with his knights in armour riding down into the water-mists – all his own magic, of course. Behind them you could see great castles lifting slow and splendid on arches of moonshine, with maidens waving their hands at the windows, which all turned into roaring rivers; and then would come the darkness of his own young heart wiping out the whole slateful. But boy's magic doesn't trouble me – or Merlin's either for that matter. I followed the Boy by the flashes and the whirling wildfire of his discontent, and oh, but I grieved for him! Oh, but I grieved for him! He pounded back and forth like a bullock in a strange pasture – sometimes alone – sometimes waist-deep among his shadow-hounds on a hawk-winged horse to rescue his shadow-girls. I never guessed he had such magic at his command; but it's often that way with boys...'

2

AESTHETICS

*

From 'The Story of Mohammad Din'*

Mohammad Din never had any companions. He used to trot about the compound, in and out of the castor-oil bushes, on mysterious errands of his own. One day I stumbled on some of his handiwork far down the garden. He had half buried the polo-ball in dust, and stuck six shrivelled old marigold flowers in a circle round it. Outside that circle again, was a rude square, traced out in bits of red brick alternating with fragments of broken china; the whole bounded by a little bank of dust. The *bhistie*-man from the well-curb put in a plea for the small architect, saying that it was only the play of a baby, and did not much disfigure my garden.

From 'False Dawn'*

No man will ever know the exact truth of this story; though women may sometimes whisper it to one another after a dance, when they are putting up their hair for the night and comparing lists of victims. A man, of course, cannot assist at these functions. So the tale must be told from outside – in the dark – all wrong.

Preface to *Under the Deodars**

Strictly speaking there should be no preface to this because it deals with things that are not pretty and uglinesses that hurt. But it may be as well to

Figures 2a and 2b Simla ladies: doodles from the autograph manuscript 'Ten Poems from a Notebook', pp. 20 and 29. Mrs Hauksbee, Mrs Reiver or one of their originals?

try to assure the ill-informed that India is not entirely inhabited by men and women playing tennis with the Seventh Commandment;* while it is a fact that very many of the lads in the land can be trusted to bear themselves as bravely, on occasion, as did my friend the late Robert Hanna Wick.* The drawback of collecting dirt in one corner is that it gives a false notion of the filth of the room. Folk who understand and have knowledge of their own, will be able to strike fair averages. The opinions of people who do not understand are somewhat less valuable.

In regard to the idea of the book I have no hope that the stories will be of the least service to anyone. They are meant to be read in railway trains and are arranged and adorned for that end. They ought to explain that there is no particular profit in going wrong at any time, under any circumstances or for any consideration. But that is a large text to handle at popular prices; and if I have made the first rewards of folly seem too inviting, my inability and not my intention is to blame.

RUDYARD KIPLING

Preface to *The Phantom Rickshaw and other Eerie Tales**

This is not exactly a book of downright ghost-stories, as the cover makes belief. It is rather a collection of facts that never quite explained themselves. All that the collector is certain of is, that one man insisted upon dying because he believed himself to be haunted; another man either made up a wonderful lie, or visited a very strange place; while the third man was indubitably crucified by some person or persons unknown, and gave an extraordinary account of himself.

The peculiarity of ghost-stories is that they are very seldom told first-hand. I have managed, with infinite trouble, to secure one exception to this rule. It is not a very good specimen, but you can credit it from beginning to end. The other three stories you must take on trust; as I did.

RUDYARD KIPLING

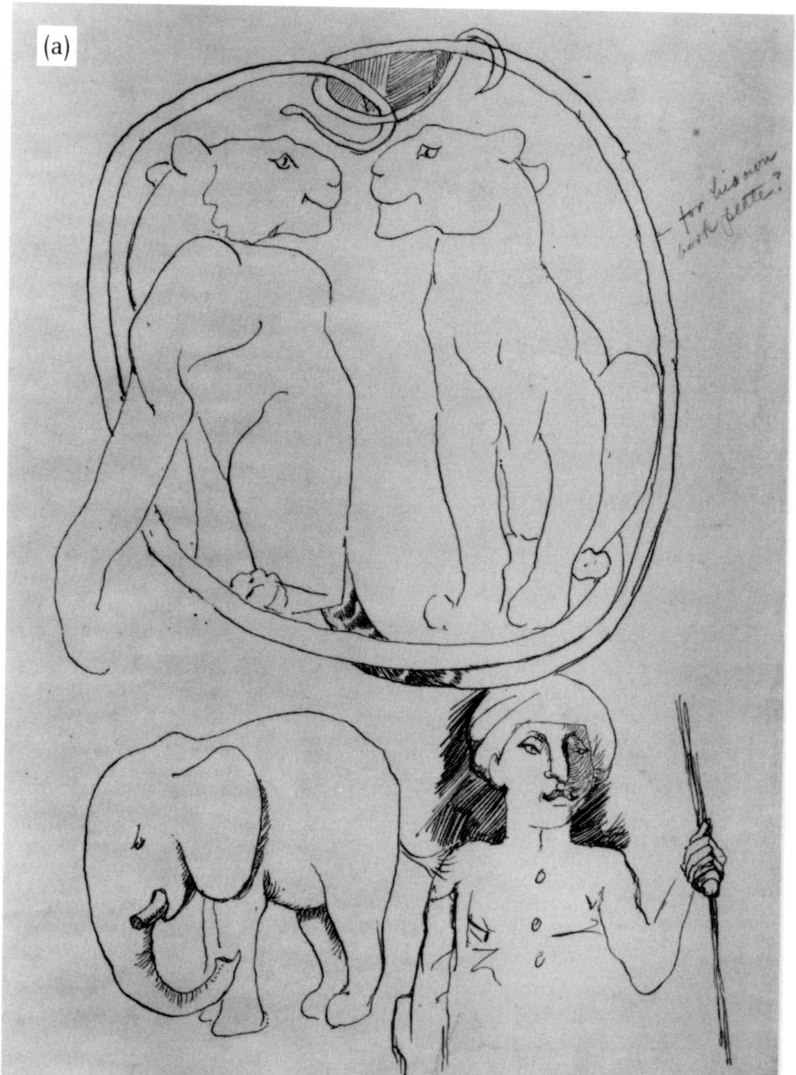

Figures 3a, 3b, 3c and 3d Tied up in tails: four original sketches for his bookplate. Manuscript caption reads 'Tied up in Tails! (or Tales) or is it Tales of Tails'.

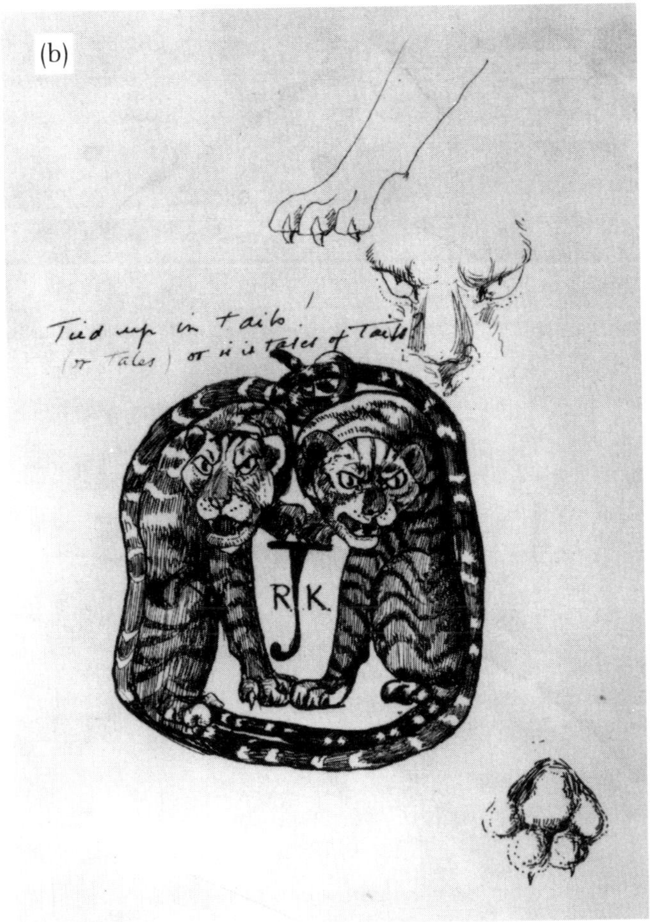

(b)

'The Last of the Stories'*

Whereof I perceive that there is nothing better, than that a man should rejoice in his own works; for that is his portion. Ecclesiastes III: 22.

'Kench* with a long hand, lazy one', I said to the punkah-coolie. 'But I am tired', said the coolie.

'Then go to Jehannum and get another man to pull', I replied, which was rude and, when you come to think of it, unnecessary.

'Happy thought – go to Jehannum!' said a voice at my elbow. I turned and saw, seated on the edge of my bed, a large and luminous Devil.

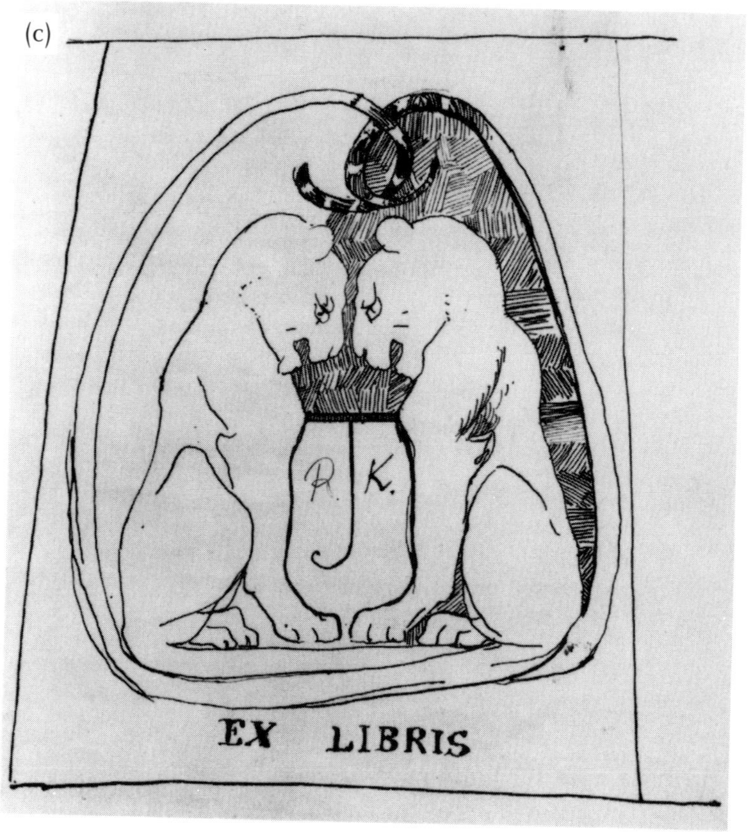

Figures 3c and 3d

'I'm not afraid', I said. 'You're an illusion bred by too much tobacco and not enough sleep. If I look at you steadily for a minute you will disappear. You are an *ignis fatuus*.'

'Fatuous yourself!' answered the Devil blandly. 'Do you mean to say you don't know *me*?' He shrivelled up to the size of a blob of sediment on the end of a pen, and I recognised my old friend the Devil of Discontent, who lives in the bottom of the inkpot, but emerges half a day after each story has been printed with a host of useless suggestions for its betterment.

'Oh, it's you, is it?' I said. 'You're not due till next week. Get back to your inkpot.'

'Hush!' said the Devil. 'I have an idea.'

'Too late, as usual. I know your ways.'

'No. It's a perfectly practicable one. Your swearing at the coolie suggested it. Did you ever hear of a man called Dante? – charmin' fellow, friend o'mine.'

'Dante once prepared to paint a picture,'* I quoted.

'Yes, I inspired that notion – but never mind. Are you willing to play Dante to my Virgil? I can't guarantee a nine-circle Inferno, any more than *you* can turn out a cantoed epic, but there's absolutely no risk and – it will run to three columns* at least.'

'But what sort of Hell do you own?' I said. 'I fancied your operations were mostly above ground. You have no jurisdiction over the dead.'

'Sainted Leopardi!'* rapped the Devil, resuming natural size. 'Is *that* all you know? I'm proprietor of one of the largest Hells in existence – the Limbo of Lost Endeavour, where the souls of all the Characters go.'

'Characters? What Characters?'

'All the Characters that are drawn in books, painted in novels, sketched in magazine articles, thumb-nailed in *feuilletons** or in any way created by anybody and everybody who has had the fortune or misfortune to put his or her writings into print.'

'That sounds like a quotation from a prospectus. What do you herd Characters for? Aren't there enough souls in the Universe?'

'Who possess souls and who do not? For aught you can prove, man may be soulless and the creatures he writes about immortal. Anyhow, about a hundred years after printing became an established nuisance, the loose Characters used to blow about Interplanetary Space in legions which interfered with traffic. So they were collected, and their charge became mine by right. Would you care to see them? *Your own are there.*'

'That decides me. But *is* it hotter than Northern India?'

'On my Devildom, no. Put your arms around my neck and sit tight. I'm going to dive!'

He plunged from the bed head-first into the floor. There was a smell of floor-cloth* and damp earth; and then fell the black darkness of night.

We stood before a door in a topless wall, from the further side of which came faintly the roar of infernal fires.

'But you said there was no danger!' I cried in an extremity of terror.

'No more there is', said the Devil. 'That's only the Furnace of First Edition. Will you go on? No other human being has set foot here in the flesh. Let me bring the door to your notice. Pretty design, isn't it? A joke of the Master's.'

I shuddered, for the door was nothing more than a coffin, the backboard knocked out, set on end in the thickness of the wall. As I hesitated, the silence of space was cut by a sharp, shrill whistle, like that of a live shell, which rapidly grew louder and louder. 'Get away from the door', said the Devil of Discontent quickly. 'Here's a Soul coming to its place.' I took refuge under the broad vans of the Devil's wings. The whistle rose to an ear-splitting shriek and a naked Soul flashed past me.

'Always the same,' said the Devil quietly. 'These little writers are so anxious to reach their reward. H'm, I don't think he likes *his'n,* though.' A yell of despair reached my ears and I shuddered afresh. 'Who was he?' I asked. 'Hack-writer for a pornographic firm in Belgium, exporting to London – you'll understand presently – and now we'll go in', said the Devil. 'I must apologise for that creature's rudeness. He should have stopped at the distance-signal for line-clear. You can hear the Souls whistling there now.'

'Are they the souls of men?' I whispered.

'Yes – writer-men. That's why they are so shrill and querulous. Welcome to the Limbo of Lost Endeavour!'

We passed into a domed hall, more vast than visions could embrace, crowded to its limit by men, women and children. Round the eye of the dome ran, a flickering fire, that terrible quotation from Job: 'Oh, that mine enemy had written a book!'

'Neat, isn't it?' said the Devil, following my glance. 'Another joke of the Master's. Man of *Us*,* y'know. In the old days we used to put the Characters into a disused circle of Dante's Inferno, but they grew overcrowded. So Balzac and Théophile Gautier* were commissioned to write up this building. It took them three years to complete, and is one of the finest under earth. Don't attempt to describe it unless you are *quite* sure you are equal to Balzac and Gautier in collaboration. Look at the crowds and tell me what you think of them.'

I looked long and earnestly, and saw that many of the multitude were cripples. They walked on their heels or their toes, or with a list to the right or to the left. A few of them possessed odd eyes and parti-coloured hair; more threw themselves into absurd or impossible attitudes; and every fourth woman seemed to be weeping.

'Who are these?' I said.

'Mainly the population of three-volume novels that never reach the six-shilling stage.* See that beautiful girl with one grey eye and one brown, and the black-and-yellow hair? Let her be an awful warning to you how you correct your proofs. She was created by a careless writer a month ago, and he changed all the colours in the second volume. So she came here as you see her. There will be trouble when she meets her author. He can't alter her now, and she says she'll accept no apology.'

'But when will she meet her author?'

'That's not in *my* department. Do you notice a general air of expectancy among all the Characters? They are waiting for their authors. Look! That explains the system better than I can.'

A lovely maiden, at whose feet I would willingly have fallen and worshipped, detached herself from the crowd and hastened to the door through which I had just come. There was a prolonged whistle throughout, a Soul dashed through the coffin and fell upon her neck. The girl with the parti-coloured hair eyed the couple enviously as they departed arm-in-arm to the other side of the hall.

'That man', said the Devil, 'wrote one magazine story, of twenty-four pages, ten years ago when he was desperately in love with a flesh-and-blood woman. He put all his heart into the work, and created the girl you have just seen. The flesh-and-blood woman married someone else and died – it's a way they have – but the man has this girl for his very own, and she will everlastingly grow sweeter.'

'Then the Characters are independent?'

'Slightly! Have you never known one of your Characters – even yours – get beyond control as soon as they are made?'

'That's true. Where are those two happy creatures going?'

'To the Levels. You've heard of authors finding their levels? We keep all the Levels here. As each writer enters, he picks up his Characters, or they pick *him* up, as the case may be, and on to the Levels he goes.'

'I should like to see –'

'So you shall, when you come through that door a second time – whistling. I can't take you there now.'

'Do you only keep the Characters of living scribblers in this hall?'

'We should be crowded out if we didn't draft them off somehow. Step this way and I'll take you to the Master. One moment, though. There's John Ridd with Lorna Doone, and there are Mr Maliphant and the Bormalacks* – clannish folk, those Besant characters – don't let The Twins talk to you about Literature and Art. Come along. What's here?'

The white face of Mr. John Oakhurst, gambler*, broke through the press. 'I wish to explain', said he in a level voice, 'that had I been consulted I should never have blown out my brains with the Duchess and all that Poker Flat lot. I wish to add that the only woman I ever loved was the wife of Brown of Calaveras.' He passed his hand behind him suggestively. 'All right, Mr Oakhurst', I said hastily, 'I believe you.' '*Kin* you set it right?' he asked, dropping into the Doric of the Gulches. I caught a trigger's cloth-muffled click. 'Just Heavens!' I groaned. 'Must I be shot for the sake of another man's Characters?'

Oakhurst levelled his revolver at my head, but the weapon was struck up by the hand of Yuba Bill. 'You durned fool!' said the stage-driver. 'Hevn't I told you no one but a blamed idiot shoots at sight *now*? Let the galoot go. You kin see by his eyes he's no party to your matrimonial arrangements.' Oakhurst retired with an irreproachable bow, but in my haste to escape I fell over Caliban,* his head in a melon and his tame orc under his arm. He spat like a wild-cat.

'Manners none, customs beastly', said the Devil. 'We'll take the Bishop with us. They all respect the Bishop.' And the great Bishop Blougram* joined us, calm and smiling, with the news, for my private ear, that Mr Gigadibs despised him no longer.

We were arrested by a knot of semi-nude Bacchantes kissing a clergyman. The Bishop's eyes twinkled, and I turned to the Devil for explanation.

'That's Robert Elsmere* – what's left of him', said the Devil. 'Those are French *feuilleton* women and scourings of the Opéra Comique. He has been lecturing 'em, and they don't like it.'

'He lectured *me*!' said the Bishop with a bland smile.

'He has been a nuisance ever since he came here. By the Holy Law of Proportion, he had the audacity to talk to the Master! Called him a "pot-bellied barbarian"! That is why he's walking so stiffly now', said the Devil. 'Listen! Marie Pigeonnier* is swearing deathless love to him. On my word, we ought to segregate the French Characters entirely. By the way, your regiment came in very handy for Zola's importations.'

'My regiment?' I said. 'How do you mean?'

'You wrote something about the Tyneside Tail-Twisters,* just enough to give the outline of the regiment, and of course it came down here – one thousand and eighty strong. I told it off in hollow squares to pen up the Rougon-Macquart series. There they are.' I looked and saw the Tyneside Tail-Twisters ringing an inferno of struggling, shouting, blaspheming men and women in the costumes of the Second Empire. Now and again the shadowy ranks brought down their butts on the toes of the crowd inside the square, and shrieks of pain followed. 'You should have indicated your men more clearly; they are hardly up to their work', said the Devil. 'If the Zola tribe increase, I'm afraid I shall have to use up your two companies of the Black Tyrone and two of the Old Regiment.'*

'I am proud –' I began.

'Go slow', said the Devil. 'You won't be half so proud in a little while, and I don't think much of your regiments, anyway. But they are good enough to fight the French. Can you hear Coupeau* raving in the left angle of the square? He used to run about the hall seeing pink snakes, till the children's story-book Characters protested. Come along!'

Never since Caxton pulled his first proof and made for the world a new and most terrible God of Labour had mortal man such an experience as mine when I followed the Devil of Discontent through the shifting crowds below the motto of the Dome. A few – a very few – of the faces were old friends, but there were thousands whom I did not recognise. Men in every conceivable attire and of every possible nationality, deformed by intention, or the impotence of creation that could not create – blind, unclean, heroic, mad, sinking under the weight of remorse or with eyes made splendid by the light of love and fixed endeavour; women fashioned in ignorance and mourning the errors of their creator, life and thought at variance with body and soul; perfect women such as walk rarely upon this earth, and horrors that were women only because they had not sufficient self-control to be fiends; little children, fair as the morning, who put their hands into mine and made most innocent confidences; loathsome, lank-haired infant-saints, curious as to the welfare of my soul, and delightfully mischievous boys, generalled by the irrepressible Tom Sawyer,* who played among murderers, harlots, professional beauties, nuns, Italian bandits and politicians of state.

The ordered peace of Arthur's Court was broken up by the incursions of Mr John Wellington Wells,* and Dagonet, the jester, found that his antics drew no attention so long as the 'dealer in magic and spells', taking Tristram's harp, sang patter-songs to the Round Table; while a Zulu *impi*, headed by Allan Quatermain,* wheeled and shouted in sham fight for the pleasure of Little Lord Fauntleroy.* Every century and every type was jumbled in the confusion of one colossal fancy-ball where all the Characters were living their parts.

'Aye, look long', said the Devil. 'You will never be able to describe it, and the next time you won't have the chance. Look long, and look at' – Good's passing with a maiden of the Zu-Vendi* must have suggested the idea – 'look at their legs'. I looked, and for the second time noticed the lameness that seemed to almost universal in the Limbo of Lost Endeavour. Brave men and stalwart to all appearance had one leg shorter than the other; some paced a few inches above the floor, never touching it, and others found the greatest difficulty in preserving their feet at all. The stiffness and laboured gait of these thousands was pitiful to witness. I was sorry for them. I told the Devil as much.

'H'm', he said reflectively, 'that's the world's work. Rather cockeye, ain't it? They do everything but stand on their feet. *You* could improve them, I suppose?' There was an unpleasant sneer in his tone, and I hastened to change the subject.

'I'm tired of walking', I said. 'I want to see some of my own Characters, and go on to the Master, whoever he may be, afterwards.'

'Reflect', said the Devil. 'Are you certain – do you know how many they be?'

'No – but I want to see them. That's what I came for.'

'Very well. Don't abuse me if you don't like the view. There are one-and-fifty of your make up to date, and – it's rather an appalling thing to be confronted with fifty-one children. However, here's a special favourite of yours. Go and shake hands with her!'

A limp-jointed, staring-eyed doll was hirpling towards me with a strained smile of recognition. I felt that I knew her only too well – if indeed it were she.

'Keep her off, Devil!' I cried, stepping back. 'I never made *that*!'

'"She began to weep and she began to cry, Lord ha' mercy on me, this is none of I!"* You're very rude to – Mrs. Hauksbee,* and she wants to speak to you', said the Devil. My face must have betrayed my dismay, for the Devil went on soothingly: 'That's as she is, remember. I *knew* you wouldn't like it. Now what will you give if I make her as she ought to be? No, I don't want your soul, thanks, I have it already, and many others of better quality. Will you, when you write your story, own that I am the best and greatest of all the Devils?' The doll was creeping nearer. 'Yes', I said hurriedly. 'Anything you like. Only I can't stand her in that state.'

'You'll *have* to when you come next again. Look! No connection with Jekyll and Hyde!' The Devil pointed a lean and inky finger towards the doll, and lo! radiant, bewitching, with a smile of dainty malice, her high heels clicking on the floor like castanets, advanced Mrs Hauksbee as I had imagined her in the beginning.

'Ah!' she said. 'You are here so soon? Not dead yet? That will come. Meantime, a thousand congratulations. And now, what do you think of me?' She put her hands on her hips, revealed a glimpse of the smallest foot in Simla, and hummed: 'Just look at that . . . just look at this! And then you'll see I'm not amiss.'

'She'll use exactly the same words when you meet her next time', said the Devil warningly. 'You dowered her with any amount of vanity, if you left out – Excuse me a minute! I'll fetch up the rest of your menagerie.' But I was looking at Mrs Hauksbee.

'Well?' she said. '*Am* I what you expected?'

I forgot the Devil and all his works,* forgot that this was not the woman I had made, and could only murmur rapturously: 'By Jove! You *are* a beauty!' Then, incautiously: 'And you stand on your feet!'

'Good Heavens!' said Mrs Hauksbee. 'Would you, at my time of life, have me stand on my head?' She folded her arms and looked me up and down.

I was grinning imbecilely – the woman was so alive. 'Talk', I said absently. 'I want to hear you talk.'

'I am not used to being spoken to like a coolie', she replied.

'Never mind', I said. 'That may be for outsiders, but I made you and I've a right –'

'You have a right? You made me? My dear sir, if I didn't know that we should bore each other so inextinguishably hereafter I should read you an hour's lecture this instant. You made me! I suppose you will have the audacity to pretend that you understood me – that you *ever* understood me. Oh, man, man – foolish man! If you only knew!'

'Is that the person who thinks he understands us, Loo?' drawled a voice at her elbow. The Devil had returned with a cloud of witnesses, and it was Mrs Mallowe* who was speaking.

'I've touched 'em all up', said the Devil in an aside. 'You couldn't stand 'em raw. But don't run away with the notion that they are your work. I show you what they ought to be. You must find out for yourself how to make 'em so.'

'Am I allowed to remodel the batch – up above?' I asked anxiously.

'*Litera scripta manet.** That's in the Delectus* and Eternity.' He turned round to the semicircle of Characters: 'Ladies and gentlemen, who are all a great deal better than you should be by virtue of *my* power, let me introduce you to your maker. If you have anything to say to him, you can say it.'

'What insolence!' said Mrs. Hauksbee between her teeth. 'This isn't a Peterhof* drawing-room. I haven't the slightest intention of being levéed by this person. Polly, come here and we'll watch the animals go by.' She and Mrs Mallowe stood at my side. I turned crimson with shame, for it is an awful thing to see one's Characters in the solid.

'Wal', said Gilead P. Beck* as he passed, 'I would not be you at this *precise* moment of time, not for all the ile in the univarsal airth. *No*, sirr! I thought my dinner-party was soul-shatterin', but it's mush – mush and milk – to your circus. Let the good work go on!'

I turned to the company and saw that they were men and women, standing upon their feet as folks should stand. Again I forgot the Devil, who stood apart and sneered. From the distant door of entry I could hear the whistle of arriving Souls, from the semi-darkness at the end of the hall came the thunderous roar of the Furnace of First Edition, and everywhere the restless crowds of Characters muttered and rustled like wind-blown autumn leaves. But I looked upon my own people and was perfectly content as man could be.

'I have seen you study a new dress with just such an expression of idiotic beatitude', whispered Mrs Mallowe to Mrs Hauksbee. 'Hush!' said the latter. 'He thinks he understands.' Then to me: 'Please trot them out. Eternity is long enough in all conscience, but that is no reason for wasting it. *Pro*-ceed, or shall I call them up? Mrs Vansuythen, Mr Boulte, Mrs Boulte, Captain Kurrell, and the Major!'

The European population in Kashima in the Dosehri hills, the actors in the Wayside Comedy,* moved towards me; and I saw with delight that they were human. 'So you wrote about us?' said Mrs. Boulte. 'About my confession to my husband and my hatred of that Vansuythen woman? Did you think that you understood? Are *all* men such fools?'

'That woman is bad form', said Mrs Hauksbee, 'but she speaks the truth. I wonder what these soldiers have to say.' Gunner Barnabas and Private Shacklock* stopped, saluted and hoped I would take no offence if they gave it as their opinion that I had not 'got them down quite right'. I gasped.

A spurred Hussar succeeded, his wife on his arm. It was Captain Gadsby and Minnie,* and close behind them swaggered Jack Mafflin, the Brigadier-General in his arms. 'Had the cheek to try to describe our life, had you?' said Gadsby carelessly. 'Ha-hmmm! S'pose he understood, Minnie?' Mrs Gadsby raised her face to her husband and murmured: 'I'm sure he didn't, Pip', while Poor Dear Mamma, still in her riding-habit, hissed: 'I'm sure he didn't understand *me*.' And these also went their way.

One after another they filed by – Trewinnard, the pet of his Department; Otis Yeere,* lean and lanthorn-jawed; Crook O'Neil* and Bobby Wick* arm in arm; Janki Meah,* the blind miner in the Jimahari coal-fields; Afzul Khan,* the policeman; the murderous Pathan horse-dealer;* Durga Dass,* the *bunnia*; Boh da Thone, the dacoit; Dana Da,* weaver of false magic; the Leander of the Barwhi ford;* Peg Barney,* drunk as a coot; Mrs Delville,* the dowd; Dinah Shadd,* large, red-cheeked and resolute; Simmons, Slane and Losson;* Georgie Porgie* and his Burmese helpmate; a shadow in a high collar, who was all that I had ever indicated of the Hawley Boy* – the nameless men and women who had trod the Hill of Illusion* and lived in the Tents of Kedar,* and last, His Majesty the King.*

Each one in passing told me the same tale, and the burden thereof was:

'You did not understand.' My heart turned sick within me. 'Where's Wee Willie Winkie?' I shouted. 'Little children don't lie.'

A clatter of pony's feet followed, and the child appeared, habited as on the day he rode into Afghan territory to warn Coppy's love against the 'bad men'. 'I've been playing', he sobbed, 'playing on ve Levels wiv Jackanapes and Lollo,* an' *he* says I'm only just borrowed. I *isn't* borrowed. I'm Willie Wi-*inkie*! Vere's Coppy?'

'Out of the mouths of babes and sucklings',* whispered the Devil, who had drawn nearer. 'You know the rest of the proverb. Don't look as if you were going to be shot in the morning! Here are the last of your gang.'

I turned despairingly to the Three Musketeers, dearest of all my children to me – to Privates Mulvaney, Ortheris and Learoyd. Surely the Three would not turn against me as the others had done! I shook hands with Mulvaney. 'Terence, how goes? Are *you* going to make fun of me, too?'

''Tis not for me to make fun of you, sorr', said the Irishman, 'knowin' as I *du* know fwhat good frinds we've been for the matther av three years.'

'Fower', said Ortheris. ''Twas in the Helanthami barricks, H block, we was become acquaint, an' 'ere's thankin' you kindly for all the beer we've drunk twix' that and now.'

'Four ut is, then', said Mulvaney. 'Me an' Dinah Shadd are your frinds, but –' he stood uneasily.

'But what?' I said.

'Savin' your presince, sorr, an' it's more than onwillin' I am to be hurtin' you; you did not ondhersthand. On my sowl an' honour, sorr, you did not ondhersthand. Come along, you two.'

But Ortheris stayed for a moment to whisper: 'It's Gawd's own trewth, but there's this 'ere to think. 'T'ain't the bloomin' belt that's wrong, as Peg Barney sez, when he's up for bein' dirty on p'rade. 'Tain't the bloomin' belt, sir; it's the bloomin' pipeclay. 'Ere I could seek an explanation he had joined his companions.

'For a private soldier, a singularly shrewd man', said Mrs Hauksbee, and she repeated Ortheris's words. The last drop filled my cup, and I am ashamed to say that I bade her be quiet in a wholly unjustifiable tone. I was rewarded by what would have been a notable lecture on propriety, had I not said to the Devil: 'Change that woman to a d – d doll again! Change 'em all back as they were – as they are. I'm sick of them.'

'Poor wretch!' said the Devil of Discontent very quietly. 'They are changed.'

The reproof died on Mrs Hauksbee's lips, and she moved away marionette-fashion, Mrs Mallowe trailing after her. I hastened after the remainder of the Characters, and they were changed indeed – even as the Devil had said, who kept at my side.

They limped and stuttered and staggered and mouthed and staggered round me, till I could endure no more.

'So I am the master of this idiotic puppet-show, am I?' I said bitterly, watching Mulvaney trying to come to attention by spasms.

'*In saecula saeculorum*',* said the Devil, bowing his head; 'and you needn't kick, my dear fellow, because they will concern no one but yourself by the time you whistle up to the door. Stop reviling me and uncover. Here's the Master.'

Uncover! I would have dropped on my knees, had not the Devil prevented me, at sight of the portly form of Maitre François Rabelais, sometime Curé of Meudon. He wore a smoke-stained apron of the colours of Gargantua. I made a sign* which was duly returned. 'An Entered Apprentice in difficulties with his rough ashlar, Worshipful Sir', explained the Devil. I was too angry to speak.

Said the Master, rubbing his chin: 'Are those things yours?'

'Even so, Worshipful Sir', I muttered, praying inwardly that the Characters would at least keep quiet while the Master was near.

He touched one or two thoughtfully, put his hand upon my shoulders and started. 'By the Great Bells of Notre Dame, you are in the flesh – the warm flesh! – the flesh I quitted so long – ah, so long! And you fret and behave unseemly because of these shadows! Listen now. I, even I, would give my Three, Panurge, Gargantua and Pantagruel, for one little hour of the life that is in you. And *I* am the Master!'

But the words gave me no comfort. I could hear Mrs Mallowe's joints cracking – or it might have been merely her stays.

'Worshipful Sir, he will not believe that', said the Devil. 'Who live by shadows lust for shadows. Tell him something more to his need.'

The Master grunted contemptuously. 'And he is flesh and blood! Know this, then. The First Law is to make them stand upon their feet, and the Second is to make them stand upon their feet, and the Third is to make them stand upon their feet. But, for all that, Trajan is a fisher of frogs.'* He passed on, and I could hear him say to himself: 'One hour – one minute – of life in the flesh, and I would sell the Great Perhaps thrice over!'

'Well', said the Devil, 'you've made the Master angry, seen about all there is to be seen, except the Furnace of First Edition, and, as the Master is in charge of that, I should avoid it. Now you'd better go. You know what you ought to do?'

'I don't need all Hell –'

'Pardon me. Better men than you have called this Paradise.'

'All *Hell*', I said, 'and the Master to tell me what I knew before. What I want to know is *how?*'

'Go and find out', said the Devil.

We turned to the door, and I was aware that my Characters had grouped themselves at the exit. 'They are going to give you an ovation. Think o' that, now!' said the Devil. I shuddered and dropped my eyes, while one-and-fifty voices broke into a wailing song, whereof the words, so far as I recollect, ran:-

But we, brought forth and reared in hours
Of change, alarm, surprise,
What shelter to grow ripe is ours –
*What leisure to grow wise?**

I ran the gauntlet, narrowly missed collision with an impetuous Soul (I hoped he liked his Characters when he met them), and flung free into the night, where I should have knocked my head against the stars. But the Devil caught me.

The brain fever bird was fluting across the grey, dewy lawn, and the punkah had stopped again. 'Go to Jehannum and get another man to pull', I said drowsily.

'Exactly', said a voice from the inkpot.

Now the proof that this story is absolutely true lies in the fact that there will be no other to follow it.

Figure 4a and b Inspiration: two caricature self-portraits. The writer and his Daemon – or the Devil of Discontent?

Unpublished Prefaces to *Departmental Ditties,** 1st English edition

[In holograph on title-page] This is *all* faked and a lie. R.K.
[In holograph on first page] Both prefaces *cancelled* by author.
Preserve this. (RK).

Preface

To my Anglo-Indian Public

Dear Folk,

They have put these verses into a fourth edition; but you knew and were good to them when they were a brown paper docket, a limp-back pink, and a hard-board blue. I have added some more verses, and now we are quite respectable and fat in the sides. Also the English public are buying us, and trying to find out what in the world it means. They still believe that all white men in India sleep for three or four hours in the middle of the day and spend most of their waking moments in 'kicking the poor dear native downstairs'. They are quite certain that the Indian administrator is much too near to affairs to be able to form impartial judgements, and every gentleman and every other lady who has bought curiosities in the verandah of Watson's Hotel* knows exactly how India ought to be governed. This has nothing to do with the verses; but it is interesting on general grounds.

You, however, can read between the lines I have written and know exactly how far the ditties tell truth, and by how much they err in describing the frivolous, gilded, idle, irresponsible life. Over here, they insist upon regarding my sermons and moralities as the diversions of an Oriental jester. Therefore I want your sympathy, and now and again just one small sign across the seas – a wink would do – to show that you understand. You can put it into any of the Indian newspapers.

RUDYARD KIPLING.

[In holograph:] January, 1890

Preface

This is a book of verses on Anglo-Indian subjects. An Anglo-Indian subject is a person who was once an Englishman, but who through the effects of climate, overfeeding and underwork becomes something quite different. His duties are to live luxuriously on the money wrung from the teeming millions of India, who are all very highly educated, peaceful, and open-minded folk, more than capable of administering a government of their own. The Anglo-Indian is vastly inferior to the real Englishman in physique, endurance and mental power. He drinks *brandy-panee*,* which is a rare Oriental beverage, also wrung from the teeming millions, travels in a palanquin, lolls under a punkah while nautch-girls sing to him, and is never seen in public without a *kuga** – the silver and jewelled water-pipe of the East.

I dare not hope that you will take any interest in an effete product of the tropics, who only exists by the forbearance of your statesmanlike, far-seeing, and dispassionate Houses of Parliament.

RUDYARD KIPLING.

From a letter to William Canton,* 5 April 1890

. . . I am not one bit grateful for the Thibetan story.* It came like a drawn sword slick across a mass of other work and I cursed it for a superb Notion. It's got to be worked out somehow and it seems just the sort o' thing that lies within my grip. But I *mustn't* take it up red-handed though I'd dearly like to do so. Send more and much and often. You understand what I want. . .

'Home'*

The longing began at least a league off shore from Colombo, when the *Chusan*, Calcutta bound, swung out round the breakwater under the *Valletta*'s nose, and we who were Anglo-Indians* separated ourselves a little from the crowd. A smell came up over the sea – a smell of damp earth, coconut oil, ginger, onions and mankind.

It spoke with a strong voice, recalling many things; but the most curious revelation to one man was the sudden knowledge that under these skies lay home and the dearest places in all the world. Even the first sniff of London had not caused so big a choke in the throat, or so strict a tightening over the heart.

There was a most urgent necessity to get away to Lahore swiftly. The *Valetta* ploughed on to Aden; a big B.I.* boat took charge of me to Tuticorin,* and at the first turn of her screw, the first glimpse of the *khitmatgars** on deck, Australia, the Cape, New Zealand, and the British Isles dropped under the sea. I was going home for Christmas, largely and expansively, as an Anglo-Indian should go – by train for the better part of a week, as soon as the *Nerbudda* should make Tuticorin.

With me, sole survivor of a scattered card-party, was the Post Officer of Vizagapatam,* and he promised me breakfast on shore in the old casual Anglo-Indian fashion. 'I know the Post Officer here', he said, 'met him once. No, I didn't, by Jove – he was out when I came – but I can put up at his house. He'll give us breakfast.' By this I knew where I was, and rejoiced.

Then we stepped on to Indian soil under the green fig trees that face the beach, where the cotton trains go to and fro, and the Tamil women weave onion baskets of green reeds while their babies hang like cocoons in the bight of a loin-cloth flung over a branch. Allah be praised, we stepped straight into India again. It was not quite the real India, but the India that the English know – the *Little Henry and his Bearer** country, all paddy, palmyra, and coconut palms, as the books draw it. Hindu temples jostled old Dutch-built Roman Catholic Churches where the Virgin, I believe, has twelve arms and the saints are rather like Krishnas. The people, too, were hereditary Christians, and spoke English, many of them. Small wonder that the South Indian papers point out that one writer at least does not describe India – their India. Could a Swede from the Baltic write of Algiers?

But the beautiful smell was there, the brown, slow-moving crowds were there (white is rather a leprous tint when you come to think of it, and it doesn't match backgrounds), the crumbling *kutcha** walls and the deep-bowed bungalows were all waiting there. Best of all there was the Port Officer, first met of our breed, a khaki-clad Anglo-Indian, not one whit disturbed because two utter strangers from the sea demanded breakfast.

Oh! that breakfast, eaten under the slow-swinging punkahs with the white-robed butlers behind our chairs – the fish fresh from the sea that was lapping twenty yards away outside in the glare, the teal bagged yesterday, the Madras curry with its rich allowance of spices, and the first long pull of Pilsener, the ice clinking in the tall glass. Afterwards – this was even more perfect – there came the self-assured and confident flop into the long chair – our long chair – where you put up your feet by right and not by permission, and jamming a black rank Dawson No. 1* between your teeth puff the well remembered incense and thank Heaven you are back among your fellows once more. There were no 'Misters' in that bungalow after the first introductions; we keep 'Mister' for the Globe-Trotter.

Even then, with two thousand four hundred miles to cover before I got home, it was manifestly absurd to pretend that I had been away for a day.

The *Nerbudda*, just visible on the horizon, was an accident I could not explain. She probably came from Colombo. I was from the North, the men on the long chairs were talking shop – cotton and harbour improvements, with allusions to sick friends and a fever stricken householder in the station. They talked in their own way, but as I listened a memory came up through the tobacco smoke 'touching the life I led before this life'* – a worritsome gabbling life somewhere overseas. In that life surely there was a man – a reviewer – who whiningly wanted to know y'know, whether anywhere in the world men talk as they are represented in certain books – that is to say, like telegraph forms. I think his words were 'cynically, brusquely and like telegraph forms'.* Oh, reviewer they do, indeed they do. That is why I made it so. Probably they would not talk to you in that fashion, because you are not of their household, but among themselves they speak – they are speaking now of a man down with smallpox – word for word, as these hands have written before. It is all one big family and if you do not know the catchwords of the family, you must stand outside.

We loafed through the bazaar to the train, paralysed booking and telegraph clerk by trying to get a ticket and send a telegram in under half-an-hour, and at noon in the brilliant moist sunshine slouched off by the S.I.R.* on a four-hundred mile run to Madras. The warm rain began to fall steadily, and in an hour or two the flat red soil was under water as far as the eye could reach. Then came the perfect tropical moon, turning the embankment aloes to frosted silver, and the frogs sang songs at the stations where we halted, and the palms dripped heavily and gave out all their smell. Moreover Asia, taking me back without reserve, threw her mantle over me from head to foot. To think that a man should be thankful for prickly heat!

After interminable hours – twenty-eight of them – and flood all the way, there was Arconum* and a parting. The Port officer of Vizag went his way to his harbour and I to mine, hopping from train to train and wrestling with booking clerks who denied the existence of Lahore. One fat Madrassi pinned me in a corner – indeed I wanted no more than a ticket to Khundwa* – and waving a triplicate form-book over my head, shouted: 'Do you know what work is?'

In free America or enlightened England he would have been badly injured, but the brutal and overbearing Anglo-Indian – who talks, as you will know, of the 'damned nigger' all day and kicks his servant all night – takes this sort of thing as part of the day's work. I would have given a month's pay to have turned one or two howling philanthropists of my England acquaintance loose among the booking offices. Nay, more, I would have paid their fines for assault with intent to kill.

Then north to Raichur and Wadi* where the look of the land changed and there was a prophecy of drought in the air. Two men entered, one a Major of seventeen years' service and the other a Subaltern of two. He was on transfer to the Staff Corps, had bagged his five tigers, desired more *shikar** and more than *shikar* lusted for active service. The elder man got out at some unholy hour of the night for a twenty-mile tonga* drive and a fifty-mile ride; and the last we saw of him was a figure in the moonlight suavely assuring the tonga driver that never since the British Raj was founded had an officer travelled with less kit. 'And it will all go into the tonga – because it must all go into the tonga' he said. It was sound logic and the principle upon which the Government servant is administered.

Then did the Subaltern and myself, climbing into our bunks on the Dhond-Manmar* line seriously discuss the ordering of a young man's future. Was it better for a man who had just entered the Staff Corps – 'and that means India all my life' – to try for the Guides, the Goorkhas or Bengal Cavalry.* After much argument, we agreed to refer the matter unofficially to any man over ten years' service whom we might catch. At Manmar junction we found that man by the simple process of falling over his feet in the dawn. He was guarded by a rampart of kit and two superb bull terriers. Over the dogs and the tea we fraternised in the blessed Anglo-Indian custom.

Fancy waking up an Englishman in his pyjamas on the Edinburgh Express let us say, and expecting him to be amiable. Presently we laid the Subaltern's difficulty before him, and he said 'Cavalry of course – Go for the horses by all means.' He was in the Cavalry himself and prejudiced. He, well knowing me to be a Punjabi, told me how some Hyderabadi troopers came up to Muridki camp last year for *dugabashi*,* and 'knocked spots out of your Pathans, by Jove!' Now everybody knows that one Punjabi is worth five down-country *sowars*.* I hate a prejudiced man.

We talked together and apart while the red-eyed bull-terriers fawned upon us, and the Subaltern whose arms were splashed with the red sun tar, far up the elbows, showed us his guns and told me how there was no one in the world so wise, so full of resource and such a 'ripping good man all round' as his Skipper. He, the Subaltern, had been learning the mystery of managing men, and getting to know his half-company as an officer should. The subject was a fascinating one – 'it's an awful grind, though' and it ended all too soon when he packed up his things and went eastward to his first Staff Corps Regiment. God be very good to him, for those square shoulders may have to uphold the weight of an Empire's honour alone in some lone outpost before a year is done.

One vision of the night-time stays with me. There was a Globe trotter with his neatly locked bag of washing fresh from the steamer. He came and slept and went but [I was] awake when he climbed into the upper bunk, and behold he wore a night-gown, a beautiful ample-tailed slashed and lily white English night-gown! See a man manoeuvre into an upper bunk with a night-gown, and die, as I nearly did.

All this time India was rolling back behind the wheels – level, burned and dusty. We ploughed through the Asseerghur jungle,* in company with a Forest Officer and a young 'Stunt* two months out from home, a little bewildered at the new life, but very resolute to make the best of it. The Forest Officer melted nearly to tears at the sight of an English half crown, handled it lovingly and offered three rupees in exchange.

Now, was it yesterday, or ten years ago, that in a railway carriage by Neemuch* I found a Globe trotter and sighed when he showed me an English penny? It must have been the better part of ten years; and to-day it is our poor one and four-penny rupee that makes me home-sick.

The first suggestion of the cold weather – our own real cold weather – began at Bhopal,* where the train ran through the dank white layers of evening wood smoke and there came a smell of dried earth and burned cowdung. Morning – a clear dry morning – brought 'the hottest town, in all this land of Ind' – Agra, with her red Fort and disreputable monkeys. There was a 'homey' look about the fields; the village boundary-pillars were familiar, and the cattle such as one knows.

But the people on the platform were only North-West men – down country folk and they did not carry the proper kind of *huqqa*.* By noon we should be in our proper territories, and it was more than likely that some old faces . . . Now observe the kindness of Providence! Three years ago it was the Lord of the Iron Horses* of the North-Western Railway who saw me off the premises in his inspection carriage. Therefore it was right and proper that the first train into Ghaziabad* – Ghaziabad with its awful tiffins and vault-like refreshment rooms – should bring up from Ajmir on his way to Lahore, that same Lord of the Iron Horses.

'Back again?' said he. 'Back again', said I. 'Well, you're a nice sort of a globe-trotter!' said he. I pocketed the insult, for there were three years arrears of news to make good of what had happened up at home? Who was dead, married, transferred, promoted or gone under? In the evening light, flying up to Meerut, my questions were answered simply and monosyllabically as is our custom. Thus: – 'A?' 'He's dead. Didn't you hear?' 'B?' 'Transferred – Poona.' 'C?' 'Still at Gurdaspore.' 'D?' 'He married Miss Such-an-one. They've both gone home on six months.'* 'Mrs E.?' 'Dead – died of typhoid last July. It was a bad hot weather.'

'And you yourself?' I said, knowing he had had no leave for eleven years.

'Oh, I don't care. I know that the weather can't be worse than I've known it, so I stick it out. I say, though, what a fuss you kicked up at Home about that Manipur business;* might have thought all India was being sacked.'

'You at Home' sticks unpleasantly in the throat; confound the Lord of the Iron Horses. What have I to do with the people at 'Home'. I am here, and the North-Western Railway is running disgracefully late as usual.

'Don't you fret' he answers calmly. 'She'll leg it in the night. Look at Meerut. There's a Cavalry camp on.'

A line of white tents and a cloud of dust fringes the station of the Race Course. Another young Subaltern – keen as mustard on his profession, who has stolen a few days and travelled a few hundred miles to see the show – leans forward intently. He is going to the camp. Everybody will be there, and General Luck, or whoever it is, will bucket them about royally. Only . . . Only I am out of it, no camp for me.* Officers in wonderful *khaki* undress* are walking about the platform. Their *putties* are white with the beautiful dust and their noses are skinned by the sun. The Subaltern goes away, and the last stretch of rail begins.

'S – if you love me, make her go. We shall be late at Lahore to-morrow.'

'She'll leg it in the night' is the answer. 'What's the good of getting into Lahore in the dawn?'

She legs it. After Saharanpur she lies down to her work in earnest with an hour and a half to make up. The Jhelum bridge rings and rattles under her heels. There is a glimpse of lean, dry sand under the moon, and with a whistle she sails into the Punjab. The rest is easy. How do the Stations run? Umballa, Phillour, Beas East, Jullundur, Amritsar and Ataree, and then Lahore. Colder and colder grows the Northern night. Somebody shouts Umballa through my dreams – Umballa of a hundred Simla memories in the days before you went to Kalka by rail.* Now that I know every tie and fish plate from here to home I will sleep . . .

* * * *

'Hi! Ho! We're past Amritsar. Here's Ataree.* There's *chota hazri** in K's carriage!'

It is the diamond clear cold weather dawn – dawn among the ferashes, the creaking well-wheels and the *Jats** – the huge thighed *Jats* – each man head-blanketted from the cold and each trailing his lumbering *Huqqa*. The land looks sick and drouthy. But it is home – every dusty inch of it.

We invade K's carriage, and finding him defenceless in his *pyjamas* make a mock of him. The elephant lines and a couple of rocking tethered *hathis** show grey through the last patches of the morning mist, and rattling over the facing points, past the back of the railway theatre – who remembers *Plot and Passion** there eight years ago, when the locomotives whistled down all the love-scenes? – pull up at Lahore platform. Four and a half days from Tuticorin. One can move in the Empire.

Now, certainly, I have never been one day absent. There was an agricultural exhibition at Jullundur yesterday, which I was sent to describe, and after breakfast there will be just time to get back to office, send in the report and take the day's mail. The old life will begin again . . . after breakfast. Up start the brown faces in the familiar verandah that takes the dust of Mozung.* 'Yes, by the Sahib's favour we be all well. Other of the Sahib's household be coming to make salutations after breakfast. Yes. He that was the scullion is now promoted to be the butler by the Honoured one's favour and' – Kadir Buksh,* pearl among khitmatgars, the voice was thine! – 'There is *Hussaini Kabab* for *hazri*.'*

A pious Musalman would be shocked if he were violently hugged by a Kafir.* None the less, I should like to dance sarabands with Kadir as he grins and hands the curry. There is only one curry in the world, and Kadir Buksh makes it, and – oh the forgotten decency, that the English cannot understand! – sets out the finger-bowls after meat. For the rest, looking round the old home there is not much of the luxury we read about in the books. How would an English *memsahib* approve white-washed walls, raw-timbered roofs split and cracked with old summers, the whitewash splashed impartially over the timbers, doors that never shut, and glass puttied as for an outhouse. But these things, with the old jail *dhurries*, the ruggled *chitai* in the verandah, the cock-eyed *almirahs*, the *choukuts** that catch a forgetful foot on the threshold, and the rude printed cloth dadoes make homes. To clinch every thing, the Very Dearest Dog in All the World recognises a long-lost master, and behaves accordingly. Vixen,* do you remember the hot weathers we shared together when you lay in the thermantidote* and penked? Do you remember the wet tonga-drives to Simla, and rat-catching in the office? Vixen, it's nearly seven years since I bought you at the sale of a dead man's kit, and you are getting old. 'Take me out', says Vixen, 'show me a squirrel and see.'

No chaprassi* comes with an office box; there is no dogcart for Vixen to direct and – all the world is going off to its work except myself.

Vixen, we will to the old duftar* and pretend that we belong there? Therefore, in the morning sunshine, sifted through the dusty ferashes,* we take stock of the land. As usual they have been excavating old graveyards, and then they wonder Lahore is unhealthy. You and I used to dig out skulls, Vixen, scrape them up with a fire shovel all round the foundations of the new Law Courts.

Now who in the exercise of his discretion has been splitting the Mall length ways with brick paths? What is the use of *surki** on the side walks? That was the only soft place to ride on. Central lamp posts invite a man to drive his dog cart into them, and Lahore Mall will never be a boulevard. It's just the Mall – the old *thunda suruk** – and even in the morning sunshine it is packed with ghosts. We've seen it in every light, Vixen – muddy and frosted and bare, drenched with the warmth of the rains, and hot as a station rail in June when the dust clouds danced down it like devils, and you wallowed, poor little beastie, in the spillage of the wells. It looks pretty enough now to a globe-trotter's eye. He couldn't guess that we have had no rain to speak of for twelve months. The frost has touched the roses a little too, and there are crowds of dead people driving up and down.

'Sahib, this is indeed the office of the *chappar kargaz** and I was your old chaprassi, but the paper itself is printed at another office and elsewhere.' This is really pleasant. It reminds you who you are, to go to your own office and find that it isn't there any longer, and that you don't know where it is. Once before, the mother-paper changed her place, but then one knew all about it. Now, one is only a rank outsider – a globe-trotter who must be piloted about Lahore. Yet it is good to think that the paper has prospered. To the new office, therefore, with a big, big lump in one's throat. No man can put in his seven years on an Indian journal when he is half the staff, and the sheet is part of his being without loving her dearly. The smell of the office comes out through the orange trees, and there is the thump of an old columbiad* (I think I know which one it is) running off the galley proofs for the editor. Then, through a cautiously lifted *chick*,* the old scene stands revealed, and there rush back on the memory the names of a score of natives buried for a time under the drift of the months. The brown comps.*

are bending over the cases, the little distributing boys are sitting cross-legged on the floor and – Yes! *He* has not changed in the least – the man who broke my heart daily for years is getting together the standing matter. What would happen if one called out:-'*Kitna* in hand *hai, kul se*?'*

The lemon and green turbans shake like a bed of tulips in a high wind, and they come up by the dozen, from the foreman, whom nothing could flurry, to the man who locks up the formes and has a detestable trick of doing it at least ten minutes too soon. One cannot say much, but one thinks a good deal. Of the old Staff of '82, the foreman, perhaps three other hands and myself are the sole survivors. And now I am on the Staff no longer. No word of mine can make the old wheels spin, and Mahmud would only grin if I rated him for his sins. It isn't a nice feeling, but I know it will be worse this evening among the men at the Hall and the Club.

Into the office and the piles of the dusty exchanges, to fall over the eternal *duftri* and to watch with envy the loaded and littered tables. There is a long talk here – talk of the old days, reminiscence of catchwords, bygone practical jokes, and all the intimacies, squabbles and crises between two yoke mates for years and then – it had to come, but it hurt – 'Well I must get through the *dak** old man. Can you give us something while you're here?'

'"*You* give *us*." Yes, I think so. An epic if I had it in hand.' 'There is no demand for epics in the Punjab; men live them: but anything else will do.' So, back again with the 'You give us' rankling in my breast. Yet, it was absurd to think that a man would sit down and get back to work for a day or two, feel the snap of the shears again, stir up the 'Kingdom of Bombay'* with irreverent jests, battle with the *Englishman* over Capua and the Exodus,* and ask Madras whether it had an army,* and if so, how many. That time is over, rightly and properly so; but one can still do a little work for one's own country otherwhere than on the old staff. I comforted myself with that thought, and went off to the happy hunting grounds in the city.

The Lahore Municipality have sold the Taksali Gate for brickwork, leaving an ugly scar in the city wall. Gentlemen, whose souls would be dear at one brick a piece, you have done a sin; for that gate was built like the Pyramids. It had little beauty save of age and time, but while it stood it was full of beautiful light and shade, corners where an idle man could plant his charpoy* and dream, niches where the burnished doves sat in the hot hours and the kine of the city used to troop under its arch twice a day making a golden haze of dust without before they plunged into the cool darkness within. You could have bought bricks from the potter, but you will never build another Taksali Gate.

As second wind to a runner, or wine to a wearied man, was this second view of the city of Lahore – the oldest and surely the most picturesque city in the world. Thomas – of the K.O.S.B.'s* – was on guard at the main gate of the Fort (I wonder which of us two best knew the guardroom on the wall)* and the sunlight was splashing the mouldering tile work of the main face – the gay tile-wrought angels and elephants of Akbar.* The minars of Shadera where Jahangir* lies dead, and with him the memories of many moonlight picnics and wild words under the roses, showed above the belt of green by the Ravi. Thomas – a spot of vermillion – was loafing down the sunk way to the gate, his dog at his heels. Thomas with a *chilumchee** and bare headed – will nothing teach Thomas that he must not play even with the cold weather sun? – was scuffling from barrack to barrack, and Thomas (fever stricken Thomas) in his great coat was hanging over the balcony of the hospital, half a dozen superb Pathan soldiers in undress were swinging across the path by the glaring native guard room where Sikh sepoys rested near their speckless rifles, rising to salute and standing one bar of blood red against the whitewashed wall. It is awful to think that in England they have never seen any of the primary colours, and that they know nothing of drapery, the folds of well worn unsewn clothing that falls in great laps and curves, and gathered round the neck and under the armpit in robes of richest deep shadowed wrinkles. The square of the Naulakha pavilion* ached in the sunshine, and there tramping across the white marble, his belt well down over his hips, his coat open and his helmet at the back of his head, was Thomas – affable and a citizen of the world – Thomas with four years service and very pronounced views on men and things. We talked together sitting under the painted, mirror-inlaid ceilings till he said with cheerful irrelevance that it was near canteen opening time. O Thomas, Thomas! to think that I should have been taken in by that stale old trick. But it was Simla beer, and no muddy English porter.

There was a glimpse of the fort barrack room with its monstrous understrutting of masonry – and the spider-legged cots disposed in the hall of dead kings, the pillars of black and white marble defiled with whitewash, and the marvellous painted relief work daubed out of all knowledge. In the vast cool silence of this echoing hall, Thomas in every stage of undress came and went; and Thomas's dog lay on the cot and barked. The verandah arches showed pure raw sunlight and blue, and Thomas stood there in red, the points of light twinkling off his accoutrements as he went to relieve guard. It was home indeed!

Out of the fort into the city, across the ground, where the cavalry camped on the night of the Mohurrum riots* – how long ago? Is there 'Captain, Colonel or knight at arms'* who remembers a scandalous night on an open gallery when the swords of fifteen skylarking subalterns came near to being thrown into the Fort ditch? Here, by the dusty outskirts was the spot where the troopers cut across the track of an infuriated procession of Muslims. Here at the corner of the Roshnai Gate* they headed off a *tazia*,* and it was at the Soneri Musjid* that horse and foot stuck fast in the roaring press – that was a night among many nights and of those who were there, none remain except – a Globe Trotter.

If the Civil station hinted at the memories of years, the city shouted them aloud. House upon piled house, the time worn wood tracery standing askew on the rotten brickwork, well gulley mouth, ruinous dead wall and crumbling heap of sheer stark red-rotten rubbish overrun by the crowd, the cattle and the asses – all spoke with the voice of the years. Here lived the Jews of Shushan,* there, arrogant and unashamed was Lalun's naughty little house,* Azizan of the Douri Bagh* was a little beyond, and the house of Suddhoo was not far off the ringing roaring gulley of the coppersmiths, where the lean traders sat by piles of beaten gold vessels selling the splendour of the East for a few annas. Here were the Pathan horse-dealers chattering with the seal cutters for a new signet ring. Not till one understands in some small measure the heart of the city, does one realise how much the poorest country in the world has to spend on fripperies – four anna embroidered caps for the babies, cheap jewellry, bats and stumps (a new industry since my time – cricket* is more than ever naturalised with us), kites, cheap lithographs of the gods, tinsel-stuck shoes and slippers, necklaces, beads, mirror-rings and a hundred other toys. Here and there through the jostling crowd where buffalo calves and led ponies share all the rights of way with men, a face passes that I know, and once or twice an old friend stops me to give greeting. The Dubbi Bazaar is full of old friends, from the fat bunnia* among the turmeric heaps to the policeman with the *kullam** and the green-glazed inkpot in his hand. They don't know me, but I know them.

How shall one describe the sun-lit river bed of people whose daily passage has oil polished the wooden posts of the shop boards, smoothed the angles of the brickwork and faced the very ground with glair as a glacier polishes a rock. As if its own beauty were not enough, the dyers have spread filmy muslins of palest blue and pink across the street, and you look upon the old witchery of the old life through the pearl tinted mists of dawn. It is noon and past, and high overhead a boy's yellow paper kite is sawing and jigging into the restful blue like a big sulphur butterfly. Below there is the hurry and the shouting, the broken waves of colour, the deep shadows that heighten colour as velvet displays the diamond, and above all, and apart from all, as a prayer from a tortured heart, the mosque of Wazir Khan flings up its four minars to heaven? What need to cry five times a day that God is great?

At the shadow of the Delhi Gate* the picture of the city ends for the sight – to be graven deeper on the mind. Again comes the memory of the murmurs of a little city called London – a city where there is neither colour nor light nor air. Who was the particular *pagal** over there who wrote of extravagance of description and the Lord knows what else? If he were here now – between that broken-hatted, unbuttoned English loafer slinking red nosed in the sunshine and the dusty swaying plantain leaves of the Badami Bagh* – here when I stand looking at the heaped-up roofs of the city, the proud arch of the gateway and the torrent of turbulent colour that rolls beneath it, what would he write? And if he had seen that Jubilee night in '87, when the city of Lahore flamed out of the dusk as a jewelled queen from the door of the palace of night – dome, minaret, bastion, wall and house-front drawn in dotted fire, what he would have said of extravagance then? But who can show a blind man colour?

From 'A Matter of Fact'*

'What are you going to do?'

'Tell it as a lie.'

'Fiction?' This with the full-blooded disgust of a journalist for the illegitimate branch of the profession.

'You can call it that if you like. I shall call it a lie.'

And a lie it has become; for Truth is a naked lady, and if by accident she is drawn up from the bottom of the sea, it behoves a gentleman either to give her a print petticoat or to turn his face to the wall and vow that he did not see.

From a letter to Edward Lucas White,* 10–17 December 1893

. . . I've been scandalously neglecting my duties to follow – Euterpe,* I think, but it is one anyway of the nine harlots – these few weeks past experimenting with divers metres and various rhymes. The results serve excellent well to light fires and the work amuses me while it goes on. There's a heap in verse though apt to get out of hand – some of it – very. Do you know to the extent you ought the poems of Donne* who was Browning's great-great grandfather? I've been reading him again for the health of my spirit and – he is no small singer. Must have been a haughty and proud stomached individual in his life – with R.B.'s temperament for turning his mind clean upside down as it were a full bottle and letting the ideas get out as they best could. He is not very accessible – all of him – by reason of his statements which are occasionally free. There were giants in those days and it is profitable to read 'em – even Fletcher* who sat down before the human carcass and hammered out God knows how many thousand lines of high and disposed allegory – or Drayton – or Drummond.* These are not of the first ranks you say? No but they worked largely and gave all they had to their verses. Read 'em again and yet again.

Somewhere in the blue beyonds there's a big poem waiting for the man who can do it – the last supper at St. Julian's wasn't it – the sacrament supper when Drake got ready to slay his traitorous friend where Magellan had hanged certain of his mutineers – away down in the south, beyond the reach of God or man. The sailors of the *Pelican* looking on; Doughty cracking his very courteous jests;* the crazy ships rocking at the world's end and the block and the headsman.* Think of it! Why can't a man do everything he has a mind to by the mere wishing of it instead of having to dig like a badger before he can get out a decent couplet. I cannot work with ease or fluency worse luck: and the fluenter the thing looks from the outside the more worriment and sweat is it to me to evolve.

Don't you go a theorising. Concreteness in expression is all very well if you happen to like it but consider how it may be a stumbling block to another make of mind. For myself I love not to hear a spade called a spade because there are so many varieties of spade; and so by preference I say when writing of such: – a balance handle, cutting edge, Beaver Falls finishing or sod spade, as the case may be, but I can easily conceive how maddening that must be to a fellow who doesn't care two damns for anything except agricultural implements in the mass. Every man is too apt to make the law of his temperament the fly wheel of all creation. I confess I love accuracy of detail, inaccuracy being the besetting sin of a man I know pretty well;* and since my life has been mainly spent among men who have to be accurate in describing the things with which they deal – guns, horses, machines, canals, roads and the steps of judicial procedure – I assume all the world is equally concerned. Which it isn't! There's room for all manner and kind of expression in this Wale* but as things and lives and surroundings get more specialised I shouldn't wonder if there wasn't a drift towards saying things more clearly than the old laws allowed...

'The Last Rhyme of True Thomas'*

The King has called for priest and cup
    The King has taken spur and blade
To dub True Thomas a belted knight,
    And all for the sake o' the songs he made.

They have sought him high, they have sought him low,
    They have sought him over down and lea;
They have found him by the milk-white thorn
    That guards the gate o' Faerie.

'Twas bent beneath and blue above,
    Their eyes were held that they might not see
The kine that grazed beneath the knowes,
    Oh, they were the Queens o' Faerie!

'Now cease your song', the King he said,
    'Oh, cease your song and get you dight
To vow your vow and watch your arms,
    For I will dub you a belted knight.

'The Last Rhyme of True Thomas'

For I will give you a horse o' pride,
    Wi' blazon and spur and page and squire;
Wi' keep and tail and seizin and law,
    And land to hold at your desire.'

True Thomas smiled above his harp,
    And turned his face to the naked sky,
Where, blown before the wastrel wind,
    The thistle-down she floated by.

'I ha' vowed my vow in another place,
    And bitter oath it was to me,
I ha' watched my arms the lee-long night,
    Where five-score fighting men would flee.

My lance is tipped o' the hammered flame,
    My shield is beat o' the moonlight cold;
And I won my spurs in the Middle World,
    A thousand fathom beneath the mould.

And what should I make wi' a horse o' pride,
    And what should I make wi' a sword so brown,
But spill the rings o' the Gentle Folk
    And flyte my kin in the Fairy Town?

And what should I make wi' blazon and belt,
    Wi' keep and tail and seizin and fee,
And what should I do wi' page and squire
    That am a king in my own countrie?

For I send east and I send west,
    And I send as far as my will may flee,
By dawn and dusk and the drinking rain,
    And syne my Sendings return to me.

They come wi' news of the groanin' earth,
    They come wi' news o' the roarin' sea,

Wi' word of Spirit and Ghost and Flesh,
    And man, that's mazed among the three.

The King he bit his nether lip,
    And smote his hand upon his knee:
'By the faith o' my soul, True Thomas', he said,
    'Ye waste no wit in courtesie!

As I desire, unto my pride,
    Can I make Earls by three and three,
To run before and ride behind
    And serve the sons o' my body.'

'And what care I for your row-foot earls
    Or all the sons o' your body?
Before they win to the Pride o' Name,
    I trow they all ask leave o' me.

For I make Honour wi' muckle mouth,
    As I make Shame wi' mincin' feet,
To sing wi' the priests at the market-cross,
    Or run wi' the dogs in the naked street.

And some they give me the good red gold,
    And some they give me the white money,
And some they give me a clout o' meal,
    For they be people o' low degree.

And the song I sing for the counted gold
    The same I sing for the white money,
But best I sing for the clout o' meal
    That simple people given me.'

The King cast down a silver groat,
    A silver groat o' Scots money,
'If I come wi' a poor man's dole', he said,
    'True Thomas, will ye harp to me?'

'The Last Rhyme of True Thomas'

'Whenas I harp to the children small,
They press me close on either hand.
And who are you', True Thomas said,
'That you should ride while they must stand?

'Light down, light down from your horse o' pride,
I trow ye talk too loud and hie,
And I will make you a triple word,
And syne, if ye dare, ye shall 'noble me.'

He has lighted down from his horse o' pride,
And set his back against the stone.
'Now guard you well', True Thomas said,
'Ere I rax your heart from your breast-bone!'

True Thomas played upon his harp,
The fairy harp that couldna lee,
And the first least word the proud King heard,
It harpit the salt tear out o' his e'e.

'Oh, I see the love that I lost long syne,
I touch the hope that I may not see,
And all that I did o' hidden shame,
Like little snakes they hiss at me.

The sun is lost at noon – at noon!
The dread o' doom has grippit me.
True Thomas, hide me under your cloak,
God wot, I'm little fit to dee!'

'Twas bent beneath and blue above –
'Twas open field and running flood –
Where, hot on heath and dyke and wall,
The high sun warmed the adder's brood.

'Lie down, lie down', True Thomas said.
'The God shall judge when all is done.

But I will bring you a better word
And lift the cloud that I laid on.'

True Thomas played upon his harp,
That birled and brattled to his hand,
And the next least word True Thomas made,
It garred the King take horse and brand.

'Oh, I hear the tread o' the fighting-men,
I see the sun on splent and spear,
I mark the arrow outen the fern
That flies so low and sings so clear!

Advance my standards in that war,
And bid my good knights prick and ride;
The gled shall watch as fierce a fight
As e'er was fought on the Border side!'

'Twas bent beneath and blue above,
'Twas nodding grass and naked sky,
Where, ringing up the wastrel wind,
The eyass stooped upon the pye.

True Thomas sighed above his harp,
And turned the song on the midmost string;
And the last least word True Thomas made,
He harpit his dead youth back to the King.

'Now I am prince, and I do well
To love my love withouten fear;
To walk wi' man in fellowship,
And breathe my horse behind the deer.

My hounds they bay unto the death,
The buck has couched beyond the burn,
My love she waits at her window
To wash my hands when I return.

For that I live am I content
(Oh! I have seen my true love's eyes)
To stand wi' Adam in Eden-glade,
And run in the woods o' Paradise!'

'Twas nodding grass and naked sky,
'Twas blue above and bent below,
Where, checked against the wastrel wind,
The red deer belled to call the doe.

True Thomas laid his harp away,
And louted low at the saddle-side;
He has taken stirrup and hauden rein,
And set the King on his horse o' pride.

'Sleep ye or wake', True Thomas said,
'That sit so still, that muse so long;
Sleep ye or wake? – till the latter sleep
I trow ye'll not forget my song.

I ha' harpit a shadow out o' the sun
To stand before your face and cry;
I ha' armed the earth beneath your heel,
And over your head I ha' dusked the sky.

I ha' harpit ye up to the throne o' God,
I ha' harpit your midmost soul in three;
I ha' harpit ye down to the Hinges o' Hell,
And – ye – would – make – a Knight o' me!'

From a letter to Robert Barr,* 1 July 1894

. . . Now, how can a man give what he hasn't got? If a Mulvaney tale* were written just for folk to read and not because I *had* to write it, it wouldn't be a Mulvaney tale anyway and I'd be deliberately firing at an old target for the sake of making bulls eyes. That way lies death. But the other business is purely delightful. With two whole years wherein to work your wicked will on the Idler and only a 50% raise to see, it ought to be as easy as falling off a log (though, at this point, I hear you swear aloud). I perceive I must pay good heed to my tales. Apropos, there's a thing on the market (about 5000) called 'Leaves from a Winter Notebook'* which, mark you, is the *only* authentic account up to date of my surroundings in Brattleboro' – written by these lily fingers. It's all about the snow and the seasons and the choppers. A. P. W[att] knows where the copy is. I took a deal of trouble over it; and if you can meet him I'll send our photos of Brattleboro' for reproduction. . .

From a letter to Edward Everett Hale,* 16 January 1895

. . . Praise from you is praise to be proud of and henceforward I shall look upon the *Jungle Book* with respect. There is to be a companion collection* issued this fall if all goes well and I can only hope that it will please you.

The idea of beast-tales seems to me new in that it is a most ancient and long forgotten idea. The really fascinating tales are those that the Bodhisat tells* of his previous incarnations ending always with the beautiful moral. Most of the native hunters in India today think pretty much along the lines of an animal's brain and I have 'cribbed' freely* from their tales. . .

From a letter to Mary Mapes Dodge,* 30 November 1895

Dear Mrs Dodge,

I have written a childs tale* for *St Nick* and it has turned out a man's tale and I am very mad at it. It is very much of a man's tale and that makes me even madder. I don't want to play in anybody's yard just now, and I feel that I am not likely to have anything for the March number. One doesn't – at least *I* don't – say 'I will write a tale for *St Nick* of so many words.' One waits till a golden notion arrives and then the Saint is pleased. I want to do a tale in several parts* but it won't come out good and so I have to sit still. . .

Letter to Miss Welman,* 14 August 1897

Dear Miss Welman,

Thank you very much for your note from Newquay saying that you liked the Jungle-Books. But really and truly I *can't* write any more of them – at least not just now and if I wrote a third Jungle-Book and a Fourth

Jungle-Book why then I should have to write a Fifth Junglebook [sic] and perhaps my own little daughter would ask me to write a sixth and my own other little daughter would make me write a Seventh. I should be writing nothing but Jungle-books and some of them would be dull and some would be flat and some would be stuffy and you would not care for them.

That is why I don't write any more Jungle-books but I hope some day to do some stories not about the Jungle* but about other animals that may make you laugh, and I am

Yours very sincerely
Rudyard Kipling

Preface to 'The Just So Stories',* December 1897

Some stories are meant to be read quietly and some stories are meant to be told aloud. Some stories are only proper for rainy mornings, and some for long, hot afternoons when one is lying in the open, and some stories are bedtime stories. All the Blue Skalallatoot* stories are morning tales (I do not know why, but that is what Effie says). All the stories about Orvin Sylvester Woodsey,* the left-over New England fairy who did not think it well-seen to fly, and who used patent labour-saving devices instead of charms, are afternoon stories because they were generally told in the shade of the woods. You could alter and change these tales as much as you pleased; but in the evening there were stories meant to put Effie to sleep, and you were not allowed to alter those by one single little word. They had to be told just so; or Effie would wake up and put back the missing sentence. So at last they came to be like charms, all three of them, – the whale tale, the camel tale and the rhinoceros tale. Of course little people are not all alike, but I think if you catch some Effie rather tired and rather sleepy at the end of the day, and if you begin in a low voice and tell the tales precisely as I have written them down, you will find that Effie will presently curl up and go to sleep.

Now, this is the first tale, and it tells how the whale got his tiny throat:– . . .

From *A Fleet in Being,** Note VI: 'The Beauty of Battleships'

Do not believe what people tell you of the ugliness of steam, nor join those who lament the old sailing days. There is one beauty of the sun and another of the moon, and we must be thankful for both. A modern man-of-war photographed in severe profile is not engaging; but you should see her with the life hot in her, head-on across a heavy swell. The ram-bow draws upward and outward in a stately sweep. There is no ruck of figure-head, bow-timbers or bowsprit-fittings to distract the eye from its outline or the beautiful curves that mark its melting into the full bosom of the ship. It hangs dripping an instant, then, quietly and cleanly as a tempered knife, slices into the hollow of the swell, down and down till the surprised sea spits off in foam about the hawse-holes. As the ship rolls in her descent you can watch curve after new curve revealed, humouring and coaxing the water. When she recovers her step, the long sucking hollow of her own wave discloses just enough of her shape to make you wish to see more. In harbour, the still waterline, hard as the collar of a tailor-made jacket, hides that vision; but when she dances the Big Sea Dance, she is as different from her Portsmouth shilling photograph as is the matron in a macintosh from the same lady at a ball. Swaying a little in her gait, drunk with sheer delight of movement, perfectly apt for the work in hand, and in every line of her rejoicing that she is doing it, she shows, to these eyes at least, a miracle of grace and beauty. Her sides are smooth as a water-worn pebble, curved and moulded as the sea loves to have them. Where the box-sponsioned, over-hanging, treble-turreted ships of some other navies hammer and batter into an element they do not understand, she, clean, cool, and sweet, uses it to her own advantage. The days are over for us when men piled baronial keeps, flat-irons, candlesticks and Doré towers on floating platforms. The New Navy offers to the sea precisely as much to take hold of as the trim level-headed woman with generations of inherited experience offers to society. It is the provincial, aggressive, uncompromising, angular, full of excellently unpractical ideas, who is hurt, and jarred, and rasped in that whirl. In other words, she is not a good sea-boat and cannot work her guns in all weathers.

Epigraph to ch. viii of *Kim**

Something I owe to the soil that grew –
More to the life that fed –
But most to Allah Who gave me two
Separate sides to my head.

'Literature'

I would go without shirts or shoes,
Friends, tobacco or bread
Rather than for an instant lose
Either side of my head.

'Literature'*

I am Earth, overtaking all things except Words. They alone escape me. Therefore, I lie heavy on their makers.*

A great and, I frankly admit, a somewhat terrifying honour has come to me; but I think, compliments apart, that the most case-hardened worker in letters, speaking to such an assembly as this, must recognise the gulf that separates even the least of those who do things worthy to be written about from even the best of those who have written things worthy of being talked about.

There is an ancient legend which tells us that when a man first achieved a most notable deed he wished to explain to his Tribe what he had done. As soon as he began to speak, however, he was smitten with dumbness, he lacked words, and sat down. Then there arose – according to the story – a masterless man, one who had taken no part in the action of his fellow, who had no special virtues, but who was afflicted – that is the phrase – with the magic of the necessary word. He saw; he told; he described the merits of the notable deed in such a fashion, we are assured, that the words 'became alive and walked up and down in the hearts of all his hearers'.* Thereupon, the Tribe seeing that the words were certainly alive, and fearing lest the man with the words would hand down untrue tales about them to their children, took and killed him. But, later, they saw that the magic was in the words, not in the man.

We have progressed in many directions since the time of this early and destructive criticism, but, so far, we do not seem to have found a sufficient substitute for the necessary word as the final record to which all achievement must look. Even today, when all is done, those who have done it must wait until all has been said by the masterless man with the words. It is certain that the overwhelming bulk of those words will perish in the future as they have perished in the past; but it is true that a minute fraction will continue to exist, and by the light of these words, and by that light only, will our children be able to judge of the phases of our generation. Now we desire beyond all things to stand well with our children; but when our story comes to be told we do not know who will have the telling of it. We are too close to the tellers; there are many tellers and they are all talking together; and, even if we know them, we must not kill them. But the old and terrible instinct which taught our ancestors to kill the original story-teller warns us that we shall not be far wrong if we challenge any man who shows signs of being afflicted with the magic of the necessary word. May not this be the reason why, without any special legislation on its behalf, Literature has always stood a little outside the law as the one calling that is absolutely free – free in the sense that it needs no protection? For instance, if, as occasionally happens, a Judge makes a bad law, or a surgeon a bad operation, or a manufacturer makes bad food, criticism upon their actions is by law and custom confined to comparatively narrow limits. But if a man, as occasionally happens, makes a bad book, there is no limit to the criticism that may be directed against it. And this is perfectly as it should be. The world recognises that little things like bad law, bad surgery and bad food, affect only the cheapest commodity that we know about – human life. Therefore, in these circumstances, men can afford to be swayed by pity for the offender, by interest in his family, by fear, or loyalty, or respect for the organisation he represents, or even by a desire to do him justice. But when the question is of words – words that may become alive and walk up and down in the hearts of the hearers – it is then that this world of ours, which is disposed to take an interest in his future, feels instinctively that it is better that a thousand innocent people should be punished rather than that one guilty word should be preserved, carrying that which is an untrue tale of the Tribe. The chances, of course, are almost astronomically remote that any given tale will survive for so long as it takes an oak to grow to timber size. But that guiding instinct warns us not to trust to chance a matter of the supremest concern. In this durable record, if anything short of indisputable and undistilled truth be seen there, we all feel, 'How shall our achievements profit us?' The Record of the Tribe is its enduring literature.

The magic of Literature lies in the words, and not in any man. Witness, a thousand excellent, strenuous words can leave us quite cold or put us to sleep, whereas a bare half-hundred words breathed upon by some man in his agony, or in his exaltation, or in his idleness, ten generations ago, can still lead whole nations into and out of captivity; can open to us the doors of the Three Worlds, or stir us so intolerably that we can scarcely abide to look at our own souls. It is a miracle – one that happens very seldom. But secretly each one of the masterless men with the words has hope, or has had hope, that the miracle may be wrought again through him.

And why not? If a tinker in Bedford Gaol;* if a pamphleteering shopkeeper,* pilloried in London; if a muzzy Scot;* if a despised German Jew;* or a condemned French thief,* or an English Admiralty official* with a taste for letters can be miraculously afflicted with the magic of the necessary word, why not any man at any time? Our world, which is only concerned in the perpetuation of the record, sanctions that hope just as kindly and just as cruelly as Nature sanctions love.

All it suggests is that the man with the Words shall wait upon the man of achievement, and step by step with him try to tell the story to the Tribe. All it demands is that the magic of every word shall be tried out to the uttermost by every means, fair or foul, that the mind of man can suggest. There is no room, and the world insists there shall be no room, for pity, for mercy, for respect, for fear, or even for loyalty between man and his fellow-man, when the record of the Tribe comes to be written. That record must satisfy, at all costs to the word and to the man behind the word. It must satisfy alike the keenest vanity and the deepest self-knowledge of the present; it must satisfy also the most shameless curiosity of the future. When it has done this it is literature of which it will be said, in due time, that it fitly represents its age. I say in due time because ages, like individuals, do not always appreciate the merits of a record that purports to represent them. The trouble is that one always expects just a little more out of a thing than one puts into it. Whether it be an age or an individual, one is always a little pained and a little pessimistic to find that all one gets back is just one's bare deserts. This is a difficulty as old as Literature.

A little incident that came within my experience a while ago shows that that difficulty is always being raised by the most unexpected people all about the world. It happened in a land where the magic of words is peculiarly potent and far-reaching, that there was a Tribe that wanted rain, and the rain-doctors set about getting it. To a certain extent the rain-doctors succeeded. But the rain their magic brought was not a full driving downpour that tells of larger prosperity; it was patchy, local, circumscribed and uncertain. There were unhealthy little squalls blowing about the country and doing damage. Whole districts were flooded out by waterspouts, and other districts annoyed by trickling showers, soon dried by the sun. And so the Tribe went to the rain-doctors, being very angry, and they said, 'What is this rain that you make? You did not make rain like this in the time of our fathers. What have you been doing?' And the rain-doctors said, 'We have been making our proper magic. Supposing you tell us what you have been doing lately?' And the Tribe said, 'Oh, our head-men have been running about hunting jackals, and our little people have been running about chasing grasshoppers! What has that to do with your rain-making?' 'It has everything to do with it', said the rain-doctors. 'Just so long as your head-men run about hunting jackals, and just so long as your little people run about chasing grasshoppers, just so long will the rain fall in this manner.'

'The Claims of Art'*

> I sought beauty, but men would not see. May their eyes now fall sometimes upon my wife and babe.

Some few years ago – in fact, before the Artists' General Benevolent Institution was founded – King Solomon, speaking of things in general, said that the race was not to the swift,* nor the battle to the strong. Speaking of Art in particular, he said: 'Nor yet favour to men of skill; but Time and Chance happeneth to them all.' Solomon was a generous patron of the arts, and the original man of letters. Nobody has improved on his remark; and you may have noticed that nobody has improved on the state of affairs that gave rise to it. There must be as many men nowadays as there were in Solomon's time whose skill has not found favour, and I should like to try and interest you in the fate of a few of them.

In an enlightened and democratic age like ours, it is possible to say that, if a man's skill has not found favour with the public, the blame must lie with the man, or with the skill. This is a pretty doctrine. I wish I could subscribe to it myself. There are, however, men who devote their skill to producing things and expressing ideas for which the public has no present need. Being artists, these men must needs do the work that is laid upon them to do, and while they are doing it they are apt to overlook a number of important worldly considerations. It is reprehensible, of course – and, worse than reprehensible, it is unbusinesslike – but it happens; and it happens more frequently than people would imagine. The Callings are unlike the Professions. No one embraces the career of Art, any more than one enters Science or the Services, with the direct idea of making money. The material rewards of Art are oftenest so small that men may be forgiven if they sacrifice themselves and their belongings to make an appeal to the next generation, while they neglect their own. These, then, are the men who do not very greatly care whether their skill finds immediate favour or not. They have elected to take their chance with time to come; but the records of the Institution and the Orphan Fund will tell you that their descendants have to take certain or uncertain chances *now*.

Besides these, there are the others whose skill, however much they may desire it, has not found favour. Time has not given them their chance; their skill has not found favour; and by the world's verdict they have not achieved success.

The world's verdict is, of course, of great financial value. The verdict of our fellow-craftsmen is a little nearer the facts of the case. Thank goodness, we all count among our friends delightful men and women whose skill has not found favour, but to whose skill, sympathy, humour and, above all, knowledge, we owe more than we realise. It may be that the very generosity of soul which impelled them to lavish themselves so unstintingly upon their associates has stood in the way of their more evident advancement, and that some of these good spirits are now facing – I won't say defeat: there is no abiding defeat in Art – but the outer appearance of defeat. If this be so, it is a comfortable thought that an organisation exists which, by our good-will, can help them as quietly and as unostentatiously as they helped us. For their lot is hard!

It is much pleasanter to contemplate the man whose skill has found favour and keeps it. One is almost hypnotised into the belief that here, at least, Time and Chance have been eliminated by the progress of modern civilisation. Unluckily, last year's report of the Institution shows that time and chance are as uncontrolled a brace of Impressionists as ever they were – rather brutal in their methods, but deadly sure in their effects. The report for last year is, quite rightly, a discreetly veiled document. It is a twelvemonth's casualty-list among a very small proportion of those who set out to make life beautiful, and found it very bitter. You can see that it covers several of the calamities that can overtake a working-man – want, disease, break-down, madness and death. Your imagination can fill in the background.

And, talking of imagination, do you know the Black Thought, gentlemen? I am loth to remind you of it in this fenced and pleasant place, but it is the one emotion that all men of imagination have in common. It is a horror of great darkness that drops upon a man unbidden, and drives him to think lucidly, connectedly, with Cruikshank* detail, of all the accidents whereby, through no fault of his own, he may be cut off from his work, and forced to leave those he loves defenceless to the world. You know the Black Thought, gentlemen? It possesses some men in the dead of night; some in the sunshine; some when they are setting their palettes; some when they are stropping their razors; but only the very young, the very sound, and the very single, are exempt.

If we look at this report again, we shall see that our blackest forebodings about our eyes, and our brain, and our hand, and our body, and our soul by which we live and work, have been realised last year in the case of these two hundred and two fellow-workers. *We* have only heard the bullets of Time and Chance. These others have had to stop them with their bodies.

Gentlemen, I have to propose Prosperity to the Artists' General Benevolent Association. Will you please respond to it?

Unpublished speech at Trinity College,* Cambridge, 17 June 1908.

Several of those who have been honoured today* are sons or nephews of this university but there remain some of us who were not so fortunate as* to pass through the Schools where learning is to be had unmixed. We have been compelled to make our small and unscientific purchases of it in the open market where it is often grossly adulterated with expediency and prejudice.

Yet we have all known and proved and even tried certain men who have been trained under your more enviable dispensation. We have worked with or against* such men, well taught not to respond too immediately or too unreservedly to every external impulse; so that in time of crisis their actions might be regulated rather by reason than by the more obvious emotions.

Normally we can know but little at first hand of the atmosphere* which bred this habit of mental continence or – I speak for myself – of the classic influences which underlie that atmosphere. But the men who have profited through* both atmosphere and influence have shown us through their lives as much as by their conversation* that in those same classics are to be found a great store of startlingly modern facts collected and illustrated a very long time ago, by persons of large experience and no small literary powers. The facts include all the things* which are at first emphatically denied, and at last unwillingly admitted by each succeeding generation of mortals. The facts are that if a man thrusts his* hand into a fire his hand will be burnt; that if he grasps a naked sword* by the blade his hand will be cut and that no body of men (or women) however large or large minded are any more exempt from the consequences of their own acts than the loneliest* figure in a Greek play. The acceptance of these facts and all that acceptance implies is knowledge which has always been confined to the few. It is possible though that the stored wisdom of the schools and the rough and ready reckoning of the marketplace come* at long last to much the same – that by different roads men of diverse* temperament and activities may reach the same end. Certainly the roads that have led us here are widely divergent. One of us has spent his days in making life more beautiful; others have equally striven to make death more instant and unlovely; and others again according to their lights have chased rainbows. We can one and all rejoice to find that the hard conclusions we were forced to come to at our own charges were fearlessly set out very long ago and for ages have been unbrokenly taught here to such as were worthy to understand them. It is a source of great pride and gratitude to us that your ancient fortress of discipline, where mens [sic] souls are set and tempered, against Life, should have seen fit to bestow upon us such signal marks of her favour.

From a letter to Miss M. Hooper* [March 1910]

My dear Miss Hooper,

In reply to your exceedingly interesting letter *re* the reference to Norse mythology in *The Knife and the Naked Chalk** – I am free to admit that when I originally wrote the tale I did not allude specifically to Thor and Fenris.* But a low friend of mine from London (her name was Maggie something or other) had the tale read to her and certain remarks which *she* made on the subject decided me, in vulgar language, to go nap on Thor and the Fenris legend!!

My dear Maggie, fancy not remembering that *you* nursed the (o)pinion that impelled that steal!!* And there's reason when you come to think of it that the flintworkers should hold their deliverer to be Thor. Put the flint age, as we honestly can, some few score thousand years back – before Norse mythology had grown, when man's deadliest foe was 'The Beast'. What was the greatest thing a Hero could do? Obviously sacrifice himself to the Beast in some fashion for the good of his tribe and I assume that the Flintworkers had legends of one dim and distant hero (always 'up yonder' as heroes are) who in binding the Beast, the incarnation of all evil – lost his hand. Naturally when *my* man parts with his eye he is compared to Thor – Tyr – Tir – Thu – the great one up North – and when he *also* produces a veritable knife that goes through and into the Beast like a pin into a pat of butter, the next most obvious step is to cry:– 'This *is* Tyr himself!' or as the tribe sang, walking over the downs in the evening, all clanking their new knives together –

> Room for his shadow on the grass – let it pass!
> 	To left and right stand clear!
> This is the buyer of the Blade! Be afraid!
> *This* is the great God Tyr! . . .*

'The Uses of Reading'*

A. 'When I heard thy words, my Father, I almost fell asleep through weariness.' B. 'Had I foreseen that sleep, my Son, I would have put aside all else to have pleased thee alone.'

You have done me the honour of asking me to read a paper to your Society this evening. Before I begin, I may as well confess that this is the first time I have ever read a paper in school since I was a member of the Natural History Society at my old school, when, for reasons which I need not explain to you, I had to read a paper whether I liked it or not.

It is one thing to write and quite another to read. And that brings me directly to what I wanted to speak about – which is the use and value of a little reading.

There is, or there was, an idea that reading in itself is a virtuous and holy deed. I can't quite agree with this, because it seems to me that the mere fact of a man's being fond of reading proves nothing one way or another. He may be constitutionally lazy; or he may be overstrained, and so take refuge in a book to rest himself. He may be full of curiosity and wonder about the life on which he is just entering; and for that reason may plunge into any and every book he can lay hands on, in order to get information about things that are puzzling him, or frightening him, or interesting him.

Now I am a very long way from saying that Literature ought to be a chief or a leading interest in most men's lives, or even in the life of a nation. But a man who goes into life with no knowledge of the literature of his own country and without a certain acquaintance with the classics and the value of words, is as heavily handicapped as a man who takes up sports or games without knowing what has been done in these particular sports or games, before he came on the scene. He doesn't know the records and so he can't have any standards. I have a book at home that gives a summary, with diagrams, of practically every attempt at perpetual-motion machines that have ever been invented for the last two hundred years. It was compiled for the purpose of saving inventors trouble; and the compiler says in his preface: 'One of the grossest fallacies of the mind is that of taking for granted that ideas of mechanical construction, apparently the result of accident, must of necessity be quite original. The most doubtful originality is that which the inventor attributes to his ignorance of all previous plans coupled with his isolated position in life.'*

There you have precisely the position of the man who has no knowledge of Literature – ignorant, that is, of all previous plans. Such a man is more likely than not to waste his own time and the patience of his friends – perhaps even to endanger the safety of the community – by inventing schemes for the conduct of his own, or his neighbours' affairs, which have been tried, found wanting, and laid aside any time these thousand years; and the record of which – the diagram and specification, so to say, of which – he could turn to if he had only taken the trouble to read.

One of the hardest things to realise, specially for a young man, is that our forefathers were living men who really knew something. I would go further and say they knew a very great deal. Indeed, I should not be surprised if they knew quite as much as we do about the things that really concern men. What each generation forgets is that, while the words which it uses to describe ideas are always changing, the ideas themselves do not change so quickly, nor are those ideas in any sense new.

If we pay no attention to words whatever, we may become like the isolated gentleman who invents a new perpetual-motion machine on old lines in ignorance of all previous plans, and then is surprised that it doesn't work. If we confine our attention entirely to the slang of the day – that is to say, if we devote ourselves exclusively to modern literature – we get to think the world is progressing when it is only repeating itself. In both cases we are likely to be deceived, and what is more important, to deceive others. Therefore, it is advisable for us in our own interests, quite apart from considerations of personal amusement, to concern ourselves occasionally with a certain amount of our national literature drawn from all ages. I say from all ages, because it is only when one reads what men wrote long ago that one realises how absolutely modern the best of the old things are.

About fifteen hundred years ago some early Anglo-Saxon writer* saw, or heard about (I imagine in those days men had generally seen what they wrote about), the ruins of an old Roman city half buried and going to pieces in the jungle somewhere in the south of England; with its walls split and falling; its roofs stripped of its tiles; its towers fallen, and all its luxurious baths and heating arrangements open to the air. The man begins to wonder about the people who built all this magnificence and he says:

Earth's grasp holdeth
The mighty workmen
Worn away, lorn away [geworen forloren]
In the grip of the grave.

Then he thinks of the strong man who commanded the place when it was first built – most likely it was a Roman prefect – and he describes him:

Gorgeous and gold-bright,
Gaudily jewelled,
Haughty and wine-hot,
Shining in armour.

And as the poem goes on, we can almost see the band of Anglo-Saxon hunters or raiders, who have scrambled through the bushes, and stand, picking the thorns out of their legs, in the presence of this great, mysterious dead city. There is one touch which is exactly what hot and dirty men *would* think, when they saw all the paraphernalia of the old Roman baths:

There stood courts of stone.
The steam hotly rushed,
With a wide eddy,

Between shut walls.
There were the baths
Hot to bathe in.
That was a boon indeed!

The whole thing is as modern as to-day's evening paper – but with a freshness and a directness and a simplicity that isn't common in modern work.

I'll take another instance. About five hundred years ago, Chaucer wrote a poem* on how a man ought to manage his life. The last verse of it – it is only three verses long – runs:

That thee is sent receive in buxomnesse [be thankful for what you get];
The wrestling of this world asketh a fall.
Here is no home – here is but wildernesse:
Forth pilgrime – forth beast from out thy stall!
Look up on high and thanke the God of all.
Weive thy lusts and let thy ghost lead thee [That means, keep yourself
in hand and trust your spirit]
And truth shall thee deliver, it is no drede.

The whole thing absolutely covers the few facts in life that really matter.

A last instance. In the course of his wonderful career, Sir Walter Raleigh* had occasion to write his opinion, as you may have to some day, on the value of forts for coast and harbour defence. Well, his practical experience showed him, what we forgot and only realised a few years ago, that mere forts on the land aren't enough to maintain an effective defence or blockade, unless they are supported by ships. And he says so. But he doesn't say it as you and I would. For some inscrutable reason Elizabethans, apparently, could not put pen to paper without producing uncommonly good prose. So he gives his reasons and his experiences thus: 'In this age a valiant and judicious man-of-war will not fear to pass by the best appointed fort of Europe, with the help of a good tide and a leading gale of wind; no, though forty pieces of great artillery open their mouths against him, and threaten to tear him in pieces. It was not long since, that the Duke of Parma, besieging Antwerp and finding no possibility to master it otherwise than by famine, laid his cannon on the bank of the river so well to purpose that he thought it impossible for the least boat to pass. Yet the

Hollanders and Zeelanders, not blown up by any wind of glory, but coming to find a good market for their butter and cheese – even the poor men attending their profit, when all things were extreme dear at Antwerp – passed in boats of ten or twelve tun, by the mouth of the duke's cannon in despight of them, when a strong westerly wind and flood favoured them. As also, with a contrary wind and ebbing tide they returned back again. So he was forced in the end to build his stockade overthwart the river, to his marvellous trouble and charge. It is true, that where a fort is so set that there is no passing along beside it, or that ships are driven to turn upon a bow-line towards it, wanting all help of wind and tide; there, and in such places, it is of great use and fearful. Otherwise not.'

Here I have given you three specimens of not exactly modern literature in three different keys; the first dealing with a concrete thing seen and brought home to a man's mind; the second describing a man's thoughts on the conduct of his own soul; and the third a practical man's plans for dealing with an actual situation – a piece, that is, of pure intellect.

But it is very possible that when you come to read them, these three specimens may not appeal to you. No matter. That is just a question of temperament; and a man is no more to be blamed for not caring for certain forms of literature than he is for not thriving on certain forms of food.

But your choice is practically illimitable; for the Literature of our England is strewn from end to end with a prodigality that almost frightens one – strewn with gems and jewels and glories and beauties fitted to every conceivable need that can arise in the course of any human being's life. But we make very little use of them. That again is quite natural. If we could buy knowledge, prudence, forethought, and all the elementary virtues out of seven-penny editions of standard authors, we should long ago have become a race of unbearably perfect archangels. And we are still quite a little lower than the angels. None the less, it is possible that our reading, if so be we read wisely, may save us to a certain extent from some of the serious forms of trouble; or if we get into trouble, as we most certainly shall, may teach us how to come out of it decently . . .*

If a man brings a good mind to what he reads he may become, as it were, the spiritual descendant to some extent of great men, and this link, this spiritual hereditary tie, may help to just kick the beam in the right direction at a vital crisis; or may keep him from drifting through the long slack times when, so to speak, we are only fielding and no balls are coming our way.

You know those curious half-waking dreams that one dreams, about one's future – a sort of story without words of the things we mean to do later on? They shade off into a vision of a gloriously successful career in our chosen line with all the world at our feet, recognising at last what splendid fellows we were.* Then we forgive all our enemies, after we've got our feet on their necks; take our seat either as a Viceroy or a legislator or a Field-Marshal or some insignificant trifle of that kind – and then we wake! Sometimes the dreams have a knack of coming true. A man does achieve something out of the ordinary; finds himself saddled with tremendous responsibilities and expected to play up to a new part. Well, that is the time that he should have provided himself with all the knowledge and strength that can be drawn from noble books, so that whatever has happened to him may not be overwhelming nor unexpected. And to do that, to keep his soul fit for all chances, a man should associate at certain times in his soul (there is no need to tell everyone about it) with the best, the most balanced, the largest, finest and most honourable and capable minds of the past. It may be a snobbish way of putting it, but a man should know 'the right people' in the great world of books, and they'll help to show him what the world really means. Men will tell you that the days are over when one can suddenly be called to power and glory. Don't you believe it! A chance may open suddenly in front of one at a minute's notice. A man's superior may die and leave him in temporary charge of a district half the size of France with ten million people in it. A flood, a storm, an outbreak of sickness may change a man's position and outlook and responsibility between breakfast and lunch. One never knows one's luck; but one ought always to be ready for it. I have seen men very little over twenty get one chance and take it. To give you an instance, I happened to be in Bloemfontein after a 'regrettable incident' called Sanna's Post* – where we lost five or six hundred men and several guns in a little ambush. I met one of the survivors a few hours after the thing had happened. He had done very well in a losing game, and he had come out of it, looking exactly like a man after the last half of a really hectic footer game. His clothes were ripped to bits, but his temper was quite good. After he'd told his tale I said to him: 'What are we going to do about it?' He said: 'Oh, I don't know. "Thank Heaven we have within the land five hundred as good as they."'

Then he went off to report himself, and see if he could get on to the column that was going out in support. But not half an hour before I met him, I'd seen an agitated gentleman flogging a horse along the veldt and he had told me that the 'flower of the British Army had been destroyed'. Here were two men, under severe strain and excitement. One of them threw up a steadying quotation from the ancient, but quite modern, ballad of 'Chevy Chase'* and went on with his job. The other made bad worse by shouting what was nothing better than a newspaper scare head-line; and, judging by the rate he was travelling, I don't think he reported for duty that night.

And that brings me to what I fear you will find more than usually dull.

I have spoken already of the advisability of a man knowing something about the classics. I have no Greek. Mine stopped at a little Greek Testament on Monday morning by gaslight before breakfast, and I depend for the rest of my knowledge on Bohn's cribs.* But I got the ordinary allowance of Latin, ending with Virgil and Horace – specially Horace. I don't pretend that I liked it, any more than I should have liked anything else that purported to be education; but looking back at it now, it strikes me as valuable. I believe in the importance of a man getting some classics ground in to him in his youth even though, as far as his elders can see (but I don't think one's elders are quite the judges), there is no visible result. Men tell us that what we want nowadays is a modern and scientific education – something that will be of immediate use to a man in 'the battle of life'. They say that you could teach a child of twelve in a couple of terms as much Latin as the average public schoolboy carries away at the end of seven years; and the rest of the time could be devoted to studying modern languages and science and the things that are of immediate use to him. I haven't the least doubt you could. Any child of twelve could kodak any masterpiece of Greek sculpture in less time than the cleverest artist in the world could begin to get ready to draw it. Any bright-minded intelligent pride of a prep.-school could in two terms learn the twenty or thirty odds and ends of quotations, the half-remembered Latin tags, which represent what the bulk of us carry away from our schools. I know a man who did much better than this. He was a wonderful Greek scholar and at school and college he took every scholarship and gold medal that was in sight, and before he was twenty-five he was appointed lecturer to his own College. Then he called on one of the dons who was a bit of a philosopher as well as a scholar. The old man asked him a few polite questions. Then he said: 'You know Plato of course.' My friend in a modest way said he thought he did. He had an idea at the back of his head that he knew Plato rather better than most men of his time. 'Well', said the old man, 'what's it all about?'

My friend scratched his head a little. Then it slowly dawned on him that he literally and absolutely did not know what Plato was all about. He knew pretty much everything else connected with the gentleman, but to put it roughly, what Plato was after, what Plato's game was in the world, my friend did *not* know. Then he sat down and began to think what Plato was all about. He's still thinking.

I have a notion that our intelligent child of twelve would be rather like my college friend without my friend's willingness to go back and think. He would know his quotations probably more accurately than we do for a while; but I doubt if he would know what they were about. They would not be part of his system, incorporated into him in seven years. They would not come back to him unconsciously, and most certainly their spirit would not.

I attach a certain amount of importance to the spirit of a few old Latin tags and quotations. Some of them, not more than three lines long, give one the very essence of what a man ought to try to do. Others, equally short, let you understand, once and for all, the things that a man should not do – under any circumstances. There are others – bits of odes from Horace, they happen to be in my case – that make one realise in later life as no other words in any other tongue can, the brotherhood of mankind in time of sorrow or affliction. But men say that one can get the same stuff in an easier way and in a living tongue. They say there is no sense in dragging men up and down through grammar and construe for years and years, when at the last all they can produce ('produce' is a good word) is a translation that would make Virgil, Horace, or Cicero turn in their graves. Here is my defence of this alleged wicked waste of time. The reason why one has to parse and construe and grind at the dead tongues in which certain ideas are expressed, is *not* for the sake of what is called intellectual training – that may be given in other ways – but because only in that tongue is that idea expressed with absolute perfection. If it were not so the Odes of Horace would not have survived. (People aren't in a conspiracy to keep things alive.) I grant you that the kind of translations one serves up at school are as bad and as bald as they can be. They are bound to be so, because one cannot re-express an idea that has been perfectly set forth. (Men tried to do this, by the way, in the revised version of the Bible. They failed.) Yet, by a painful and laborious acquaintance with the mechanism of that particular tongue;

by being made to take it to pieces and put it together again, and by that means only; we can arrive at a state of mind in which, though we cannot re-express the idea in any adequate words, we can realise and feel and absorb the idea. To put it in this way. No one can play cricket like Ranji* at his best. But to appreciate Ranji's play; to pick up enough from it to try and improve your own with; you *must* have played cricket for more than two terms.

Our ancestors were not fools. They knew what we, I think, are in danger of forgetting – that the whole background of life, in law, civil administration, conduct of life, the terms of justice, the terms of science, the value of government, are the everlasting ramparts of Rome and Greece – the father and mother of civilisation. And for that reason, before they turned a man into life at large, they arranged that he should not merely pick up, but absorb into his system (through his hide if necessary) the fact that Greece and Rome were there. Later on, they knew, he would find out for himself how much and how important they were and they are, and that they still exist.

Some time ago I had the honour to meet a statesman who had been in charge of a great portion of the Empire. He was an old man, trained in the old school, and, talking about this very subject, he said something like this: 'All I took away from school and college was the fact that there were once peoples who didn't talk our tongue and who were very strong on sacrifice and ritual, particularly at meals, whose gods were different from ours, and who had strict views on the disposal of the dead. Well, you know, all that is worth knowing if you ever have to govern India.'*

I have never had to govern India, but I quite agree with him.

A certain knowledge of the classics is worth having, because it makes you realise that all the world is not like ourselves in all respects, and yet in matters that really touch the inside life of a man, neither the standards nor the game have changed.

I suppose I ought to apologise for the attitude I've taken. I certainly *do* apologise for taking so long to explain it. We will now revisit calmer scenes. Let me assure you for your comfort that Literature can't be taught, unless a man really wants to know something about it. Pieces or periods can be set and studied with notes, but that, thank goodness, is the worst that can happen.

One can't prescribe books, even the best books, to people unless one knows a good deal about each individual person. If a man is keen on reading, I think he ought to open his mind to some older man who knows him and his life, and to take his advice in the matter, and above all, to discuss with him the first books that interest him.

This idea applies only to what are called the standard authors – and – this is only my own theory; I don't know how it would work with you – the Elizabethan dramatists. You mustn't be afraid of fashions. The thing to remember is that all first-class stuff is as good and as new and as fresh now as in the day it was made.

But there are some things a man can't discuss with any one, and it isn't right that he should. We have times and moods and tenses of black depression and despair and general mental discomfort which, for convenience sake, we call liver or sulks. But so far as my experience goes, that is just the time when a man is peculiarly accessible to the influence of a book, as he is to any other outside influence; and, moreover, that is just the time when he naturally and instinctively does not want anything of a mind-taxing soul-stirring nature. Then is the time to fall back on the books that neither pretend to be nor are accepted as masterpieces, but books whose tone and temper soothe your trouble for the time being. A man who knows you and your life may be able to recommend such books. Ask him.

The thing to be careful of when you are in this mood is to come out of it as soon as it lifts, and not to continue dreaming over books because they suit that mood or because they minister to your own vanity. There have been a few great dreamers in the world who have achieved great things for the world; but for every dreamer whose dreams have been good, or at least not harmful, there are thousands who have been a hindrance to themselves, an expense to their families, and a nuisance to mankind. Books used intemperately to excess become most dangerous drugs, and there is a type of book – modern, I regret to say, as Mr. Pecksniff did *not* say about the Sirens* – which is to be avoided when one's mind is a little off colour. One reads in a newspaper occasionally of the bold youth of ten who goes off with a knife and sevenpence-halfpenny in coppers, to become a demon chauffeur or to lariat Red-Indians or shoot cowboys, and is then brought into court, weeping, by a policeman. And the magistrate says it's the sad result of reading – *Deadwood Dick* or *The Terror of Bloody Gulch*. It's hard to realise that there is a mass of modern stuff which is practically no more than *Deadwood Dick* and the penny dreadful disguised and flavoured to modern taste. They fill the mind, they are meant to fill the mind, with a lot of vague and windy ideas that one can start off to do miracles or benefit one's fellow-men (which is the fashion just now), without training or equipment of any kind except a desire to astonish the world and show one's independence – exactly like the kid with the penknife and the stolen coppers. It is not probable that you'll come much in the way of these books, but if you do, before you read them, watch the men who discuss 'em and recommend 'em to you. If they strike you as the kind of men you'd like to be with in a tight place, or to go to if you were in trouble, then read them. Otherwise, as Sir Walter Raleigh said – 'Otherwise not.'

Many of you are going to enter what is called the life of action, in which you will discover that you will have to think harder, closer and quicker than the bulk of men who take up what is so kindly called 'the intellectual life'. Harder, because you will be thinking against men, not books; closer, because your thoughts will be translated, several times a day perhaps, into action that may affect the lives and interests of men; quicker, because, even if you don't eventually make ghastly mistakes, you may have to alter your plans at a minute's notice to meet a changed situation. Incidentally, you will have to express your thoughts, wants, and orders both in speech and writing with much more clearness than the average literary man, and under circumstances that will not exactly lend themselves to clear thinking or easy writing. It is almost worse for a C.O. not to have expressive written (not spoken) words at his command than not to have men. With luck you can always scratch together a few men out of the hospitals or the Army Service Corps; but if you send in a report that nobody can make head or tail of, because you haven't the words to tell your case, you can lose a thousand men in half an hour. So you *must* get your words, and a working knowledge of the use of words. And words come out of Literature – even if you make no other use of it.

Those of you who go into the Service will find out that, in spite of aeroplanes, you will have to guess, most of your time, at what is going on behind the next hill; and this is not only the whole business of war but of life. And those who have read *The Green Curve*,* which is a splendid book, know that you will have to think what is in the mind of the man who is opposed to you. And you must do that in life as well as in the Service.

Well, half of Literature is placing fields that aren't there, and the rest of it is recording how every conceivable kind of ball that can be bowled by the Fates or life or circumstances has, at one time or another, been bowled at some wretched or happy man; and how he has played it. Life is too short to hunt up the individual record in each case; but, over and above all the help we can get from our ordinary training, association with our betters, and our very limited experience, we can pick up from Literature a few general and fundamental ideas as to how the great game of Life has been played by the best players.

'Some Aspects of Travel'*

'The life of wanderers is ill to live?' 'Credit it not. I have entered and possessed new lands daily for many days. Whether their earth or their water now possesses my carcass, they are welcome to it.'

I must begin by asking your forgiveness where I touch on matters of which you know much more than I.

I cannot claim to have travelled widely, but I have met many travellers, and I have noticed what they tell the public in print of their experiences is one thing, and what they tell their friends by word of mouth is another. So I would like to try to deal with some of the more intimate and personal aspects of travel. They may be trivial or absurd, but one must remember that in a few years, most of our existing methods of transport, together with the physical and mental emotions that accompany them, will be profoundly changed. The time is near when men will receive their normal impressions of a new country suddenly and in plan, not slowly and in perspective; when the most extreme distances will be brought within the compass of one week's – one hundred and sixty-eight hours' travel; when the word 'inaccessible' as applied to any given spot on the surface of the globe will cease to have any meaning. I present myself tonight, then, as in some sort a recorder of experiences which are on the eve of being superseded.

Many years ago a friend of mine was engaged on a survey in a little-known part of Asia. When he came back, I asked him what he used to think about while he was at work. He told me that, as soon as his party had settled to camp-routine, his mind moved in an uneasy triangle – he traced it in the air as he spoke – between Supplies, possible Sickness and Mileage. The figure was as real to him as one on a blackboard. It was an isosceles triangle with a narrow base, in the centre of which he felt himself to be walking, between Supplies on the one hand and Sickness on the other, always looking forward to the always retreating point M. When his work was ended, and the survey had connected up, the point M, he said, 'opened and let him through'. Till then he had felt himself constricted – 'harnessed up' was his word – between these imaginary lines. I remember we discussed the matter at some length, and in our interest to discover why his thoughts had cast themselves into a triangle, we missed, I think, the main point – that the phenomenon did not show itself till the boy had been worked rather hard.

That roused my interest in what one might call the psychology of moving bodies under strain. Most of the men I was brought in contact with, knew something about the strain of travel, and I asked them – as I have asked many men since – how they realised their experiences to themselves. Few things are more doubtful than any man's, especially any Englishman's, evidence as to his own feelings; and in the rare cases where one meets a man who can or cares to testify, one finds that a very few days of baths, clean clothes and mixed society blur the clearness of his record. Travellers, like sea-trout, should be caught fresh-run, with their experiences still sticking to them.

Yet it seemed to me, from what I was told, that a number of the men who work under strain and responsibility, as leaders of expeditions – survey, prospecting, exploration or scientific – come to evolve a more or less definite image of their work within the limits of which, or with reference to which, they accomplish that work. For the sake of brevity, let us call those images pressure-lines.

I have no knowledge of any other case except the one I have given, of pressure-lines taking the form of a complete mathematical figure. One man, who had led a rather trying expedition, told me that his pressure-line showed itself, after a few days' hard marching, as a diagonally shaded bar or line a little above and to the right of his right eyebrow. It was a distinct mental image almost as insistent as a scratch on the glass of one's spectacles; and he felt himself to be constantly pushing in or shouldering towards it. After a good day's work the bar was clear and firm in outline. A bad day, with lost loads and delayed transport, broke it up into ragged curdled flecks. He carried the bar with him for the first few mornings after his return to civilisation, exactly as one carried the memory of the school-bell for the first few mornings of one's holidays.

Many of the pressure-lines, of course, cannot be defined in words. One man has written to me: 'I had the picture of my job at the back of my head all the time. For the life of me I couldn't tell you what it was like, but it was there and it was quite real. I kept it by me, or rather it kept by me, till I had had a week's sleep between sheets.' And another man told me that his pressure-line appeared to him as an amorphous lump – a cross between a monthly calendar and a porter's load. That gives an idea of complicated pressure and its attendant horrors. And yet another, who suffered from malaria, compared his pressure-line to that indescribable sensation of swelling and thickening of the hands at the beginning of a bout of fever, which, as you know, is sometimes accompanied by a consciousness of indefinitely protracted parallel ruled lines in the head.

In every case, I noted that the pressure-lines did not show themselves till the man was physically tired out – and a little more. When the pressure of work was removed and the man was fed again, the lines gradually faded, and could only be recalled by an effort of will.

And I remember, too, when I was a young man, listening to Stanley,* who was talking, half to himself, of some work he had done in his early days. He had been under the necessity of covering a certain distance in a certain time, and he ended his monologue with an abrupt fore-reaching movement of his first finger, as though he were pegging down or hooking up something, and he said: 'Of course, it was the mileage that worried me!' I often wondered whether that gesture of Stanley's was characteristic, and what form *his* pressure-lines took.

Several men have told me that their mental idea of their day's work, as distinguished from the responsibility of leadership, was a ribbon or tape unrolling behind them or being dropped from their hands as they marched. In one case my informant said that he thought of distance actually covered as a clear white tape; distance to the next halting-place ran forward along the ground like a misty web or skein. These men were not leaders, but subordinates responsible for making good so many miles per diem. One can see the reason for their linear conception of progress. Expeditions, as a rule, string out in single file, and any movement of the leaders is seldom to a flank, but up and down the line.

Speaking from my own experience of the one march I ever had to make in a hurry, my impression at the time, as well as the memory that stayed with me afterwards, was that of the unrolling ribbon. Luckily I had not to worry about supplies, but my single object was to get myself and my coolies out of a certain district as soon as possible. My mind projected itself along an imaginary straight line – in this instance white against dull green. It would be interesting if any of the Polar men who work against white backgrounds would tell us how the idea of their work presents itself to them while they are engaged in it. I have heard that the dog-train mailrunners of Alaska and Northern Canada sometimes see their winter-trails as short straight lines strung with beads – that is to say, as a diagram of the taut sleigh-traces with dogs attached.

But I think that most travellers do not cast, or do not recall that they cast, their thoughts into mathematical outlines. They retain more or less accurate pictures of incidents that have impressed them personally. I knew one man who said he could run any road that he had marched over, backward between his eyelids like a cinematograph film before he went to sleep. His companions told me that his diary and written work were quite bad; but that they always took his word for the time and place of any event that had happened on the road. Such a gift as this – and some motorists have the rudiments of it – stands at the top of a scale that ends in those disappointing men who, after months of experience, can communicate no more than a hazy recollection of the places where they got food or water or warmth or shelter. *Punch* has described this type in the man who said: 'Rome – Rome. Wasn't that the place where I bought the shocking bad cigars?' It is not at all a bad type to travel with, because it generally gives all its attention to its own duties. A man who carries too many pictures in his head is apt to forget vital things like straps and kettle-lids when the loads are being packed. On the other hand, I have been assured by competent authorities that the camp-cook, if white, ought to be of a sentimental and imaginative disposition. It makes him more generous. I seem to have read lately of a cook whose notion of a twelfth course of a dinner to some returned voyagers was ten boxes of sardines made into a pile with bacon and pastry to match. May one take it that he was imaginative?

I have, not exactly a theory, but an idea, that first-class leaders of expeditions, however definite and urgent their conception of their work, either do not visualise too much or keep their powers of visualisation under control. At least, I do not remember to have heard any men who have led me into a tight place and out again, say to me: 'I could see exactly what was going to happen when the canoe swamped or the bridge broke.' They usually put it:

'*When* the bridge broke or *when* the hippo charged, I did so and so, or gave such and such orders.' And there is reason for that, too. An old prospector once warned me: 'As long as you've only got yourself to think about, you can think as much as you damn-well please. When you've other folks' hides to answer for, you must quit thinking for your own amusement.' So I should be inclined to say that, however great the strain, responsibility does not encourage detailed imaginative excursuses on the road – or on any road – while the work is in hand. Later, when a man is boiling down his log and notes into book-form, he falls back on his store of mental pictures, but, in the actual stress of travel, the first-class man as distinguished from the very first-class second-class man – and this is an important distinction – does not, or decides not to, visualise.

There is another useful gift of visualisation not necessarily connected with the executive capacity that may be worth noting: for the reason that it must deal with new material in the years to come. I do not assert that it is impossible to hold intelligent conversation without the help of an atlas. But I *do* say that as soon as men begin to talk about anything that really matters, some one has to go and get the atlas. And when that has been mislaid or hidden, it is interesting to see how far the company can carry on, scribbling and sketching in the fork-and-tablecloth style, without it. One discovers then that most men keep a rough map in their heads of those parts of the world they habitually patrol, and a more accurate – often a boringly precise one – of the particular corner they have last come out of. Motoring has tremendously increased our powers in this respect; for a man who can read a county can learn to read a country, and so on. Many men, I find, can visualise the Empire on Mercator's projection enough for conversational purposes; and I have sat at the feet of one or two superior men who seemed to be able to spin the 24-inch globe, with steamer-distances, in their heads as required. Ideally, of course, every average man ought to be able to do this. Myself, I am like the rest. I only see the atlas, and that roughly, as far as I have used it. Everything outside those limits is a cloudy blur; and the atlas that I see in my mind is based on the first atlas – a little cheap blue-and-yellow one – that I was forced to study. Other men have told me much the same thing about their mental atlases, and they all agree that we visualise our imaginary travels as from sea-level, with specially vivid pictures of certain capes and ports and land-falls. Naturally, so long as we travel by sea, we must embark from a port and look out for land-falls. But the time is not far off when the traveller will know and care just as little whether he is over sea or land as we to-day know and care whether our steamer is over forty-fathom water or the Tuscarora Deep. Then we shall hear the lost ports of New York and Bombay howling like Tarshish and Tyre. Incidentally, too, we shall change all our mental pictures of travel.

The other day I asked half-a-dozen men at random what picture or diagram the words, 'He went down to the Cape', called up in their minds. Three or four of them, who had not been there, said it evolved a mind-picture of what they called the 'veld' – probably a cloudy composite photograph from illustrated papers. One said he could see the brownish-red outline of Cape Colony as coloured in his private atlas. But one man, who took the road regularly, answered at once by indicating the long curve of the liner's southerly descent, as that is laid down in the chart. It was his mental sign-talk or way-signal. Assuming identical experience and temperament, if that man's grandfather had been asked the same question in the days of the sailing-ship, he would have swung his curve westward to within sight of the Brazil coast, and would have made his southing on the long slant. When that man's son is asked the same question, he will not describe any curve at all. It will have no more meaning for him than the old coach-road over the downs to Salisbury has for the modern motorist. His way-sign will be one straight line slightly inclined from left to right – from fifty-one nothing North to thirty-three South, and fifteen, whatever it is, East; and his time-conception – that indescribable diagram of time which rises in each man's mind at the mention of a voyage of known length – will be shrunk to a little block or bead or shadow representing forty-eight or fifty hours. And so it will be with all voyages. At present, most men's mental shorthand of the run to India is a zigzag of four: London – Gibraltar; Gibraltar – Port Said; Port Said – Aden; Aden – Bombay; of the Australian voyage, a zigzag of three: the line running straight from Aden to the southern continent generally. These will be all straightened out into single lines, each carrying its own vastly shortened time-conception.

But all this, as you will say, is in the air. Let us leave it there, and consider for a while the illimitable, the fascinating subject of smells in their relation to the traveller. We shall soon have to exchange them for blasts of petrol and atomised castor-oil. Have you noticed wherever a few travellers gather together, one or the other is sure to say: 'Do you remember that smell at such and such a place?' Then he may go on to speak of camel – pure camel

– one whiff of which is all Arabia; or of the smell of rotten eggs at Hitt on the Euphrates, where Noah got the pitch for the Ark; or of the flavour of drying fish in Burma. Then the company begin to purr like cats at valerian, and, as the books say, 'conversation becomes general'.

I suggest, subject to correction – there are only two elementary smells of universal appeal – the smell of burning fuel and the smell of melting grease. The smell, that is, of what man cooks his food over and what he cooks his food *in*. Fuel ranges from coal to cow-dung – specially cow-dung – and coconut husk; grease from butter through *ghi* to palm and coconut oil; and these two, either singly or in combination, make the background and furnish the active poison of nearly all the smells which assault and perturb the mind of the wayfaring man returned to civilisation. I rank wood-smoke first, since it calls up more, more intimate and varied memories, over a wider geographical range, to a larger number of individuals, than any other agent that we know. My powers are limited, but I think I would undertake to transport a quarter of a million Englishmen to any point in South Africa, from the Zambezi to Cape Agulhas, with no more elaborate vehicle than a box of matches, a string or two of rifle cordite, a broken-up biscuit-box, some chips of a creosoted railway sleeper, and a handful of dried cow-dung, and to land each man in the precise spot he had in his mind. And that is only a small part of the world that wood-smoke controls. A whiff of it can take us back to forgotten marches over unnamed mountains with disreputable companions; to day-long halts beside flooded rivers in the rain; wonderful mornings of youth in brilliantly lighted lands where everything was possible – and generally done; to uneasy wakings under the low desert moon and on tops of cruel, hard pebbles; and, above all, to that God's own hour, all the world over, when the stars have gone out and it is too dark to see clear, and one lies with the fumes of last night's embers in one's nostrils – lies and waits for a new horizon to heave itself up against a new dawn. Wood-smoke magic works on every one according to his experience. I live in a wood-smoke country, and I know how men, otherwise silent, become suddenly and surprisingly eloquent under its influence.

And next to wood-smoke for waking rampant 'wanderlust' comes the smell of melting grease – such a smell or bouquet of smells as one may gather outside a London fried-fish shop. It is less sentimental and vague in its appeal than wood-smoke, but it hits harder. Where grease is melting, something is being cooked, and that means a change from tinned food for one night at any rate. It is an opulent, a kaleidoscopic, a semitic smell of immense range and variety of colour. Sometimes it reconstructs big covered bazaars of well-stocked cities with the blue haze hanging in the domes; or it resurrects little Heaven-sent single stalls picked up by the road-side, where one can buy penny bottles of sauce or a paper of badly needed buttons. It implies camels kneeling to unload; belts and straps being loosened; contented camp-followers dodging off to buy supplies – turmeric, assafoetida, curry-stuffs; men washing their hands in sand before dipping them into the greasy pewter platters. And the next gust or surge of it may be pure Central Asia – thick and choking as butter-lamps before a Tibetan shrine – a Tibetan shrine, with frost in the air, one star on the tip of a mountain, and a brown-cloaked Bhotyali rustling up through dry maize-stalks to sell a chicken. Or it may thin out to a mere echo of an appeal that calls up all the pulse and thrill and clamour of the true tropic night – blazing moonlight, black shadow, the roar of the tree-toads, a touch of Chinese matting, a gust of jasmine or champak,* and the languid puff of a warm phosphorescent sea.

To me, as to others, a fried-fish shop can speak multitudinously for all the East from Cairo to Singapore; and I have heard West Coast* men say that, when the smell turns bitter, it will sometimes duplicate the smell of their palm-oil chop, and cause them to relive horrible depressing evenings by the light of kerosene lamps, hung under corrugated iron roofs of factories beside brown rivers that bubble. It does not cover the South Seas, that wonderful fifth quarter of the world, where, I believe, the smell of first appeal is burning coconut husk, a heavy loading of coco-nut oil, and a dash of salt coral-reef. But it is no mean magician, as we all know.

And so much for universals. Coming now to smells of particular appeal, what would most vividly remind a Polar explorer of past experiences? I suggest that ether-like smell given off by the flame of a big spirit-lamp when it is flattened out against the heated metal cooking-plate above – an unmixed smell, simple of itself, like Falstaff's sack.* I should put the limits of this appeal roughly as from the Seventies to either Pole. From the Seventies to the Sixties runs that belt of unsanctified latitudes which are the stamping-ground of the winds, the wilderness and the fringes of the restless ice, all linked together, in the minds of men who know it, by the desolate smell of the stranded berg as it piles up reeking with ooze gouged off the sea-floors. Melville, of the *Jeannette,** once told me that it would 'send your heart into your boots – if you hadn't eaten them already'. At the Sixties and down to Labrador, it seems to me we reach kindly timber and a suggestion of meat on the hoof. The smell of stranded ice is mixed with the clear breath of seas that are not always frozen, and the acrid tang of a raw moose-hide being passed back and forth through wood-smoke to cure it – this last as characteristic as the smell of home-made rimpje on a Dutch farm* at the other side of the world. A little lower, the appeals thicken and become more complex. I suggest evergreens sweating in the sun; birchwood smoke; the oily bark itself; pine-gums, resin and tallow melted together; the clean-swept smell of milky-green snow-water pouring over pebble bars; and not so far in the background, a suspicion, or a camp-shifting certainty, of skunk. Here – say 50° N. and 65° W. – we meet our friend the horse, or rather he pushes his way into the rotten-wood smudge (that is an awakening smell, too) beside us. He keeps us company west through the grass-scented prairie air till we are more conscious of him and his saddlery than any other flavour in the landscape.

There is a heart-searching little motif of five notes – horse; old saddlery; coffee; fried bacon; and tobacco (from cut-plug to maize-leaf cigarettes) that can carry a man down from high dry camps in the Selkirks,* or wet ones in Oregon, down and down over red spicy dust and dead white dust, through the scent of sage-brush and sharp peppery euphorbias, down to the torrid goat-scented South where fried beans, incense and the abominable brassy smell of pulque will pass him on to all the forlorn brood of mangrove, foreshore and yellow-fever stinks, until he leaves his horse on the beach, and the Tropics lift up his heart with the wholesome rasp of sun-baked coral and dried fish.

Forgive me, ladies and gentlemen! I will not go on with the catalogue, though I feel like the commercial traveller in the story, who said: 'If you don't care to look at my samples, d'you mind *my* having a look at 'em? It's so long since I've seen them.'

It is probable that the future will have no place for these links with past delights and labours – that they will be forgotten like the labours themselves – as we have forgotten the smell of home-made soap or the whistle and rap of the flails on a threshing-floor. Only a little while ago a man wrote me from Northern Canada: 'We have broken into a new belt of wheat 40 miles wide – and we have left the horse behind!' Even now one can charge by rail in less than a week through the exquisitely graduated and significant series of smells, that lie like iridescence on an oyster-shell, over the last 2500 miles of South Africa, and one can return with no more than a general impression of sunshine and coal-smoke. And, as people always say in the middle of a revolution: 'We are only at the beginning of things.'

Conceive for a moment a generation wholly divorced from all known smells of land and sea-travel – a generation which will climb into and drop down from the utterly odourless upper airs, unprepared in any of its senses for the flavour, which is the spirit, of the country it descends upon! Everything that we have used till now has allowed us time for a little mental adjustment of horizons – time and contact with the changing earth and waters under us. In the future, there will be neither mental adjustment nor horizons as we have understood them: not any more of the long days that prove and prepare, nor the nights that terrify and make sane again, neither sweat nor suffering, nor the panic knowledge of isolation beyond help – none, so far as we can guess, of the checks that have hitherto conditioned all our travels.

And hitherto our life has only taught us to love what we have suffered for or with. One loves a stray dog after one has had to sit up with him for a night or two. How much more that corner of the Earth to which we have given our very hide and health and reputation!

And it is the same on the human side. Men like a man who has shown himself a pleasant companion through a week's walking-tour. They worship the man who over thousands of miles for hundreds of days, through renewed difficulties and efforts, has brought them without friction, arrogance or dishonour, to the victory proposed, or to the higher glory of unshaken defeat. Anything like a man can bustle hounds after a sinking fox, but it takes something like a man to bring them home with their sterns up after they have lost him, or – seen him run into by another pack! It is one of the mysteries of personality that virtue should go out of certain men to uphold – literally to ennoble – their companions even while their own nerves are like live wires, and their own mouths are full of the taste of fever and fatigue. There is no head-mark by which we can recognise such men before they have proved themselves. Their secret is incommunicable. One man, apparently without effort, inspans the human equivalent of 'three blind 'uns and a bolter'* and makes them do miracles. Another, working hard all the time, scientifically reduces half-a-dozen picked men to the level of sulky, disloyal schoolboys. And everybody wonders how it happened.

The explanations are as bewildering as the facts. A man was asked some time ago why he invariably followed a well-known man into most uncomfortable situations. He replied: 'All the years I have known So-and-so, I've never known him to say whether he was cold or hot, wet or dry, sick or well; *but* I've never known him forget a man who was.' Here is another reply to a similar question about another leader, who was notoriously a little difficult to get on with. One of his followers wrote: 'So-and-so is all you say and more, and he grows worse as he grows older; but he will take the blame of any mistake that any man of his makes, and he doesn't care what lie he tells to save him.' And when I wrote to find out why a man whom I knew preferred not to go out with another man whom I also knew, I got this illuminating diagnosis: 'So-and-so is not afraid of anything on earth except the newspapers. So I have a previous engagement.' In the face of these documents, it looks as though self-sacrifice, loyalty and a robust view of moral obligations go far to make a leader, the capacity to live alone and inside himself being taken for granted.

But then come the accidents for which no allowance is made – or can be made. A good man, who has held a disorganised crowd together at the expense of his own vitality, may be tried, slowly or suddenly, beyond his limit, till he breaks down, and, as Hakluyt says, is either 'ignominiously reported or exceedingly condemned'.* There is a limit for every man, an edge beyond which he must not go. But here at home only the doctor, the nurses, and the clergymen see what happens next – not the caravan, not the grinning coolies, and the whole naked landscape – and afterwards all the world.

However, these things, and worse, are part of the rule of the road. They have never hindered men from leading or following. Even in these days a man has but to announce he is going to gamble against death for a few months on totally inadequate cover, and thousands of hitherto honest Englishmen will fawn and intrigue and, if necessary, lie like any one you choose to think of – in order to be allotted one life-share in the venture.

But what of the future? Into what terms will this world-old, foot-pound energy of travel translate itself under the new conditions? Here is our position. Up to the present we have been forced to move in two dimensions by the help of the Three Beasts of Burden and a few live coals in a pot.

Now we perceive that we can move in three dimensions, and the possibilities of our new freedom distract and disturb us in all relations. This is because our minds are still hobbled and knee-haltered by inherited memories of what were held to be immutable facts – distance, height and depth, separation, homesickness, the fear of accident and foul weather. The sea, in spite of our attacks, is still unplumbed, salt, and estranging;* a mountain-range means so many days' delay or *detour*; so many extra rations, sure changes of heat and cold. The desert and the wilderness have still to be approached by cautious sap and mine – depot and cache. Where there is no water for 200 miles, we shake our head and limp round it. A little while ago we should have done so, humbly, glad to be excused. Now we step out of our path grudgingly, resentfully, resolute to come back again and take no refusal.

Presently – very presently – we shall come back and convert 200 miles across any part of the Earth into its standardised time equivalent, precisely as we convert 5 miles with infantry in column, 10 with cavalry on the march, 12 in a Cape cart, or 50 in a car – that is to say, into two hours. And whether there be one desert or a dozen mountain-ranges in that 200 miles will not affect our time-table by five minutes.

Month by month the Earth shrinks actually, and, what is more important, in imagination. We know it by the slide and crash of unstable material all around us. For the moment, but only for the moment, the new machines are outstripping mankind. We have cut down enormously – we shall cut down inconceivably – the world-conception of time and space, which is the big flywheel of the world's progress. What wonder that the great world-engine, which we call Civilisation, should race and heat a little; or that the onlookers who see it take charge should be a little excited, and, therefore, inclined to scold? You could witness precisely the same flurry in any engine-room on the Atlantic this evening, where a liner happens to be pitching her propellers out of water. For the moment the machines are developing more power than has been required for their duties. But just as soon as humanity can get its breath, the machines' load will be increased and they will settle smoothly to their load and most marvellous output.

Frankly, one is not so much interested in the achievements of the future as in the men of the present who are already scouting and reporting along its fantastic skyline. All, or nearly all, that can be accomplished by the old means has been won and put to general account. The old mechanism is scrapped; the moods and emotions that went with it follow. Only the spirit of man carries on, unaltered and unappeasable. There will arise – they are shaping themselves even now – risks to be met as cruel as any that Hudson or Scott faced; dreams as world-wide as Columbus or Cecil Rhodes dreamed, to be made good or to die for; and decisions to be taken as splendidly terrible as that which Drake clinched by Magellan,* or Oates a little farther south.* There is no break in the line, no loads are missing; the men of the present have begun the discovery of the New World with the same devoutly careless passion as their predecessors completed the discovery of the Old.

Epigraph to 'The Edge of the Evening'*

Ah! What avails the classic bent,
    And what the chosen word,
Against the undoctored incident
    That actually occurred?

And what is Art whereto we press
    Through paint and prose and rhyme –
When Nature in her nakedness
    Defeats us every time?

From 'A Thesis'*

By the tales told at their mother's knee do men live or die. Praise the Gods, Mother, that you told me tales of the open-breasted Gods, and not of vermin!

... the nations of the world betray their essential characteristics and ideals more intimately and more precisely in the folk-tales which they tell to their children, than through any other medium. In public assemblies, man makes use of the lie proper to the occasion; but beside his own hearth, among his own family, he reveals unconsciously the absolute truth concerning all that he desires or fears. The folk-tales of a race never lie ...

'Fiction'*

> Gold and Gems we may steal – melt down, re-cut and re-sell them. All that we need is the Fire. That we must find in ourselves.

I am sure that to-morrow every member of my craft will be grateful, Lord Balfour,* that in your many-sided career you have never thought to compete in the ranks of professed workers in fiction.

As regards the subject, not the treatment, of Lord Balfour's speech, I think we may take it, gentlemen, that the evening light is much the same for all men. When the shadows lengthen one contrasts what one had intended to do in the beginning with what one has accomplished. That the experience is universal does not make it any less acid – especially when, as in my case, one has been extravagantly rewarded for having done what one could not have helped doing.

But recognition by one's equals and betters in one's own craft is a reward of which a man may be unashamedly proud – as proud as I am of the honour that comes to me to-night from your hands. For I know with whom you have seen fit to brigade me* in the ranks of Literature. The fiction that I am worthy of that honour be upon your heads!

Yet, at least, the art that I follow is not an unworthy one. For Fiction is Truth's elder sister. Obviously. No one in the world knew what truth was till some one had told a story. So it is the oldest of the arts, the mother of history, biography, philosophy dogmatic (or doubtful, Lord Balfour)* and, of course, of politics.

Fiction began when some man invented a story about another man. It developed when another man told tales about a woman. This strenuous epoch begat the first school of destructive criticism, as well as the First Critic, who spent his short but vivid life in trying to explain that a man need not be a hen to judge the merits of an omelette. He died; but the question he raised is still at issue. It was inherited by the earliest writers from their unlettered ancestors, who also bequeathed to them the entire stock of primeval plots and situations – those fifty ultimate comedies and tragedies to which the Gods mercifully limit human action and suffering.

This changeless aggregate of material workers in fiction through the ages have run into fresh moulds, adorned and adapted to suit the facts and the fancies of their own generation. The Elizabethans, for instance, stood on the edge of a new and wonderful world filled with happy possibilities. Their descendants, 350 years later, have been shot into a world as new and as wonderful, but not quite as happy. And in both ages you can see writers raking the dumps of the English language for words that shall range farther, hit harder and explode over a wider area than the service-pattern words in common use.

This merciless search, trial and scrapping of material is one with the continuity of life which, we all know, is as a tale that is told, and which writers feel should be well told. All men are interested in the reflection of themselves and their surroundings, whether in the pure heart of a crystal or in a muddy pool; and nearly every writer who supplies a reflection secretly desires a share of immortality for the pains he has been at in holding up the mirror – which also reflects himself. He may win his desire. Quite a dozen writers have achieved immortality in the past 2500 years. From a bookmaker's – a real bookmaker's – point of view the odds are not attractive, but Fiction is built on fiction. That is where it differs from the other Arts.

Most of the Arts admit the truth that it is not expedient to tell everyone everything. Fiction recognises no such bar. There is no human emotion or mood which it is forbidden to assault – there is no canon of reserve or pity that need be respected – in fiction. Why should there be? The man, after all, is not telling the truth. He is only writing fiction. While he writes it, his world will extract from it just so much of truth or pleasure as it requires for the moment. In time a little more, or much less, of the residue may be carried forward to the general account, and there, perhaps, diverted to ends of which the writer never dreamed.

Take a well-known instance. A man of overwhelming intellect and power goes scourged through life between the dread of insanity and the wrath of his own soul warring with a brutal age. He exhausts mind, heart, and brain in that battle: he consumes himself, and perishes in utter desolation. Out of all his agony remains one little book, his dreadful testament against his fellow-kind, which to-day serves as a pleasant tale for the young under the title of *Gulliver's Travels*. That, and a faint recollection of some baby-talk in some love-letters, is as much as the world has chosen to retain of Jonathan Swift, Master of Irony. Think of it! It is like tuning-down the glare of a volcano to light a child to bed!

The true nature and intention, then, of a writer's work does not lie within his own knowledge. And we know that the world makes little allowance for any glory of workmanship which a writer spends on material that does not interest. So it would seem that Fiction is one of the few 'unsheltered' occupations, in that there is equal victimisation on both sides, and no connection between the writer's standard of life, his output or his wages.

Under these conditions has grown up in England a literature lavish in all aspects – lavish with the inveterate unthrift of the English, who are never happy unless they are throwing things away. By virtue of that same weakness, or strength, it overlaps so sumptuously that one could abstract and bestow from the mere wastage of any literary age since Chaucer's enough of abundance and enjoyment to quicken half a world. Those who study in the treasure-houses of its past know what unregarded perfection of workmanship and what serene independence of design often went to fabricate the least among those treasures. And they know, also, the insolence of the greatest Masters, who were too pressed to wait on perfection in their haste to reveal to us some supreme jewel scarcely cleansed from the matrix. Our English literature, I think, has always been the expression of a race more anxious to deliver what was laid upon it than to measure the means and methods of delivery.

And this immense and profligate range of experience, invention and passion is our incommunicable inheritance, which is drawn upon at every need, for multitudes who, largely, neither know nor care whence their need is met.

In every age some men gain temporary favour because they happen to have met a temporary need of their age. Yet, as regards their future, they stand on a perfect equality with their fellow-craftsmen. It is not permitted to any generation to know what, or how much, of its effort will be carried forward to the honour and grace of our literature. The utmost a writer can hope is that there may survive of his work a fraction good enough to be drawn upon later, to uphold or to embellish some ancient truth restated, or some old delight reborn.

Admitting this, a man may, by the exercise of a little imagination, persuade himself that he has acquired merit in his lifetime. Or, if imagination be lacking, he may be led to that comfortable conclusion by the magic of his own art heard as we have heard it from Lord Balfour to-night, on the lips of a man wise in life, and a Master not ignorant of the power of words.

From Introduction to *The Irish Guards in the Great War**

. . . As evidence is released, historians may be able to reconstruct what happened in or behind the battle-line; what motives and necessities swayed the actors; and who stood up or failed under his burden. But a battalion's field is bounded by its own vision. Even within these limits, there is large room for error. Witnesses to phases of fights die and are dispersed; the ground over which they fought is battered out of recognition in a few hours; survivors confuse dates, places and personalities, and in the trenches, the monotony of the waiting days and the repetition-work of repairs breed mistakes and false judgements. Men grow doubtful or oversure, and, in all good faith, give directly opposed versions. The clear sight of a comrade so mangled that he seems to have been long dead is burnt in on one brain to the exclusion of all else that happened that day. The shock of an exploded dump, shaking down a firmament upon the landscape, dislocates memory throughout half a battalion; and so on in all matters, till the end of laborious enquiry is too often the opening of fresh confusion. When to this are added the personal prejudices and misunderstandings of men under heavy strain, carrying clouded memories of orders half given or half heard, amid scenes that pass like nightmares, the only wonder to the compiler of these records has been that any sure fact whatever should be retrieved out of the whirlpools of war. . .

'Chartres Windows'*

Colour fulfils where Music has no power:
　　By each man's light the unjudging glass betrays
All men's surrender, each man's holiest hour
　　And all the lit confusion of our days –
Purfled with iron, traced in dusk and fire,
　　Challenging ordered Time who, at the last,
　　Shall bring it, grozed and leaded and wedged fast,
　　To the cold stone that curbs or crowns desire.

Yet on the pavement that all feet have trod –
        Even as the Spirit, in her deeps and heights.
Turns only, and that voiceless, to her God –
        There falls no tincture from those anguished lights.
And Heaven's one light, behind them, striking through
Blazons what each man dreamed no other knew.

3

HOW TO WRITE: INGREDIENTS AND METHODS

*

From a letter to Edmonia Hill,* 25–7 May 1888

... Saturday. Midnight. Whewww!

That must stand for a sigh of relief for I have just put a rabid friend of mine into his cart. Your letter of Friday noon has arrived. So many thanks – indeed 'tha'anks awf'lly' for it! The man was a fiction* was he? I've had him under the lens since 8:15 this evening. Now for wholesale breaches of confidence! His name is Beames – David Beames* – son of Beames, Commissioner of Burdwan or who was before the Babus got him jumped on. He is Adjutant and Wing Commander in the 19th B[engal]. (or P[unjabi]. L[ancers]. stationed at Mian Mir*: went up to Simla to attend the marriage of his oldest friend Captain Saunders to a Miss Temple, daughter of Dr. Temple, VC, Secretary to the Surgeon General and, while up there, fell in love with Miss Ethel Temple aetat. 17: a maiden with untidy hair, sallow complexion and large bovine eyes for I have seen her photo, which he wears about his foolish, foolish neck. I do not say that the names are fictitious. You have done me sufficient honour already in calling the whole a lie. (Nasty word that, but it takes up less space than 'fiction') and you may check 'em by the Army list.

B. is not mad. He is generally insane and to the best of my belief (who am I to pass judgements on men?) will continue to be so till the 17th or 18th of next month when by hook or by crook he goes up, so he swears with perfectly uncalled for blasphemy, to speak his mind. I have been listening to him patiently at this table and he has given me a fair amount of good material, for he was more than usually expansive. The quaintest thing –

though that I was prepared for – was to watch the boy's Pride kicking against his love, and to hear the everlasting cuckoo cry: – 'She's only a girl of seventeen – she's untidy – she isn't very pretty – but she's the only woman in the world for me.' I heard again from his lips all the extravagances that I had read of in books, and was immensely edified at his *naif* astonishment at the fact that all the world had changed for him and the glory of his old pursuits had departed. 'There's *the Duchess* going to foal' he wailed 'and I don't care – I don't care. I'd been looking forward to have the best colt in the Punjab . . . only eleven and a half days ago. I don't care for my dogs – I don't care for my horses.' Then he cussed tremendous!

I set down some of his more excruciating sentences for future use – they'll all be worth weaving in some day – but these I will forbear to bother you with. They were as mad as anything I have ever heard for he was learning Humility and a lot of other strange things and sweated and winced like a colt under the cavesson for the first time. I was in no mood to spare him for many reasons – *imprimis* because I had had my own words thrown in my teeth with an *imprimatur* more terse than flattering and less truthful than either. May be I shall be punished later on but I gave myself up to the full enjoyment of the moment and tried to see how far my words had weight on his mind. I might have worked on so much sculptor's clay. First I pointed out gravely and seriously the 'excessively ephemeral existence' of all attachments, the chances of other men mashing round the place and taking that young heart, and the Honourable Necessity of allowing a young girl her choice before forcing a hasty passion on her. Thereat he squirmed for the gift of speech came down upon me and I wanted to see what would happen if I used it. In the end he snorted which is as near as a man gets to sobbing and, while admitting the cold justice of my arguments, called me all the evil names under the sun. I had flicked him on the raw neatly and to the full of my power.

Then I changed my tune and sang a prettier song – sketching the Primrose Path of Dalliance step by step from the tonga flying up hill to the cool of the snows, to the hot-headed avowal at the back of Elysium (verily I told him the quietest spot to go to) and the end of all things – the Glassy Sea of a Perfect Matrimony. And he rejoiced – the idiot – and slapped his leg and swore just as vehemently as before (his four days abstinence from evil language seems to have sent him on with fresh zest) but this time more cheerily and having played him through the moods I let him rest and talk; though I was sorry that I had not hurt him more in the first *chukker.** I believe that I was possessed of one or two devils. I know that when I put him out on the stroke of twelve I went to my room and, as the Amer – as people say – 'kicked myself' for having been a brute and a Judas. 'It's so awfully good of you old man to let me pester you in this way' he said. But he has given me the material I want and if I can catch him after his engagement (men are entirely different to women in their almost brutal outspokenness) his carcass will give me more flesh for the dissecting. The pity is that he's a common type and unless I run a silver thread* through the web, even the cloth I shall spin will look poor and commonplace. However it's great good luck just when I'm running low for subjects. He's dining with me again on Tuesday – he, D. Beames, Lt. 19 P.L. whom I am treacherously deceiving with a false sympathy and a lying condolence...

From a letter to Augusta Tweddell,* 10 July 1888

Dear Miss Tweddell

I have read the poems and MS which you so kindly sent me and – what shall I say? You see I have hardly the right or the experience to give advice: and I pray you not to be offended with me if I speak plainly.

You have power certainly – and in one or two places, notably in the story of the Subaltern's brown paper bride a sense of humour which is not common among lady-writers. But on the other hand you, like all beginners, have not the strength of hand to carry out even one tithe of what your brain plots. For instance in the story of a mad-woman you have tried deliberately to be terrible and to fill the reader with awe. To yourself, reading the MS over, you are sufficiently ghastly because your mind goes back unconsciously to the mood which affected you when you were writing, and bridges over gaps and flaws in the work. But you must remember that the average reader is altogether beyond the influence of these considerations and regards passages which to you seem well thought out as 'stilted', and emotions which you intended to be passionate as simply 'jerky'. Am I too brutal in saying this? I wouldn't do it if I didn't think that you could do something good.

And now will you submit to be preached at for a while?

It is Longfellow who says: –

That is best which lieth nearest
Shape from that thy art.*

Don't try to invent or fly off into other worlds. That is beginning at the wrong end. If you have invention, and believe me it is a very rare faculty, all the realities of all this world won't put it out. Go simply and deliberately at the reality of this life as you see it, first. Note faces, turns of expression, and conversations, exactly as you would put down sketches of tree-boles or gate posts. Then as you feel your power to reproduce these in pen and ink, take the story of some one you know and write it out until you are assured in your own mind – 'this is the truth'. Keep on doing this – it doesn't sound nice does it? – and have no fear of attempting to describe anything and everything that lies in the pale of human life. You will fail horribly – as I fail week by week and month by month – but every failure will show you the extent of your own powers. Then if you have invention a time will come when you will find that you are no longer a copyist but a teller of tales – a writer who can make men and women move and speak and think and love like men and women. That time will not be till you have had experience larger than you at present own; and you will find that each experience through which you pass gives a broader scope to your pen. Your diction at present contains a good many German turns of speech (get rid of these by reading good models) and your poetry some very pretty German turns of thought. Keep these by all means but accustom yourself to write rhyming poetry. The restraint of dancing in fetters will teach you more thoroughly how to write prose than any thing else; and verse you know is only the stepping stone to good prose. I should recommend you to get and read thoroughly every one of Besant's novels* for he to my mind is master of the art of writing about men and women. If you don't know 'em pray ask at the Library for *Ready Money Mortiboy, This Son of Vulcan, By Celia's Arbour, With Harp and Crown, My Little Girl* and best of all, *All Sorts and Conditions of Men.* Read and reread them until you pass from mere reading to criticism and begin to see how they are put together and what means the author uses to produce certain effects. Also (this sounds queer I know) read the Bible thoroughly and see how much can be said in how few words. I regard the Book as a great help to literary composition. There is any amount of loose slipshod English in the world and its influence has affected my style incurably but do you avoid it. Write and rewrite and when you have rewritten put away the sheets even for so short a time as a fortnight and you will be surprised to see how many new ideas have grown up in that short space. If you want relaxation or amusement try a wild and mad story occasionally and you will find that the more you know of human life (which is the wildest and maddest thing of all) the more *grotesquerie* and horror will you be able to put into this sort of work.

Forgive this lofty sermon. I do not pretend to practise what I preach but that doesn't prevent me from preaching does it? From a business point of view not one of the things you have sent me is worth the paper it's written on; but some of them are valuable as showing future promise. If you care to go on writing – remember that ink once in the blood is a subtle poison and destroys a good many pretty illusions and some of the capacities for enjoyment – send me anything you like and as soon as it is fit for anything you may be assured that I will do my best to get it put into a print frock for you. I know most of the papers and weeklies in India. If you care to send me a real life tale I'll get it, at least, set up in type and you will be astonished to see how bald and crude it looks in the merciless clear speaking of print.

Yours very sincerely
Rudyard Kipling. . .

From a letter to Mary Mapes Dodge,* 21 October 1892

. . . I'm glad you like her and perhaps if the children think fit we'll try another – the tale of the Thibetan lama and Kim o' the Rishti* for I would sooner make a fair book of stories *for* children than a new religion or a completely revised framework of our social and political life.

BUT – let her Pottedness* remain for the very reason that you say. It is suggestive of canned meat. Children are pigs (little ones) in their insides. The title will stick in their tum – I mean their minds. . .

From a letter to Mary Mapes Dodge,* 12 November 1892

. . . I held over answering your letter till I had done the monkeys and the poison stick* in the rough. I send you the draft herewith. It wants at least another lick of varnish. Will you kindly get it typed for me (Brattleboro keeps no superfluous luxuries in the Remington line) and send it to me for revision. This without prejudice to what I may do to it in proof. If you accept it I have a notion that it may be about six inches over the head of the young – a lot of it but that you must decide. If it's so I must reframe it and make it a tale for the grown ups. Please let me have just a little note giving me book rights of all tales I may write for *St Nick.*

Now what do you think of a tale about an elephants' ball.* Held by moonlight in one of the great stamped down ballrooms that they make for themselves in the heart of the moist hot Assam terai.* Fancy several acres as flat as beaten clay and a midnight gathering of the great trumpeting waltzing wheeling giants as watched in fear and terror by an Assamese *Keddah** man, an elephant tracker. It was their last waltz you see for next day the lines of the elephant drive closed and they were driven into the stockade. The queer thing was that the tracker had gone off to hunt the wild elephants with his own string of four tame trained *mucknas** and they broke away from him and he saw them the big chains jingling as they twirled, dancing through the mammoth quadrilles. There's a deal more truth in this than you'd think afterwards a camel tale* might not be amiss but that's as you think best. . .

P.S. Better still. A tame tusker breaks out of his pickets at night, slings the driver's five year old son on his neck, goes forty miles into the Garo hills crashing through the underbrush to dance with his fellows and the little chap is the only living human who sees the great dance. Tell it in verse, ballad form, and charge *St Nick* untold gold!

From a letter to Mary Mapes Dodge,* 24 November 1892

. . . The elephant ball did not come out in verse at least I lathered away at it ballad fashion and it carried me out ever so far beyond a child's depth. However I bethought me of some notes that were by me on elephant capturing (the which is a great science) and putting the surroundings into a *Keddah* camp* made that which I send you now. I think it will illustrate not so badly. It's long but I fear me I can't cut much more but if you like it I will try. Perhaps the little verse* and the descent of the elephants to the plains is not needed but I got so interested I forgot brevity.

Now if that tale pleases you I will do 'Tiger-Tiger' – the tale of the man eater who was ignominiously squelched in his lair by the charge of the village buffaloes under the command of the little boy herd.* That's a true tale.

From a letter to Edward Lucas White

Also, there will be (D.V.) a wolf tale,* 'Mowgli's Brothers'. *He* was a wolf boy (we have them in India) but being caught early was civilised. His brothers the wolves followed his career respectfully and afar (but they wanted food and were used to three meals a day) from village to village till at last Mowgli's too faithful retainers became a nuisance and he took council with a holy man in a grove and the upshot was that he went out in the moonlight and explained things to those four grey wolves of Oudh* and they saw the justice of his demands and left him in peace.

Then after that (if you care to have the set of six finished) we'll do a camel tale. I haven't looked up my notes for that but it should come. Altogether the six ought to make a little book. The question is won't they be rather too much of a load for *St Nick*? Consider the invoice.

The Potted Princess
Collar Wallah and the Poison Stick
Toomai of the Elephants
'Tiger-Tiger'
Mowgli's Brothers.

And the Camel. It will be a regular Zoo. I'm interested in them and want to finish them off before my spring work sets in.† Here with I return *Collar Wallah* for proofing...

† there ought to be a regular title for all six. Noah's Ark tales? or how.

From a letter to Edward Lucas White,* 25 February 1893

Esteemed Younger Brother,

I've been busy experimenting along of those metres that you are so interested in; and now I'm through for a while. I had to hunt in the *Century* to find out what a Paeonic lilt* was and it impresses me immensely. *I* do 'em on my ten fingers or shout them into the ear of a bullock (splendid public is a steer) and lo they have arsises and crisisses and pentabolic metronomes under the hypogastrium, all the time! Seriously there was a time when I read much about the nature and properties of verses:

How the cothurns trod majestic
    Down the deep iambic lines,
And the rolling anapaestic
    Curled like vapour over shrines!*

but I have forgotten all that I read, and it comes back to me fresh. Remember me when your book is born.

You are right about the old things being revived. *Exempli gratia*, all the French talk about the 'colours of vowels' is not much older than original sin. The nigger knows it: the Afghan knows it in his love songs and if we could resurrect a mummy I daresay he'd tell us how the 'Pyramids Pilot and Nile Review of Modern Literature' discussed it in his days. But mercifully, these things are hidden from us and we go on heaving our little packs of wares into the mud and the public tucks 'em away under its feet as an elephant in a quicksand tucks the straw bundles that you throw him but unlike the elephant the public never gets out. I've been working for a month on a nine storied pagoda of a song* when I ought to have been doing decent prose. So I have now the double satisfaction of doing verse and being bad...

P.S. Here is a question for the schools? How far is a man justified in onoma – (I can't spell it) tapoeic metres reproducing the beat of engines* and so on? Where does legitimate Art end and sheer trick work begin?

From a letter to Howard Pyle,* 25 August 1894

Dear Sir:

Scribners tells me that it is my great good fortune to have you for the illustrator of some verses of mine* in the Christmas Number. Also they write that you have not yet begun on the sketches. Is it permitted to a man who knows less than nothing about art to plague you with suggestions? I haven't the shadow of a doubt you'll do the verses considerably more than justice but it may help you a little to know that the ship *McAndrew's Hymn* belongs to is the old *Doric*,* once an Atlantic White Star I think, and now an S[haw]. S[avill]. A[lbion]. boat running to New Zealand via the Cape of Good Hope and home round the horn. She'd be about the same type, in her engine fittings as the *Germanic* or the *Brittanic* [sic]* I should say – i.e. in no sense a new boat with any special gear. When I was on her her l[ow]. p[ressure]. cylinder had a play of about an inch and a half on the columns and every piece of machinery had the muffled and protected look of a long-voyage boat. Not a bit like all the shiny stuff on a racing Atlantic hotel; but lapped and swathed and junked up and all white with salt-crust.

From a letter to Robert Barr

If you use American machinery for models you'll get things much too light and graceful, for one can tell the difference between American and English engines as far as one can see them – or hear them they say who know. McAndrew also is a Scot of the Scots – clean shaven or with a torpedo beard I should say and his uniform would be pretty dingy too after a three month voyage...

From a letter to Robert Barr,* 4 November 1894

Dear Barr –

It has arrived *seriatim** in little white blocks like dominoes a form in which a book is anyhow detestable. All the same, and I am not manufacturing any polite fiction, I've been putting everything else aside to go ahead with it. Mrs Kipling was laughing over it last night and sat up late and I've gone through it again – also laughing. It fulfils the first requisite of the novel – its dead interesting.

But (a) Yates did not exist in America in the year 1866. He's of the generation that was born during the war – and you've put in the wrong slide. Think a minute and you'll see. The Fenian rebellion is ancient history – Yates* comes from today, this morning, and the 'guff' between him and his fellow special is of today and no other time to take but one instance.

Also (b) both girls are of today – as I look at it.

Unless I have forgotten my fellow countrymen, the book that has Yates for a central character *and* a cold blooded proposal to two girls in quick time* (*that* don't strike me as convincing. Maybe you haven't dwelt enough on the psychology of the same) won't go for sour apples on the London market. They don't care a cuss about America: resembling Bartlett* in that amiable particular. And yet, my wife suggests, and she has a queer foreknowledge of our business, it will probably be a great success with 'em – for the very reasons that I think will be against it.

It ought to go well this side for its thundering good – honestly: out and away the best I've seen of you (this may sound like cheek but its true). It's all the snap and drama that a first-class tale wants; and generally does not get. It's packed and built and constructed as I like 'em to be and there's all in it that I fancy poor Wolcott would have appreciated to the marrow. You've good call to be proud of it. Touching the review – I've tried and made a failure of it. It's dead off my line of work and – how the deuce am I to put through a thing as thoroughly American as that in an English paper? It's like writing of a Hebrew text in Greek for the benefit of a Central African. They wouldn't understand and I couldn't make 'em. I hope this won't annoy you as much as it has done me but – it's hopeless.

How would an extract from a private letter suit you? I admit that this is a trifle crude but – the business of publishing isn't exactly refined. I could pitch in a letter to your publishers that would give what I thought of the book in five lines – and the longest review in the P[all]. M[all]. G[azette]. wouldn't yield more than that to the most generous blue pencil. Again, one has to consider that if any casual remarks of mine in print drifted over here, it might prejudice a lot of papers against the book. I've known one case where a perfectly innocent little speech meant to serve as a bush to good wine was construed into – interference with American something or other – swelled head perhaps. However I'll be guided by you in the matter. Now (unbusinesslikely) let me thank you on my own behalf for the pure joy I got out of the reading of it...

From a letter to Richard Watson Gilder,* 25 September 1895

Dear Gilder:

I am glad to find The Brushwood Boy* interests you and I'm free to confess myself that I was not a little pleased with it when it was done.

As a matter of fact I've drawn the map of the dream-country several times but will make a clean copy for repro. in facsimile, as soon as I can. As to head and tail pieces why certainly *if* you can find any that will fit in any way from *The Second Jungle Book*: but why not a simple initial and tail piece from the office?

In regard to the boil* seeing as how the Century is a magazine and not a book; and somebody else's property and not mine, I will do what you suggest: to the extent of making the said boil, blain, pustule or tumour a cut hand or something similar. It grieves me much that you call my yarn a romance for what I prided myself on most was my grey and unflinching realism.* Thus is a man misunderstood. Please send proof as soon as possible because I am sure to need a revise and certain to cut it down a little on re-reading.

Always sincerely yours
Rudyard Kipling...

From a letter to Louisa Baldwin,* 14 December 1895

... Now, dropping the nephew, for a minute, will you let me say that what you want most is 'heap plenty blue pencil'? The tales* are good and more than good but you give the impression of wanting forty pages to turn in and there's an overlarge sprinkling of easy and accepted phrases that have been worn smooth by other pens. I don't mean journalese but more in the nature of padding stuff. It's like an etching where the central figure is bitten in clearly enough and the rest is a clutter of lines put in to make background.

The Lord he knoweth I would not counsel you to bring up your backgrounds too much (that's *my* besetting sin) but only to elaborate them cleanly and clearly in a few well chosen words that bring air and light and perspective into the show, and that, I take it, is only attained by considering every word of minor dialogue and description and most resolutely avoiding the set phrase. It's a mistake we are all of us most prone to in our business. I wish I could go through a page or two over your shoulder and show you what I mean. It wouldn't look so horribly impertinent as it does on paper...

From a letter to Robert Barr,* 10 June 1896

... I'm most through with my first genuine out and out American story* – a long one – new ground untouched even by the pious New England – and oh Rrrobert it is a beauty! You'll hear the continent sit up as one man over it and the band will begin to play. I've poached on all the down East peoples preserves, from Mary Wilkins* to Sarah Orne Jewett* and I've raided into the Pacific slope and I've run a light & masterly hand over the whole darn continent. It raises no questions: it don't criticise. There's no me in it. It's plain narrative done from the inside and I'd give a year's growth to publish anonymous. It's a corker – a daisy and more I'm sinfully proud of it. This in confidence because I always told you I would write a tale...

From a holograph note in the manuscript of *Puck of Pook's Hill*

The Runes on the Sword*

This is Puck's translation of the Runes on Weland's sword but the children could not see the meaning of them till the end of the year. They are what were called Belted Runes of three lines each. Where a line is the same for two opposite verses it is carved half on one side of the blade and half on the other and the verses run together towards the point. At the very tip, separated from the rest, are three lines that can only be read in one way – from the first to the last. With all the others you can begin any verse where you please and it will read the same...

From a letter to Ian Colvin,* 18 July 1909

Dear Colvin,

Many thanks for your kind note. The only references I have seen to *City of Brass** were, as you might say, hectic and profane – likewise coarse – but great fun.

Glad you like the metre. It's a 'sport' from an Arabian one. You can see the same sort of thing in certain passages of the *Arabian Nights.** I tried some rather jolly variations of it – with three-syllable rhymes at the end and three line stanzas instead of couplets. Also with the internal rhymes two syllable and the final a one syllable. You try and see how the thing can be expanded and contracted...

From a letter to Louisa Baldwin,* 20 November 1909

...They are all much better to my mind but I've gone over them unkindly.* The trouble is always to get not the word that suffices but *the* word and with luck one gets that about three times out of ten. Such as can find it every other time are poets. William of Stratford on Avon (you may have heard of him) did it seven times out of ten.

Now I suggest, for exercise, that you wholly change the form of your sonnet – from William's form to the clanging six line finish and double ended rhymes – or here's a copy (Lord forbid I should call it a model) of some other variety, as thus: –

From a letter to Edward Lucas White

The overfaithful sword returns the user
    His heart's desire at price of his heart's blood:
The clamour of the arrogant accuser
    Wastes that one hour we needed to make good.
This was foretold of old at our outgoing –
This we accepted who have squandered, knowing,
The wreck and rubble of our reputations
    At the day's need, as it were dross, to guard
The tender and new dedicate foundations
    Against the sea we fear – not man's award.
For – so the ark be borne to Zion, who
Heeds how they perished or were paid that bore it,
For, so the shrine abide, what shame, what pride
If we the priests were bound or crowned before it?*

You'll see here that one line is a blank ender, but that there is an inlaid rhyme in the last but one to balance it. But the fun comes in, in using the bigger, the more reverberating words at the end. Also the short words balance against the longer ones.

Get a perfectly clear thought and a conclusion at which you desire to arrive and put all you have or feel on that matter into the fourteen lines. Then we'll sit on it together and after that the ballad which will be the Deuceanall!

Ever affectionately,
Ruddy...

From a letter to Edward Lucas White,* 13 December 1910

. . .What a lordly appreciation you have sent of Rewards and Fairies. I purred when I read it – same as Moses (or Aaron?) did when the ointment ran down 'even to the skirts of his clothing'.* I confess myself to be rather fond of my last baby. In that kind of work one can stuff in, unbeknownst, all manner of allusions and references and cross-references that really don't show up at all unless you hold the texture at a certain angle. At the same time they don't hamper the narrative much. There are anagrams and cryptograms intil't too, and thefts and plagiarisms and ploughings with other folk's heifers.* Yes I *did* enjoy myself. But as to the Songs they're all mine. If you're alluding to the two verses that Philadelphia sings,* here's their genesis. Shenstone has somewhere or other, about the end I think, of a long and drearyish ode* four lines of pure tears thus: –

Yet time may diminish the pain
The flower and the bud and the tree
That I reared for her pleasure in vain
In time may bring comfort to me.

– or words to that effect. I quote without the book, but my heart knows it too well. Well, of course they were *the* words for my Philadelphia only they wouldn't have been set to music. So I had to invent a sort of parallel passage of about the same age and appearance and if you look closely you'll see that *they* in turn owe something to the Meditation of Alexander Selkirk* 'I am monarch &c.' The actual effect comes out of 'desolate' – 'rave' and 'charge'. I'm rejoiced that *you* spotted it…

From a letter to a schoolboy,* 24 February 1919

… Now as to literature generally. There's no way to learn to write verse except by writing it. A man called Tom Hood once wrote a small book called '*How I taught a youngster to write verse*'.* It's out of print now but I think any leading bookseller could try to fish up a copy for you. It gives the mere mechanics – the longs and shorts – of the business and that is always worth learning. Blank verse, of course, is the most difficult stuff in the world to write – too hard for any one to try. But the value of writing English verse is that it makes you handier in writing prose – gives you more words and better command over 'em.

As to play writing don't worry to start in too soon, but take an old well known play to pieces and study how it's done. There is any amount of books on play making. 'Q' (Quiller Couch) has just published a most interesting study of 'Shakespeare's workmanship' – really useful and interesting stuff. You'd better ask for it at the school library.

All books by Saintsbury* on English literature are sound and – what is unusual – interesting. Are you sure that his 'Peace of the Augustans' is out of print? He's written a book on Elizabethan literature which is very good.

As a general piece of advice, …, if I were you, I should simply confine myself to one section of English literature – Elizabethan or Augustan for choice – browse in it, copy it and generally soak myself in it. After a bit, if you have any real *itch* for writing, you'll find your spirit will begin to move by itself – and very likely in a direction which has nothing to do with your previous studies. The main thing is to give the mind something to start up upon. Side by side with that, accustom yourself to describing – for your own private benefit – some incident, or affair or scene that has taken your fancy. Do this about once a week simply as a 'swot' till it becomes easier and easier.

That's about all the advice that I will decant on you at present. Be thankful...

From 'The Bull that Thought'*

. . . He allowed himself to be played into the shadow or the sun, as the delighted audience demanded. He raged enormously; he feigned defeat; he despaired in statuesque abandon, and thence flashed into fresh paroxysms of wrath – but always with the detachment of the true artist who knows he is but the vessel of an emotion whence others, not he, must drink...

'"Proofs of Holy Writ"'*

Arise, shine; for thy light is come, and the glory of the Lord is risen upon thee.
2. *For, behold, the darkness shall cover the earth, and gross darkness the people: but the Lord shall arise upon thee, and his glory shall be seen upon thee.*
3. *And the Gentiles shall come to thy light, and kings to the brightness of thy rising.*

. . . .

19. *The sun shall be no more thy light by day; neither for brightness shall the moon give light unto thee: but the Lord shall be unto thee an everlasting light, and thy God thy glory.*
20. *Thy sun shall no more go down; neither shall thy moon withdraw itself: for the Lord shall be thine everlasting light, and the days of thy mourning shall be ended.*

ISAIAH LX. AUTHORISED VERSION

They seated themselves in the heavy chairs on the pebbled floor beneath the eaves of the summer-house by the orchard. A table between them carried wine and glasses, and a packet of papers, with pen and ink. The larger man of the two, his doublet unbuttoned, his broad face blotched and scarred, puffed a little as he came to rest. The other picked an apple from the grass, bit it, and went on with the thread of the talk that they must have carried out of doors with them.

'But why waste time fighting atomies who do not come up to your belly-button, Ben?' he asked.

'It breathes me – it breathes me, between bouts! *You*'d be better for a tussle or two.'

'But not to spend mind and verse on 'em. What was Dekker* to you? Ye knew he'd strike back – and hard.'

'He and Marston had been baiting me like dogs . . . about my trade as they called it,* though it was only my cursed stepfather's. "Bricks and mortar", Dekker said, and "hodman." And he mocked my face.* 'Twas clean as curds in my youth. This humour has come on me since.'

'Ah! "Every man *and* his humour"?* But why did ye not have at Dekker in peace – over the sack, as you do at me?'

'Because I'd have drawn on him – and he's no more worth a hanging than Gabriel.* Setting aside what he wrote of me, too, the hireling dog has merit, of a sort. His *Shoemaker's Holiday*. Hey? Though my *Bartlemy Fair*, when 'tis presented, will furnish out three of it and –'

'Ride all the easier. I have suffered two readings of it already. It creaks like an overloaded hay-wain', the other cut in. 'You give too much.'

Ben smiled loftily, and went on. 'But I'm glad I lashed him in my *Poetaster*,* for all I've worked with him since. How comes it that I've never fought with thee, Will?'

'First, Behemoth', the other drawled, 'it needs two to engender any sort of iniquity. Second, the betterment of this present age – and the next, maybe – lies, in chief, on our four shoulders. If the Pillars of the Temple fall out, Nature, Art and Learning come to a stand. Last, I am not yet ass enough to hawk up my private spites before the groundlings. What do the Court, citizens, or 'prentices give for thy fallings-out or fallings-in with Dekker – or the Grand Devil?'

'They should be taught, then – taught.'

'Always *that*? What's your commission to enlighten us?'

'My own learning which I have heaped up, lifelong, at my own pains. My assured knowledge, also, of my craft and art. I'll suffer no man's mock or malice on it.'

'The one sure road to mockery.'

'I deny nothing of my brain-store to my lines. I – I build up my own works throughout.'

'Yet when Dekker cries "hodman" y'are not content.'

Ben half heaved in his chair. 'I'll owe you a beating for that when I'm thinner. Meantime, here's on account. I say, *I* build upon my own foundations; devising and perfecting my own plots; adorning 'em justly as fits time, place and action. In all of which you sin damnably. *I* set no landward principalities on sea-beaches.'*

'They pay their penny for pleasure – not learning', Will answered above the apple-core.

'Penny or tester, you owe 'em justice. In the facture of plays – nay, listen, Will – at all points they must be dressed historically – *teres atque rotundus** – in ornament and temper. As my *Sejanus*, of which the mob was unworthy.'

Here Will made a doleful face, and echoed, 'Unworthy! I was – what did I play, Ben, in that long weariness? Some most grievous ass.'

'The part of Caius Silius', said Ben stiffly.

Will laughed aloud. 'True. "Indeed that place *was* not my sphere."'*

It must have been a quotation, for Ben winced a little, ere he recovered himself and went on: 'Also my *Alchemist* which the world in part apprehends. The main of its learning is necessarily hid from 'em. To come to your works, Will –'

'I am a sinner on all sides. The drink's at your elbow.'

'Confession shall not save ye – nor bribery.' Ben filled his glass. 'Sooner than labour the right cold heat to devise your own plots you filch, botch, and clap 'em together out o' ballads, broadsheets, old wives' tales, chapbooks –'

Will nodded with complete satisfaction. 'Say on', quoth he.

''Tis so with nigh all yours. I've known honester jackdaws. And whom among the learned do ye deceive? Reckoning up those – forty, is it? – your plays you've misbegot, there's not six which have not plots common as Moorditch.'*

'Ye're out, Ben. There's not one. My *Love's Labour* (how I came to write it, I know not) is nearest to lawful issue. My *Tempest* (how I came to write *that,** I know) is, in some part, my own stuff. Of the rest, I stand guilty. Bastards all!'

'And no shame.'

'None! Our business must be fitted with parts hot and hot – and the boys are more trouble than the men. Give me the bones of any stuff, I'll cover 'em as quickly as any. But to hatch new plots is to waste God's unreturning time like a –' – he chuckled – 'like a hen.'

'Ye see what ye miss! Invention next to Knowledge, whence it proceeds, being the chief glory of Art –'

'Miss, say you? Dick Burbage* – in my *Hamlet* that I botched for him when he had staled of our Kings? (Nobly he played it.) Was *he* a miss?'

Ere Ben could speak Will overbore him.

'And when poor Dick was at odds with the world in general and womenkind in special, I clapped him up my *Lear* for a vomit.'

'An hotch-potch of passion, outrunning reason', was the verdict.

'Not altogether. Cast in a mould too large for any boards to bear. (My fault!) Yet Dick evened it. And when he'd come out of his whoremongering aftermaths of repentance, I served him my *Macbeth* to toughen him. Was that a miss?'

'I grant your *Macbeth* as nearest in spirit to my *Sejanus*; showing for example: "How fortune plies her sports when she begins To practise 'em."* We'll see which of the two lives longest.'

'Amen! I'll bear no malice among the worms.'

A liveried serving-man, booted and spurred, led a saddle-horse through the gate into the orchard. At a sign from Will he tethered the beast to a tree, lurched aside and stretched on the grass. Ben, curious as a lizard, for all his bulk, wanted to know what it meant.

'There's a nosing Justice of the Peace lost in thee', Will returned. 'Yon's a business I've neglected all this day for thy fat sake – and he by so much the drunker . . . Patience! It's all set out on the table. Have a care with the ink!'

Ben reached unsteadily for the packet of papers and read the superscription: '"To William Shakespeare, Gentleman, at his house of New Place in the town of Stratford, these – with diligence from M.S." Why does the fellow withhold his name? Or is it one of your women? I'll look.'

Muzzy as he was, he opened and unfolded a mass of printed papers expertly enough.

'From the most learned divine, Miles Smith* of Brazen Nose College', Will explained. 'You know this business as well as I. The King has set all the scholars of England to make one Bible, which the Church shall be bound to, out of all the Bibles that men use.'

'*I* knew', Ben could not lift his eyes from the printed page. 'I'm more about Court than you think. The learning of Oxford and Cambridge – "most noble and most equal,"* as I have said – and Westminster, to sit upon a clutch of Bibles. Those 'ud be Geneva (my mother read to me out of it at her knee), Douai, Rheims, Coverdale, Matthew's, the Bishop's, the Great,* and so forth.'

'They are all set down on the page there – text against text.* And you call me a botcher of old clothes?'

'Justly. But what's your concern with this botchery? To keep peace among the Divines? There's fifty of 'em at it as I've heard.'

'I deal with but one. He came to know me when we played at Oxford – when the plague was too hot in London.'

'I remember this Miles Smith now. Son of a butcher? Hey?' Ben grunted.

'Is it so?' was the quiet answer. 'He was moved, he said, with some lines of mine in Dick's part. He said they were, to his godly apprehension, a parable, as it might be, of his reverend self, going down darkling to his tomb 'twixt cliffs of ice and iron.'

'What lines? I know none of thine of that power. But in my *Sejanus* –'

'There were in my *Macbeth*. They lost nothing at Dick's mouth:–

'To-morrow, and to-morrow, and to-morrow
Creeps in this petty pace from day to day
To the last syllable of recorded time,
And all our yesterdays have lighted fools
The way to dusty death –'

or something in that sort. Condell* writes 'em out fair for him, and tells him I am Justice of the Peace (wherein he lied) and *armiger*,* which brings me within the pale of God's creatures and the Church. Little and little, then, this very reverend Miles Smith opens his mind to me. He and a half-score others, his cloth, are cast to furbish up the Prophets – Isaiah to Malachi. In his opinion by what he'd heard, I had some skill in words, and he'd condescend –'

'How?' Ben barked. 'Condescend?'

'Why not? He'd condescend to inquire o' me privily, when direct illumination lacked, for a tricking-out of his words or the turn of some figure. For example' – Will pointed to the papers – 'here be the first three verses of the Sixtieth of Isaiah, and the nineteenth and twentieth of that same. Miles has been at a stand over 'em a week or more.'

'They never called on *me*.' Ben caressed lovingly the hand-pressed proofs on their lavish linen paper. 'Here's the Latin atop and' – his thick forefinger ran down the slip – 'some three – four – Englishings out of the other Bibles. They spare 'emselves nothing. Let's to it together. Will you have the Latin first?'

'Could I choke ye from that, Holofernes?'*

Ben rolled forth, richly: '"*Surge, illumare, Jerusalem, quia venit lumen tuum, et gloria Domini super te orta est. Quia ecce tenebrae operient terram et caligo populos. Super te autem orietur Dominus, et gloria ejus in te videbitur. Et ambulabunt gentes in lumine tuo, et reges in splendore ortus tui.*" Er-hum? Think you to better that?'

'How have Smith's crew gone about it?'

'Thus.' Ben read from the paper. '"Get ye up, O Jerusalem, and be bright, for thy light is at hand, and the glory of God has risen up upon thee."'

'Up-pup-pup!' Will stuttered profanely.

Ben held on. '"See how darkness is upon the earth and the peoples thereof."'

'That's no great stuff to put into Isaiah's mouth. And further, Ben?'

'"But on thee God shall shew light and on –" or "in," is it?' (Ben held the proof closer to the deep furrow at the bridge of his nose.) '"On thee shall His glory be manifest. So that all peoples shall walk in thy light and the Kings in the glory of thy morning."'

'It may be mended. Read me the Coverdale of it now. 'Tis on the same sheet – to the right, Ben.'

'Umm – umm! Coverdale saith, "And therefore get thee up betimes, for thy light cometh, and the glory of the Lord shall rise up upon thee. For lo! while the darkness and cloud covereth the earth and the people, the Lord shall shew thee light, and His glory shall be seen in thee. The Gentiles shall come to thy light, and kings to the brightness that springeth forth upon thee." But "gentes" is, for the most part, "peoples,"' Ben concluded.

'Eh?' said Will indifferently. 'Art sure?'

This loosed an avalanche of instances from Ovid, Quintilian, Terence, Columella, Seneca,* and others. Will took no heed till the rush ceased, but stared into the orchard, through the September haze. 'Now give me the Douai and Geneva for this "Get thee up, O Jerusalem,"' said he at last. 'They'll be all there.'

Ben referred to the proofs. ''Tis "arise" in both', said he. '"Arise and be bright" in Geneva. In the Douai 'tis "Arise and be illuminated."'

'So? Give me the paper now.' Will took it from his companion, rose, and paced towards a tree in the orchard, turning again, when he had reached it, by a well-worn track through the grass. Ben leaned forward in his chair. The other's free hand went up warningly.

'Quiet, man!' said he. 'I wait on my Demon!'* He fell into the stage-stride of his art at that time, speaking to the air.

'How shall this open? "Arise?" No! "Rise!" Yes. And we'll have no weak coupling. 'Tis a call to a City! "Rise – shine!" . . . Nor yet any schoolmaster's "because" – because Isaiah is not Holofernes. *"Rise – shine; for thy light is come, and – !"'* He refreshed himself from the apple and the proofs as he strode. '"And – and the glory of God!" – No! "God"'s over short. We need the long roll here. *"And the glory of the Lord is risen on thee."* (Isaiah speaks the part. We'll have it from his own lips.) What's next in Smith's stuff? . . . "See how?" Oh, vile – vile! . . . And Geneva hath "Lo?" (Still, Ben! Still!) "Lo" is better by all odds: but to match the long roll of "the Lord" we'll have it "Behold." How goes it now. *"For, behold, darkness clokes the earth and* – and –" What's the colour and use of this cursed *caligo*, Ben? – *"Et caligo populos."*'

'"Mistiness" or, as in Pliny,* "blindness". And further –'

'No – o . . . Maybe, though, *caligo* will piece out *tenebrae. "Quia ecce tenebrae operient terram et caligo populos."* Nay! "Shadow" and "mist" are not men enough for this work. . . Blindness, did ye say, Ben? . . . The blackness of blindness atop of mere darkness? . . . By God, I've used it in my own stuff many times! "Gross" searches it to the hilts! *"Darkness clokes the earth, and gross – gross darkness the people!"* (But Isaiah's prophesying, with the storm behind him. Can ye not *feel* it, Ben? It must be "shall") – *"Shall cloke the earth"* . . . The rest comes clearer. . . . "But on thee God shall arise" . . . (Nay, that's sacrificing the Creator to the Creature!) *"But the Lord shall arise on thee"*,' and – yes, we'll sound that "thee" again – "and on thee shall" – No! . . . *"And His glory shall be seen on thee."* Good!' He walked his beat a little in silence, mumbling the two verses before he mouthed them.

'I have it! Heark, Ben! *"Rise – shine; for thy light is come, and the glory of the Lord is risen on thee. For, behold, darkness shall cloke the earth, and gross darkness the people. But the Lord shall arise on thee, and His glory shall be seen upon thee."'*

'There's something not all amiss there', Ben conceded.

'My Demon never betrayed me yet, while I trusted him. Now for the verse that runs to the blast of rams'-horns.* *"Et ambulabunt gentes in lumine tuo, et reges in splendore tui."* How goes that in the Smithy? "The Gentiles shall come to thy light, and kings to the brightness that springs forth upon thee?" The same in Coverdale and the Bishops' – eh? We'll keep "Gentiles," Ben, for the sake of the indraught of the last syllable. But it might be "And the Gentiles shall draw?" No! The plainer the better! "The Gentiles shall come to thy light, and kings to the splendour of –" (Smith's out here! We'll need something that shall lift the trumpet anew.) "Kings shall – shall – Kings to –" (Listen, Ben, but on your life speak not!) "Gentiles shall come to thy light, and kings to thy brightness" – Not "Kings to the brightness that springeth –" Serves not! . . . One trumpet must answer another. And the blast of a trumpet is always *ai-ai.* "The brightness of –" *"Ortus"* signifies "rising", Ben – or what?'

'Ay, or "birth", or the East in general.'

'Ass! 'Tis the one word that answers to "light". "Kings to the brightness of thy rising." Look! The thing shines now within and without. God! That so much should lie on a word!" He repeated the verse – '*"And the Gentiles shall come to thy light, and kings to the brightness of thy rising."'*

He walked to the table and wrote rapidly on the proof margin all three verses as he had spoken them. 'If they hold by this', said he, raising his head, 'they'll not go far astray. Now for the nineteenth and twentieth verses. On the other sheet, Ben. What? What? Smith says he has held back his rendering till he hath seen mine? Then we'll botch 'em as they stand. Read me first the Latin; next the Coverdale, and last the Bishops'. There's a contagion of sleep in the air.' He handed back the proofs, yawned, and took up his walk.

Obedient, Ben began: '*"Non erit tibi amplius Sol ad lucendum per diem, nec splendur Lunae illumabit te."* Which Coverdale rendereth, "The sun shall never be thy day light, and the light of the Moon shall never shine unto thee." The Bishops read: "Thy sun shall never be thy daylight and the light of the moon shall never shine on thee."'

'Coverdale is the better', said Will, and, wrinkling his nose a little, 'The Bishops put out their lights clumsily. Have at it, Ben.'

Ben pursed his lips and knit his brow. 'The two verses are in the same mode, changing a hand's-breadth in the second. By so much, therefore, the more difficult.'

'Ye see *that*, then?' said the other, staring past him, and muttering as he paced, concerning suns and moons. Presently he took back the proof, chose him another apple, and grunted. 'Umm-umm! "Thy Sun shall never be –" No! Flat as a split viol. *"Non erit tibi amplius Sol –"* That *amplius* must give tongue. Ah!... "Thy Sun shall not – shall not – shall no more be thy light by day"... A fair entry. "Nor?" – No! Not on the heels of "day." "Neither" it must be – "Neither the Moon" – but here's *splendor* and the rams'-horns again. (Therefore – *ai – ai!*) "Neither for brightness shall the Moon –" (Pest! It is the Lord who is taking the Moon's place over Israel. It must be "thy Moon".) "Neither for brightness shall thy Moon light – give – make – give light unto thee." Ah! . . . Listen here! . . . *"The Sun shall no more be thy light by day: neither for brightness shall thy Moon give light unto thee."* That serves, and more, for the first entry. What next, Ben?'

Ben nodded magisterially as Will neared him, reached out his hand for the proofs, and read: '*"Sed erit tibi Dominus in lucem sempiternam et Deus tuus in gloriam tuam."* Here is a jewel of Coverdale's that the Bishops have wisely stolen whole. Hear! *"But* the Lord Himself shall be thy everlasting light, and thy God shall be thy glory."' Ben paused. 'There's a hand's-breadth of splendour for a simple man to gather!'

'Both hands rather. He's swept the strings as divinely as David before Saul',* Will assented. 'We'll convey it whole, too. . . . What's amiss now, Holofernes?'

For Ben was regarding him with a scholar's cold pity. 'Both hands! Will, has thou *ever* troubled to master *any* shape or sort of prosody – the mere names of the measures and pulses of strung words?'

'I beget some such stuff and send it to you to christen. What's your wisdomhood in labour of?'

'Naught. Naught. But not to know the names of the tools of his trade!' Ben half muttered and pronounced some Greek word* or other which conveyed nothing to the listener, who replied: 'Pardon, then, for whatever sin it was. I do but know words for my need of 'em, Ben. Hold still awhile!'

He went back to his pacings and mutterings. '"For the Lord Himself shall be thy – or thine? – everlasting light." Yes. We'll convey that.' He repeated it twice. 'Nay! Can be bettered. Hark ye, Ben. Here is the Sun going up to over-run and possess all Heaven for evermore. *There*fore (Still, man!) we'll harness the horses of the dawn.* Hear their hooves? "The Lord Himself shall be unto thee thy everlasting light, and –" Hold again! After that climbing thunder must be some smooth check – like great wings gliding. *There*fore we'll not have "shall be thy glory", but "*And* thy God thy glory!" Ay – even as an eagle alighteth! Good – good! Now again, the sun and moon of that twentieth verse, Ben.'

Ben read: '"*Non occidet ultra Sol tuus et Luna tua non minuetur; quia erit tibi Dominus in lucem sempiternum et complebuntur dies luctus tui.*"'

Will snatched the paper and read aloud from the Coverdale version. '"Thy Sun shall never go down, and thy Moon shall not be taken away. . . ."' What a plague's Coverdale doing with his blocking *ets* and *urs*, Ben? What's *minuetur*? . . . I'll have it all anon.'

'Minish – make less – appease – abate, as in –'

'So?' . . . Will threw the proofs back. 'Then "wane" should serve. "Neither shall thy moon wane" . . . "Wane" is good, but over-weak for place next to "moon"' . . . He swore softly. 'Isaiah hath abolished both earthly sun and moon. *Exeunt ambo*. Aha! I begin to see! . . . Sol, the man, goes down – down stairs or trap – as needs be. Therefore "Go down" shall stand. "Set" would have been better – as a sword sent home in the scabbard – but it jars – it jars. Now Luna must retire herself in some simple fashion . . . Which? Ass that I be! 'Tis common talk in all the plays. . . . "Withdrawn" . . . "Favour withdrawn" . . . "Countenance withdrawn." "The Queen withdraws herself" . . . "Withdraw", it shall be! "Neither shall thy moon withdraw herself." (Hear her silver train rasp the boards, Ben?) *"Thy sun shall no more go down – neither shall thy moon withdraw herself. For the Lord . . ."* – ay, the Lord, simple of Himself – *"shall be thine"* – yes, "thine" here – *"everlasting light, and"* . . . How goes the ending, Ben?'

'"*Et complebuntur dies luctus tui.*"' Ben read. '"And thy sorrowful days shall be rewarded thee", says Coverdale.'

'And the Bishops?'

'"And thy sorrowful days shall be ended."'

'By no means. And Douai?'

'"Thy sorrow shall be ended."'

'And Geneva?'

'"And the days of thy mourning shall be ended."'

'The Switzers have it! Lay the tail of Geneva to the head of Coverdale and the last is without flaw.' He began to thump Ben on the shoulder. 'We have it! I have it all, Boanerges!* Blessed be my Demon! Hear! *"The sun shall no more be thy light by day, neither for brightness the moon by night. But the Lord Himself shall be unto thee thy everlasting light, and thy God thy glory."'* He drew a deep breath and went on. '*"Thy sun shall no more go down; neither shall thy moon withdraw herself, for the Lord shall be thine everlasting light, and the days of thy mourning shall be ended."*' The rain of triumphant blows began again. 'If those other seven devils* in London let it stand on this sort, it serves. But God knows what they can *not* turn upsee-dejee!'*

Ben wriggled. 'Let be!' he protested. 'Ye are more moved by this jugglery than if the Globe were burned.'*

'Thatch – old thatch! And full of fleas! . . . But, Ben, ye should have heard my Ezekiel making mock of fallen Tyrus in his twenty-seventh chapter. Miles sent me the whole, for, he said, some small touches. I took it to the Bank – four o'clock of a summer morn; stretched out in one of our wherries – and watched London, Port and Town, up and down the river, waking all arrayed to heap more upon evident excess. Ay! "A merchant for the peoples of many isles" . . . "The ships of Tarshish did sing of thee in thy markets?"* Yes! I saw all Tyre before me neighing her pride against lifted heaven. . . . But what will they let stand of all mine at long last? Which? I'll never know.'

He had set himself neatly and quickly to refolding and cording the packet while he talked. 'That's secret enough', he said at the finish.

'He'll lose it by the way.' Ben pointed to the sleeper beneath the tree. 'He's owl-drunk.'

'But not his horse', said Will. He crossed the orchard, roused the man; slid the packet into an holster which he carefully rebuckled; saw him out of the gate, and returned to his chair.

'Who will know we had part in it?' Ben asked.

'God, maybe – if He ever lay ear to earth. I've gained and lost enough – lost enough.' He lay back and sighed. There was long silence till he spoke half aloud. 'And Kit* that was my master in the beginning, he died when all the world was young.'

'Knifed on a tavern reckoning – not even for a wench!' Ben nodded.

'Ay. But if he'd lived he'd have breathed me! 'Fore God, he'd have breathed me!'

'Was Marlowe, or any man, *ever* thy master, Will?'

'He alone. Very he. I envied Kit. Ye do not know that envy, Ben?'

'Not as touching my own works. When the mob is led to prefer a baser Muse, I have felt the hurt, and paid home.* Ye know that – as ye know my doctrine of play-writing.'

'Nay – not wholly – tell it at large', said Will, relaxing in his seat, for virtue had gone out of him.* He put a few drowsy questions. In three minutes Ben had launched full-flood on the decayed state of the drama, which he was born to correct; on cabals and intrigues against him which he had fought without cease; and on the inveterate muddle-headedness of the mob unless duly scourged into approbation by his magisterial hand.

It was very still in the orchard now that the horse had gone. The heat of the day held though the sun sloped, and the wine had done its work. Presently, Ben's discourse was broken by a snort from the other chair.

'I was listening, Ben! Missed not a word – missed not a word.'
Will sat up and rubbed his eyes. 'Ye held me throughout.' His head dropped again before he had done speaking.

Ben looked at him with a chuckle and quoted from one of his own plays: –

> '"*Mine earnest vehement botcher*
> *And deacon also, Will, I cannot dispute with you.*"'*

He drew out flint, steel and tinder, pipe and tobacco-bag from somewhere round his waist, lit and puffed against the midges till he, too, dozed.

4

HISTORY AND CONTEMPORARY CULTURE

*

Review in *The Pioneer*,* 5 February 1886

From Recruit to Staff Sergeant,* a Tale of the old Bengal Horse Artillery, is a modest and unpretentious little book by Mr. N. W. Bancroft, late Staff Sergeant of 2–1, Bengal Horse Artillery. It is dedicated to the Rev. G. Gregson,* the apostle of temperance in the Army; but, in spite of this fact, is not written with a purpose or a moral. Sergeant Bancroft went through the campaign of the Army of the Sutlej* forty years ago, and his book deals for the most part with the battles of Moodkee, Ferozeshah, Aliwal and Sabraon. He does not trouble himself or his readers with military criticism or fine writing, but records simply what he actually saw and heard under fire. War thus treated loses a good deal of its glamour and picturesqueness, but gains in realism. Some of the incidents of the battle of Ferozeshah should never have been told to a squeamish public – notably a conversation exchanged under the fire of the Sikh guns by two Artillery men, and now faithfully recorded in its almost heroic brutality.* Sergeant Bancroft alludes to himself when allusion is necessary, as 'the writer': and the impersonality of the reference reads very quaintly sometimes. At Ferozeshah, an officer's head is taken off by a cannon ball. 'At the same time the writer felt a dreadful shock on his right side, and his right arm involuntarily whirled round his head. He was at the time picking out a quid of tobacco from a comrade's pouch to moisten his lips withal. Feeling that he was hit, he returned the pouch with the left hand, remarking: – "here, take your pouch I've lost my arm". A cannon ball had passed between the limb and the body shattering but not carrying away the arm.' Then 'the writer' describes his drive on a gun-trail, and divers horrible scenes which took place before the Sikhs were put to flight – all in the simple and philosophical tone of one recounting a review. Stories of camp fire jests, rough banter and practical jokes alternate with the more sombre portions of the book which, in addition to its point and directness, has the merits of an interesting historical record. It is published by the Calcutta City Press.

From a letter to W. C. Crofts,* 18–27 February 1886

... I see by this week's P[all. M[all]. Gazette* that the worthy William Morris has been giving his opinion on the Hundred best books. Lord! Lord! what a lying world it is. He has gravely stuck down the Mahabarat* and I will wager everything I have that he hasn't the ghost of a conception what he means when he recommends the study of that monstrous midden. Imprimis it's a colossal undertaking even in English *and* the only translation which would be intelligible to the ordinary English reader has just begun and is coming out in monthly parts – semi occasional parts I should say – here. Well, I have patiently perused all the Mahab. I could lay my hands on and I assure you that a more hopeless, aimless, diffuse drivel (tempered with puerile obscenity) it would be hard to come across. Yet Morris gravely puts it down – and the Shah-nameh* as well. I wonder that he didn't stick in the Ramayana of Tulsi Dass* and the Rig Veda* to crown the lie. I see every now and then at home some man who hasn't touched 'em lifting up his voice in praise of 'the golden mines of Oriental Literature' and I snort. There are one or two things worth the reading but to get at them one has to wade through a muck heap, and the vast bulk of the stuff that is as a matter of duty belauded and extolled to the skies is so much waste of paper and ink. Get hold of a translation of the Rig Veda Sir and by the time you've ploughed through a few thousand verses reiterating one monotonous whine for horses, cattle, corn and strong drinks you will heave the book out of the window and go a hunting for the blood of Monier Williams.* But I suppose we must accept the dictum of William the poet and it would be flat blasphemy to hint that one decent primer on Sanitary Engineering and sewage disposal is worth more than all the tomes of sacred smut ever produced. Young India – in the shape of the educated Bengali – has a clear notion that a study of English and surveying pays better than anything else and when he is exhorted to 'study the classics of his native land' he smiles. He knows all the dirty yarns in 'em from his youth up, for they make the staple of the songs of the people and the lullabies of the mothers. What more does he want? Imagine ten folio pages filled with stuff like this: – 'I adore the toe-nails of the sacred guru whose breath is like the breath of the kine of India. I prostrate myself making the seven abasements and the four lesser genuflexions before the dust of his feet which are like unto the young lotus. Oh Indra! give us sons – fair men. I worship Indra with the prescribed ceremonies and the navel of the illustrious Guru!'* Am I exaggerating? Don't condemn me till you've tried to swallow some of the big fraud yourself Sir...

Obituary in *The Pioneer,** 14 February 1887

The Authoress of *East Lynne* and the *Johnny Ludlow Papers* is dead. Mrs Henry Wood belonged to an almost byegone generation of novelists, for her first work was before the public in the days when the 'Society' novel had scarcely come into being, and writers dealt with vigorous and distinct colours instead of the half-tones and neutral subleties of the Franco-American school or the charnel-house horrors of the shilling dreadfuls. '*The Mill on the Floss*', and '*The Woman in White*'* were new when Mrs Wood began her life's work more than a quarter of a century ago, and won herself a name among English women writers. It was through *East Lynne* that she gained her reputation – melodramatic and overstrained though the work was – and the *Johnny Ludlow Papers* fixed that reputation among the vast host of novel readers. By these two works she will be remembered.

From a letter to Edmonia Hill,* 22 April 1888

... Remind me that I bear a grudge against Mrs Ross. She has insulted by sending the English version of Madame Bovary* embellished by bad Woodbury or autotype* pictures. To mark my deep contempt I have thrown it at the lame black cat who is my constant companion and from her language I gather that she approves of Flaubert as little as I do. Happy thought! Perhaps Flaubert had indigestion and that suggested killing his crazy heroine with arsenic. You've read the thing haven't you? Didn't you resent it?

Twasn't so bad in its French but when I unearthed it in all the bald brutality of the British tongue I kicked... as the black cat knoweth.

From a letter to Edmonia Hill,* 15 May 1888

...Yes Madam I have read Cape Cod Folk* and it's what they call genre work. Can't say that I care for it much but then my taste in literature is queer. Just now it has been principally confined to blue books* of a gay and festive nature – all about export and import tonnage and the racial difference between an Aka and a Madan Kheyl* or skittles of that kind. But I've been trying once more to plough through The Descent of Man* and every fiber (observe the American way of spelling) of my body revolted against it. To believe in that it is necessary never to have – Hullo! Where is this one-idea'd pen going off to anew. Also I've been taking up some French stuff of sorts – rummy old French books written in the blanking style that I've always associated with the march of the priests in Athalie.* But I haven't much time for reading...

From 'The Children of the Zodiac'*

It was after this that Leo made the Song of the Bull who had been a God and forgotten the fact, and he sang it in such a manner that half the young men in the world conceived that they too might be Gods without knowing it. A half of that half grew impossibly conceited, and died early. A half of the remainder strove to be Gods and failed, but the other half accomplished four times more work than they would have done under any other delusion.

Letter to Robert Underwood Johnson,* 14 December 1895

Dear Johnson,

Yours of the 12th.

What you propose is an exceeding big job* and one altogether beyond my scope. I made a try at the same thing years ago in India and in turning over documents came across *one* file of John Lawrence's* ordinary office letters for the month of June 1857. That cured me. Besides '57 is the year we don't talk about and I know *I* can't. Again you overlook the little fact that it is much more difficult to catch the spirit, the hundred little shades, of society 40 years ago than of society of the middle ages or of the neolithic age for that matter. But it would be a great thing to have it properly done.

Mrs Flora Annie Steel* – she that wrote *From the Land of the Five Rivers*; *The Potters Thumb*; and so on, is I believe collecting material *in situ*, for a novel covering the same ground. Now I know that she has had at least 25 years' experience of India and knows more about certain twists of the native mind than any one I know. It seems to me that if you could get *her* novel you'd be likely to be buying something really good. She's a beautiful writer and she *knows*. Then again there is S. Levett Yeats* – *The Honour of Savelli*. When I knew him in the Punjab Club in the old days he was full of notions for a mutiny tale and he may have something up his sleeve that would be worth getting at. I throw out these here gratuitous suggestions because I very much want to see a good mutiny novel. I'd try in a minute if I felt I had a call that way but I'm rather convinced I have not. Very sincerely always

Rudyard Kipling.

'Shakespeare and *The Tempest*'*

Your article on 'Landscape and Literature'* in the *Spectator* of June 18th has the following among other suggestive passages: 'But whence came the vision of the enchanted island in *The Tempest*? It had no existence in Shakespeare's world, but was woven out of such stuff as dreams are made on.'

May I cite Malone's* suggestion connecting the play with the casting away of Sir George Somers* on the island of Bermuda in 1609? And further, may I be allowed to say how it seems to me possible that the vision was woven from the most prosaic material – from nothing more promising, in fact, than the chatter of a half-tipsy sailor at a theatre? Thus:–

A stage-manager, who writes and vamps plays, moving among his audience, overhears a mariner discoursing to his neighbour of a grievous wreck, and of the behaviour of the passengers, for whom all sailors have ever entertained a natural contempt. He describes, with the wealth of detail peculiar to sailors, measures taken to claw the ship off a lee-shore, how helm and sails were worked, what the passengers did, and what he said. One pungent phrase – to be rendered later into: 'What cares these roarers for the name of king?'* – strikes the manager's ear, and he stands behind the talkers. Perhaps only one-tenth of the earnestly delivered, hand-on-shoulder sea-talk was actually used of all that was automatically and unconsciously stored by the inland man who knew all inland arts and crafts. Nor is it too fanciful to imagine a half-turn to the second listener as the mariner, banning his luck as mariners will, says there are those who would not give a doit to a poor man, while they will lay out ten to see a raree-show – a dead Indian.* Were he in foreign parts, as now he is in England, he could show something in the way of strange fish. Is it to consider too curiously to see a drink ensue on this hint (the manager dealt but little in his plays with the sea at first hand, and his instinct for new words would have been waked by what he had already caught), and with the drink a sailor's minute description of how he went across through the reefs to the island of his calamity – or islands rather, for there were many? Some you could almost carry away in your pocket. They were sown broadcast like – like the nutshells on the stage there. 'Many islands, in truth', says the manager patiently, and afterwards his Sebastian says to Antonio: 'I think he will carry this island home in his pocket and give it his son for an apple.'* To which Antonio answers: 'And, sowing the kernels of it in the sea, bring forth more islands.'

'But what was the land like?' says the manager. The sailor tries to explain. 'It was green, with yellow in it; a tawny coloured country',* – the colour, that is to say, of the coral-beached, cedar-covered Bermuda of to-day – 'and the air made one sleepy, and the place was full of noises'* – the muttering and roaring of the sea among the islands and between the reefs – 'and there was a sou'west wind that blistered one all over'.* The Elizabethan mariner would not distinguish finely between blisters and prickly heat; but the Bermudian of to-day will tell you that the sou'west or Lighthouse wind in summer brings that plague and general discomfort. That the coral rock, battered by the sea, rings hollow with strange sounds, answered by the winds in the little cramped valleys, is a matter of common knowledge.

The man, refreshed with more drink, then describes the geography of his landing-place – the spot where Trinculo makes his first appearance. He insists and reinsists on details which to him at one time meant life or death; and the manager follows attentively. He can give his audience no more than a few hangings and a placard for scenery, but – that his lines should lift them beyond that bare show to the place he would have them – the manager needs for himself the clearest possible understanding – the most ample detail. He must see the scene in the round – solid – ere he peoples it. Much, doubtless, he discarded, but so closely did he keep to his original information that those who go to-day to a certain beach some two miles from Hamilton* will find the stage set for Act II. Scene 2 of *The Tempest* – a bare beach, with the wind singing through the scrub at the land's edge, a gap in the passage wide enough for Stephano's butt of sack, and (these eyes have seen it)* a cave in the coral within easy reach of the tide, whereto such a butt might be conveniently rolled ('My cellar is in a rock* by the seaside where my wine is hid'). There is no other cave for some two miles. 'Here's neither bush nor shrub'; one is exposed to the wrath of 'yond same black cloud', and here the currents strand wreckage. It was so well done that, after three hundred years, a stray tripper, and no Shakespeare scholar, recognised in a flash that old first set of all.

So far good. Up to this point the manager has gained little except some suggestions for an opening scene, and some notion of an uncanny island. The mariner (one cannot believe that Shakespeare was mean in these little things) is dipping to a deeper drunkenness. Suddenly he launches into a preposterous tale of himself and his fellows, flung ashore, separated from their officers, horribly afraid of the devil-haunted beach of noises, with their heads full of the fumes of broached liquor. One castaway was found hiding under the ribs of a dead whale, which smelt abominably. They hauled him out by the legs – he mistook them for imps – and gave him drink. And now, discipline being melted, they would strike out for themselves, defy their officers, and take possession of the island. The narrator's mates in this enterprise were probably described as fools. He was the only sober man in the company.

So they went inland, faring badly as they went up and down this pestilent country. They were pricked with palmettoes, and the cedar branches rasped their faces. Then they found and stole some of their officers' clothes,* which were hanging up to dry. But presently they fell into a swamp,* and, what was worse, into the hands of their officers; and the great expedition ended in muck and mire. Truly an island bewitched. Else why their cramps and sickness? Sack never made a man more than reasonably drunk. He was prepared to answer for unlimited sack; but what befell his stomach and head was the purest magic that honest man ever met.

A drunken sailor of to-day wandering about Bermuda would probably sympathise with him; and to-day, as then, if one takes the easiest inland road from Trinculo's beach, near Hamilton, the path that a drunken man would infallibly follow, it ends abruptly in a swamp. The one point that our mariner did not dwell upon was that he and the others were suffering from acute alcoholism combined with the effects of nerve-shattering peril and exposure. Hence the magic. That a wizard should control such an island was demanded by the beliefs of all seafarers of that date.

Accept this theory, and you will concede that *The Tempest* came to the manager sanely and normally in the course of his daily life. He may have been casting about for a new play. He may have purposed to vamp an old one – say *Aurelio and Isabella*.* Or he may have been merely waiting on his Demon. But it is Prosper's wealth against Caliban's pignuts that to him in a receptive hour, sent by Heaven, entered the original Stephano fresh from the seas and half-seas-over. To him Stephano told his tale all in one piece, a two hours' discourse of most glorious absurdities. His profligate abundance of detail at the beginning, when he was more or less sober, supplied and surely established the earth-basis of the play in accordance with the great law that a story to be truly miraculous must be ballasted with facts. His maunderings of magic and incomprehensible ambushings, when he was without reservation drunk (and this is just the time when a lesser-minded man than Shakespeare would have paid the reckoning and turned him out), suggested to the manager the peculiar note of its supernatural mechanism.

Truly it was a dream, but that there may be no doubt of its source or of his obligation, Shakespeare has also made the dreamer immortal!

From a letter to John St Loe Strachey,* 2 January 1899

... What you say about the 'poet as interpreter'* pleases me on one side of my head and annoys me on the other. It is too late now: but there was a happy time of some six or seven years when I was accepted as a story-teller and rhymester, in which I think I managed to get more work out of the type of man I wished to reach, than since people found out I was putting two meanings into my work. But you must always remember that I am only getting things ready for the real poet who will appear about the first quarter of the next century. He will appropriate everything he wants – perhaps six lines and half an idea – out of all that I and scores of others have done: he will add his own powers to it and then we shall have Browning's successor – not Browning but another. My own dream is that he will be born – perhaps he is born already* – in one of our colonies. The Great War between 1905 and '15 will make him find himself: and about 1925 or '30 the peoples will know who he is. I am roughing out the work for that man – as Ferguson did for Burns:* and I think if he hasn't appeared when I die I shall leave him a private letter of suggestions.

It's a great shame because if I had been born twenty years later I might have seen and understood the drift of the new century. It began in 1889, as nearly as I reckon but we are all bondslaves to our childhood and mine was mixed up with the '70s, which belong to a dead age, and I was under the care of people who drew from the '40s and '50s.* Have you ever thought how all the people who talk about 'the present' are every one of them at least thirty years behind it?

Sincerely yours
Rudyard Kipling.

P.S. Of course my real poet will not interfere with the English-bred, English trained contemplative masters. They will always persist but he will severely shake up and influence the more fluid ones.

From a letter to John St Loe Strachey,* 22 January 1899

. . .I've a friend over the sea
I don't know him and he don't know me

but he sends me clippings of Canadian verse in papers, and being a poet (His name is Sherman)* he knows what I want when I bother him. I am trying to get samples of the same kind from Australia, NZ and that disappointingly slow-to-sing country, the Cape. This batch that I enclose seems to me very encouraging and I send it on to you in the hope that it may perhaps make a 'middle' called, say: – 'The Genesis of National Poetry' which is a fine stodgy title. Now I loathe too much insistence on Nationality which is apt to degenerate into rank provincialism, but I do want you to see how these chaps are working each with his eye on the object – describing his own pines, the lights and shades of his own sun and the coming of his own spring. Out of these things, I think, a good and sane national poetry is born. Of course the men are only fore runners – *ferashes** sweeping the floor and laying the carpets till the great poets come in: but their verse says what the Canadian born thinks and feels as he goes about his own land.

Their similes are his similes and some day, may be, he will back his actions by quotation from verses like these.

There was once a beast – a Bloomsbury, bus-riding, Beast – in the *Athenaeum* who went out of his way, and did much mischief thereby, to say that songs in the English tongue introducing an 'alien flora and fauna left him cold'. I did my best to warm him up with 'The Flowers'* in *The Seven Seas*; but the harm was done and the young Colonial singers in all sorts of places were naturally hurt and discouraged.

One doesn't want to make the boys self-conscious more than they are, but don't you think that you could set forth the inner significance of the work they are doing?

I don't know who Theodore Roberts* is but his 'Hearth in the North' goes straight to the inside of people who know the snows and the return of the trappers, and Sherman's two lines

> – toward the sound of waking mills
> Swing the brown rafts in one by one –

gives the whole Canadian spring. One can smell the raw, new-sawed lumber and feel the squashy ground underfoot. Looking through the verses, one can see here and there how the men are working with a new background – and I am intensely curious to know what the upshot will be. It will differ from American poetry because there isn't the gross materialism in Canada that stains and distorts a good deal of what the Americans think noble and refined. It will be the poetry of free white men who have never had to face the actual bread-and-butter problem – men who have never laid down in the shadow of external fear (think what that means) a race with nothing but open-space and ice between them and the North Pole! I don't know whether you can see the face of the unborn child in these clippings but I do think they'll interest you . . .

From a letter to Brimley Johnson,* 28 November 1900

Dear Mr Johnson,

Many thanks for the *Wild Knight*. Of course I knew some of the poems before, notably *The Donkey* which stuck in my mind at the time I read it.

I agree with you that there is any amount of promise in the work – and I think marriage will teach him a good deal too. It will be curious to see how

From a letter to H. A. Gwynne

he'll develop in a few years. We all begin with arranging and elaborating all the Heavens and Hells and stars and tragedies we can lay our poetic hands on – Later we see folk – just common people under the heavens –

Meantime I wish him all the happiness that there can be . . .

Yours sincerely,
Rudyard Kipling

P.S. Merely as a matter of loathsome detail, Chesterton has a bad attack of 'aureoles'. They are spotted all over the book. I think every one is bound in each book to employ unconsciously some pet word but that was Rossetti's.

Likewise I notice 'wan waste' and many 'wans' and things that 'catch and cling'. He is too good not to be jolted out of that. What do you say to a severe course of Walt Whitman, or will marriage make him see people?

From '"Wireless"'*

. . . in all the millions permitted there are no more than five – five little lines – of which one can say: 'These are the pure Magic. These are the clear Vision. The rest is only poetry.'

From a letter to Sir Alfred Milner,* 26 February 1903

. . . Personally – I mean poetically – I am bound to [Chamberlain's]* chariot wheels because he is all that we have and we owe him gratitude for the past. So I have made – god forgive me – a peaceful and reconciliatory poem* ['The Settler'] of the situation as it ought to be: which perhaps you will see in the papers. That is my small contribution at the end of a very hectic week . . .

From a letter to H. A. Gwynne,* 5 December 1903

. . . I am hard at work on 'The Dream of Belligerontius'* and hope to get it ready in a few weeks. Of course it won't be a serious scheme of Army Reform, but it will, I hope, contain several suggestions at which men can peck . . .

From a letter to Mrs Edmonia Hill,* 8 March 1905

... Most of the Sahib's War* by the way was taken down from the mouth of a native officer up country during the war...

I am glad some part of Traffics interested you. It was really done for the purpose of carrying one political pamphlet – *the Army of a Dream* – and in that respect it was a failure. But what I saw during the war of our arrangements and notions of work, scared me and I thought it might be good to try and train people before a real war came. I got a good deal of *gali** for it...

From a letter to Edward Bok,* 18 July 1905

... I told Watt to send you the first four of my child-stories* (you see I hadn't forgotten my promise) and they may serve to amuse you for awhile if you're off your job. Frankly I don't myself see how they can be used for the L[adies']. H[ome]. J[ournal]. but they're part of a scheme of mine for trying to give children *not* a notion of history but a notion of the time sense which is at the bottom of all knowledge of history and history rightly understanded means love of one's fellow men and the lands one lives in...

Letter to H. S. Canby,* 9 October 1909

Dear Sir

Thank you very much for thinking to send me your study of the short story. I am specially glad that you acknowledge that loose-lipped old frump Aphra Behn* as a workwoman in her particular – or unparticular style. I've often thought that she in *Oroonokoo** and Defoe in many tales drew from the same inkpot if with different pens. In spite of all you say about Henry James* you don't seem to me to admit what I believe to be the case – that he is head and shoulders the biggest of them all and will in the end be found to be perhaps the most enduring influence. It's very amazing to see men who, so to say, blaspheme his manner unconsciously saturated with his technical methods. I should have liked a long chapter on him. Poe of course one always regards as *the* poet of America and the fact that he chose prose instead of verse for his expression in his tales was merely an accident. *Is* this an awful heresy?

But I don't believe that a short-story writer after all is any judge of the business of short-stories and I have therefore found your work specially interesting and new to me.

Very sincerely
Rudyard Kipling.

From a letter to Henry James,* 4 November 1911

Dear Henry James,

... we'd dearly love to see you. On second thoughts I don't know that I should be pleased because I've read and reread *The Out Cry** and have sat down and stolidly hated you. How do you make your dialogues solid – solid in three dimensions like a stage – with peeps and loopholes and vistas and depths and luminosity and a few trifles of that kind, which I can't? There are whole lumps of it which (without scenery) appeal directly through the eye, not as the drama of the persons concerned but as a whole setting of life. And the joyous thing to me is to see the other people imitating you and failing horribly...

From a letter to C. R. L. Fletcher,* 10 April 1915

... In my spare time at Bath I've been reading Jane Austen and the more I read the more I admire and respect and do reverence. What are *your* views? When she looks straight at a man or a woman she is greater than those who were alive with her – by a whole head. Greater than Charles:* greater than Walter* – with a more delicate hand and a keener scalpel. I have suspected it for a long time but, like my friend the South African millionaire* who discovered the Bible, in my presence, in his thirtieth year, now I am sure...

Verses in the margins of a copy of Horace's *Odes**

On Liber II, xiii ('Ille et nefasto te posuit die'):*

There was a Tree
Nigh fell on me,
And brought my wits to confusion:
For the first three stanzas
Ring like a man's, Sirs;
But the rest is classic allusion.

On Liber II, xix ('Bacchum in remotis carmina rupibus'):*

Conventions of another age
Fill us with boredom or with rage;
And that is just how later ages
Will look upon our dainty pages.

All the book-passions we were thrilled with:
All self-made wind that we were filled with:
Will whistle off: and men will say
(As I do, of this thrice-faked lay)
'Whatever made *him* write this way?'

On Liber III, xxviii ('Festo quod potius die'):*

He drank the strenuous Caecuban*
With Lyde at the close of day
And I recall another man
Whose instincts also turned that way –
A Latitudinarian
(So Deb and Mercer had to pay)
Yes! Through the age-old tale there creeps
The note – the very note of –
Pepys!*

On Liber III, xxx ('Exegi monumentum aere perennius'):*

Gods! what a breath I have blown
Through the wide world for all ages.
Praise me or damn me or let me alone,
What does it matter? My Soul is my own
And *that* is my work and my wages!
What I have done I have done.
It is first-class work and I know it.
Nothing under the sun
Shall minish or overthrow it.
(*Certified.* BC 21.)
Q. H. Flaccus, Poet.

In Liber IV, viii ('Donarem pateras grataque commodus'):*

Ah don't be too censorious for what do riches matter –
I can not send you *pateras* but I can send you patter
And tho' it sound vainglorious, your claim on after-times
May be the fact your name was tacked to my undying rhymes.

On Liber IV, xiii ('Audivere, Lyce, di mea vota, di'):*

This thing was born of dirty spite
    But that sure Daemon at his side
Allowed the vengeful one to write
    The first twelve lines – then turned the tide
Of impotent, unseemly wrath
    To Eve's eternal Hymn of Pain
When Beauty, bilked of all she hath,
    Solicits even Death in vain.

From a letter to Ian Colvin,* 17 August 1917

Dear Colvin,

I've been reading Bunyan's Holy War again – which is the most modern work that I know: and I beg you to get it as a weapon. Everything and everybody is there – from the German Emperor down to the *flammenwerfer*, the pacifists and the Pope – all the methods of fighting, all the arguments, all the labour party.

It simply bristles with quotations and comparisons that is why I commend it to you for your good uses. I'd send you my copy but that I'm busy gutting it.

Ever
R.K. . . .

'The Fabulists'*

When all the world would have a matter hid,
    Since Truth is seldom friend to any crowd,
Men write in fable, as old Aesop did,
    Jesting at that which none will name aloud.
And this they needs must do, or it will fall
Unless they please they are not heard at all.

When desperate Folly daily laboureth
    To work confusion upon all we have,
When diligent Sloth demandeth Freedom's death,
    And banded Fear commandeth Honour's grave –
Even in that certain hour before the fall
Unless men please they are not heard at all.

Needs must all please, yet some not all for need
    Needs must all toil, yet some not all for gain,
But that men taking pleasure may take heed,
    Whom present toil shall snatch from later pain.
Thus some have toiled but their reward was small.
Since, though they pleased, they were not heard at all.

This was the lock that lay upon our lips,
    This was the yoke that we have undergone,
Denying us all pleasant fellowships
    As in our time and generation.
Our pleasures unpursued age past recall.
And for our pains – we are not heard at all.

What man hears aught except the groaning guns?
    What man heeds aught save what each instant brings?
When each man's life all imaged life outruns,
    What man shall pleasure in imaginings?
So it hath fallen, as it was bound to fall,
We are not, nor we were not, heard at all.

'A Recantation'*
(To Lyde of the Music Halls)

What boots it on the Gods to call?
    Since, answered or unheard,
We perish with the Gods and all
    Things made – except the Word.

Ere certain Fate had touched a heart
    By fifty years made cold,

'A Recantation'

I judged thee, Lyde, and thy art
        O'erblown and over-bold.

But he – but he, of whom bereft
        I suffer vacant days –
He on his shield not meanly left –
        He cherished all thy lays.

Witness the magic coffer stocked
        With convoluted runes
Wherein thy very voice was locked
        And linked to circling tunes.

Witness thy portrait, smoke-defiled,
        That decked his shelter-place.
Life seemed more present, wrote the child,
        Beneath thy well-known face.

And when the grudging days restored
        Him for a breath to home,
He, with fresh crowds of youth, adored
        Thee making mirth in Rome.

Therefore, I, humble, join the hosts,
        Loyal and loud, who bow
To thee as Queen of Songs – and ghosts –
        For I remember how

Never more rampant rose the Hall
        At thy audacious line
Than when the news came in from Gaul
        Thy son had – followed mine.

But thou didst hide it in thy breast
        And, capering, took the brunt
Of blaze and blare, and launched the jest
        That swept next week the front.

Singer to children! Ours possessed
Sleep before noon – but thee,
Wakeful each midnight for the rest,
No holocaust shall free.

Yet they who use the Word assigned,
To hearten and make whole,
Not less than Gods have served mankind,
Though vultures rend their soul.

From a letter to C. R. L. Fletcher,* 12 July 1918

. . . I've been seeing 'Eminent Victorians' by Lytton Strachey.* It seems to me downright wicked in its heart.

Ever,
R.K.

Letter to Stanley Baldwin,* 13 June 1919

Bateman's Farm

To Mr Staneley Baldwin Esq. MP

Sir,

Just after you got home that Evening I rec'd enclosed from yr Mr Retrench But I think it is Walton* but I want to know why I have got to get such Things and be Woked up to be made sing songs re Lones even if I do it all comes to the Sam thing for yr Mr David* he takes it all 1 way or the other and It All goes up the Bang-Hole Sir and you can tell yr Mr French* he can go to Hele and Shak Himself befor I do him Pouemns about Loans Sir if I pay Tacxis it is a oatrag to mak Songs re them and no Reply-Paid answer either and to wit when I want to be brod-cast and pressed I bless God can do it on my Own for cash rates myself and will now suscribe Myself hoping This finds you as it leaves me yr

Obedt Servant
J. N. Shoesmith*

I oppen to Add it is Dr Brigdes's* work to sing re Lones and hes Propper Jobb as wel as he is paid Butts of Marlmesbury for doing sam annually.

Letter to James Rennell Rodd,* 1 July 1924

Dear Rennell Rodd,

Thanks for your letter and the draft, which I ought to have acknowledged before. But don't you think, perhaps, one might go light (the present generation are quite expert enough in their own sins) on Byron's* moral lapses, – and we don't know how much he dressed them up and dramatised them; – and insist more directly on his claims as a Poet and a Power to his rightful place in the Abbey. It might save some people with a taste for moral disquisitions rushing into the papers and giving us their views on his personal weaknesses.

This because I am jealous for the poet. The man must, as always, be in the hands of Allah! That's my only criticism.

Ever sincerely,
Rudyard Kipling.

Letter to E. V. Lucas,* 6 November 1930

Dear Lucas,

The date must have been my error. The first Tusser Redivivus* was D. Hilman's – 1710. I am sending you (registered insured and so forth) my own sacred 1744 edition, which is the same with a new title page. I am myself not more than indifferent honest about books – so you may guess what I think of the virtue of others. I want it back as soon as may be. I am very content that there is going to be a worthy edition of him. I expect you have discovered now that his works – *qua* volumes – are as rare as Markham's Farriery* or Pilgrim's Progress, in that they have been fairly used up in active service – 'Worn threadbare by the thumbs of men'* to alter Watson's line. I have a combined Hartlib and Tusser* (black letter) which, after all these years, still reeks faintly of the midden and the brewery. What I like about him is that he does not seem to have made much of a success of his own job – whereby he came to know what he was writing about. He was so dead keen to impart his knowledge to his neighbours (I don't think he ever thought much beyond his own county) that he rammed his maxims into his metre with a sledge-hammer. For instance, you can't get much more into a couplet than this:–

New bread is a waster but mouldie is worse,
For that which dog catcheth that loseth the purse.*

And, if you take his own profession of faith,* his Sit down Robin and rest thee,* and his Cur mundus militat translations,* he wrote some good verse. He went to his grave not knowing he had made a book which should last in the full flower of practical use (neither anthologised and classicised but *en bloc*) for two hundred and fifty years. *You* couldn't do that!

As to the bindings, the plain crushed levant looks all right but when you send me *my* copy, I would like it, please, in sheep – about the tint of a ripe chestnut. That is fittest for Tusser.

Ever sincerely,
Rudyard Kipling.

Speech to the Canadian Authors' Association*
July 1933

Strictly between ourselves, I think this is an occasion when we are justified in feeling a little proud of our calling. We know that, after all the men who do things have done them, and the men who say things about the their doings have said them, it is only words – nothing but words – that live to show the present how, and in what moods, men lived and worked in the past.

And we do not know what words they will be. That is one of the reasons why there can be neither first nor last in the kingdom – for it is not a republic – of letters.

We who use words enjoy a peculiar advantage over our fellows. We cannot tell a lie. However much we wish to do so, we only of educated men and women cannot tell a lie – in our working hours. The more subtly we attempt it, the more certainly do we betray some aspect of the truth concerning the life of our age.

It is with us as with timber. Every knot and shake in a board reveals some disease or injury that overtook the log when it was growing. A gentleman named Jean Pigeon,* who once built a frame house for me, put this in a nutshell. He said: 'Everything which a tree she has experienced in the forest she takes with her into the house.' That is the law for us all, each in his or her land.

Canadian writers and poets have dealt directly or by implication with every detail of their country's life and background.

Some have chosen the days of the first adventurers* wandering bewildered across blind forests and great waterways. Others have illuminated the distracted times of the United Empire Loyalists,* of the great famine year,* the Fenian raids,* and Riel's rebellion.* Others, again, those periods of doubt and self-distrust that followed the birth of your huge subcontinent.

And now men and women are dealing with the marvellous later years when Canada, first of the new Powers, came to her soul and strength, and, incidentally, sent four hundred thousand free men to the War.*

Directly or unconsciously, then, the splendour, the toil and the variety of your national history will have inspired or coloured all your work.

Somewhere in the mass of this work must be laid up the very lines, phrases and books which will be taken by the world of tomorrow as the authentic portrayal of your world of yesterday. But, as I said, who the people are that have already written those words, and for what reason of art or emotion their words will be accepted before all other words, we cannot tell.

Mercifully, it is not permitted to any one to foresee his or her literary election or reprobation, any more than it was permitted to our ancestors to foresee the just stature of their contemporaries, whose shrines and former dwellings you are now in the process of visiting.

You have already spent five or six fairly crowded days with us. You have before you ten more in which to look over some of the possessions, and verify some of the title-deeds, of your imperishable inheritance here.

The things that you will see, and the atmospheres you will realise, are not, as aliens might regard them, archeological curiosities or ineffective echoes out of a spent past. Whether they may be the work of men's hands, or men's souls, they bear witness to the instinct – it is more than a tradition – the immemorial racial instinct towards unbridled expenditure on matters material and spiritual for sheer joy of the exercise.

They are proof of our land's deep unconscious delight through all ages in her own strength and beauty and unjaded youth.

That same headlong surplus of effort and desire goes forward along other paths today. But our eyes are held. Like the generations before us, we cannot perceive among what new births of new wonders we now move.

And all these things, out of our past, in our present, and for our future, are yours by right.

They are doubly yours, since the dominant strains of your blood draw from those twin races – French and English – which throughout their histories have been most resolute not to be decivilised on any pretext or for any gain.

If on your journeys some of you feel inclined to faint by the wayside, you have my deepest sympathy, for it was given to me once to see Canada *en bloc*.* I had known portions of it, of course, many years before, but this was one prodigious sweep from Quebec to Victoria and back again.

Through three amazing weeks it was my turn to be shown things – to listen to prophecies which, within the next ten years, fell short of the facts, and to feel the moral pulse of a land and a people free as their own airs, and yet set in most ancient and sane practices of justice, honour and self-control.

I tried to grasp all these things because they were just as much mine as everything here is yours. Not till long after my return did the significance of them begin to break in upon me. Then my experiences and impressions clarified and arranged themselves, and as I sorted them out in my head I found that I had the key to them all the time in my heart.

It will be the same with you on your return, because one's own heart is the best place to store the few things in life that really matter.

From a letter to Sir Herbert Baker,* 17 March, 1934

... That was a queer life those 'Home-keepers'*, as you rightly call 'em kept in the old days. I was a boy and, later, a very young man when it was in full blast. The significance of it didn't hit me till much later. They were all purveyors of luxuries – utterly dependent on the fabric round them being kept safe. *But* (and this was their starting-point) all the *décor* of the civilization that they knew was horrible. (Horse-hair chairs, red lambrequins – you remember? – giving way to Jap fans and vases. See Punch of those days!) They fought tooth and nail and, in the general revolt, as I think, the Fabian Society was spawned. One knew the heads of it, and I remember one illuminating sentence launched by not the least of 'em – apropos 'wicked' wars. 'We must snatch away their arms when they aren't looking – as you snatch a knife from a child – so that when they want to fight, they will find that they can't.' And of war, or its necessity, they knew as little as they did of any life which did not directly touch their own emotions and prettinesses. But now we can see how much they helped to bring and to continue trouble. It was a immensely curious atmosphere in its beginnings, and all, so one felt – mixed up with a general and sustained falsity of speech and bearing – presently to become almost integral – that made one physically fatigued.

But, you can believe, that to a youngster, it was intensely interesting – for a while. And, naturally half the harm was done, as it always is, by the women playing up to their men. B[urne].-J[ones]. was in all ways the biggest. He had the most glorious sense of humour. Morris had none. It annoyed him as flies annoy cattle. But to hear the two together, discussing the workshop side of their art – fabrication of colours; design of glass windows and the inlay of the little bits, and how the lines cut each other, as they loafed in the studio between whiles was a thing to be grateful for, even though one did not comprehend it...

From a letter to Nicholas Murray Butler,* 1935

...To my mind [Mark Twain] was the largest man of his time; both in the direct outcome of his work, and, more importantly still, as an indirect force in an age of iron Philistinism. Later generations do not know their debt, of course, and they would be surprised if they did...

5

THE COMMERCE OF LITERATURE

*

From a letter to Thacker Spink & Co.,* Publishers, 30 June 1887

Gentlemen

I forward today in one packet the whole of the copy of the Plain Tales from the Hills.*

The index explains the order in which I wish the tales to go. I am sorry to say that the sheets are in a disgracefully messy condition. This comes of keeping them for retouching. You will see that each story has a few lines of quotation or poetry to go in small (minim?) type between the title and the body of the story.

The make up, spacing and binding of the book I leave entirely in your hands; only suggesting again that the Plain Tales and the third Edition of the Departmental Ditties should be uniform. The price also I leave to you as I suppose you will try to make it as cheap a publication as is consistent with decent binding. But don't make this latter too good to be dirtied. I have noticed that a book one can eat buttered toast over without any special pangs of conscience, gets on well in the world and has a ready sale.

In conclusion may I ask you to put the thing through as soon as may be. I want to catch the people at Simla before they are scattered at the end of the season. We have three clear months before us, up to the end of September to do this in.*

I am afraid that I shall have to ask you for a second revise. It is on this account that I am recommending speed. If I could get my first proofs within six weeks I should be grateful.

Yours very sincerely
Rudyard Kipling...

From a letter to Thacker Spink & Co.,* Calcutta, 9 August 1888

... To the 25% commission* I most strongly protest and beg you to see your way to withdrawing it.

We will now talk business. I am a little bit too well known to continue this extravagant rate of buying publicity. Therefore as soon as the first edition runs out I will resume my property and publish elsewhere, using and altering the book as I please. The second series to which you refer is one of five books* which are being got ready for the Home market,* and therein I do not think that I need trouble you.

If you are anxious to secure any lien upon the P.T's you are welcome to the copyright for the sum of Rs 10,000 (Rupees ten thousand) or in other words the price of three editions. I feel sure that when you look over your books and see what the DDs and the Plain Tales have done for your profit you will admit that it has been a pleasant and profitable connection between us.

Yours sincerely,
Rudyard Kipling.

From a letter to Thacker Spink & Co.,* Calcutta, 31 August 1888

... I am prepared to accept the offer for the first Edition, conditionally on your allowing 1–12 (one twelve) royalty per copy on the second, the cost of producing which will be much less for you both in setting it and advertisements.

If you care to accept these terms and to be content with only four or five thousand rupees profit on the two editions, I am willing on receipt of whatever sums may be up to date, my share, to forward you my revised and corrected copy of the book* with the press notices by whatever time you may choose to name, as I have no special desire to break with you if I am treated with moderate fairness. In regard to what you say about warehousing, bad debts, trade commissions and the absence of charges for heavy corrections I can only remind you that I also am in a fairly large printing office where we do a good deal of publishing and in these matters am more or less behind the scenes. The other books we may perhaps discuss when matters are more settled. At present I can give you no definite details.

Yours sincerely
Rudyard Kipling.

From a letter to Thacker Spink & Co.,* Calcutta, October 1888

. . . I have now by me for outright sale a volume of verse* – mostly ballads of incident and action, entirely or almost entirely Anglo-Indian and certain to take with the public if they haven't changed their minds. Also it is a likely volume for home consumption as it would introduce the Englishman to a life that he knows very little about. . .

P.S. . . . They write me from home that Edwin Arnold has said* some very pleasant things both about the P.T.'s and the D.D.'s. R.K.

From a letter to Caroline Taylor,* 2 November 1889

. . . By the way, English publishers live in regal – nay imperial luxury. I begin to see now why authors were created and where go the profits that should rightly be theirs. This makes me sad because I am just now being chased by several publishers. The last firm are very funny. They are a sort of Literary Supply Association* and they want me to write tales of adventure suitable for youths. Just at present I reply with great sweetness that my engagements are *complet** and that they had better go and take a walk. Publishers are not used to being treated in this manner and they return to the charge like Jew hawkers with proffers of ready money down. See'st thou the drift of this? It is to make the new man write as swiftly and as largely as possible on the novel subject. Then when he is squeezed dry they heave him away and call the newspapers to witness that there is no originality in the present writers.*

I did not come to England to write myself out at first starting – not by a very long sight. This seemeth to me the more perfect way. To go slowly and only do sufficient magazine work to enable me to rub along comfortably while I turn my attention to the novels and the books. A man can fritter himself away on piece work and be only but a very little the richer for it. Whereas if he holds his hand the money and what is of more importance the power of doing fresh and original work comes to him. What thinkest thou? I have burned more than one solitary pipe over the question. Even regarding it from a business point of view the latter method pays better in the long-run. Wherefore I have refused in a brief poem of five stanzas* the St James's Gazette offer of a permanent engagement. Catch me putting my head into that old noose again – and me hardly recovered from the constant surprises of seven years' journalism.

The situation stands thus. I hold work on Macmillan's Magazine up to £300 a year: The Lahore paper stands me for £100 (and that's four hundred); on those two alone therefore without turning my attention to the St James's, the Spectator, Longmans and Punch (who all want me) I could devote myself to building up the American connection and going on straight with the books and the poetry. Have I your sanction for these things?...

From a letter to S. S. McClure,* January 1890

I have had the pleasure of dealing with your association while in charge of a weekly in India, but if possible I should much like to see some of the printed schedules, tariffs and general arrangements of the Press. I am afraid short tales from my pen are all disposed of but I fancy the 'fiction for youth notion' is workable. Thus, I have the notes and scaffolding of a book for boys, to be called 'An Officer and a Gentleman'. It is merely the history of a lad serving the Queen in India – his troubles, war experiences* . . . He fights on the Northern frontier, in Burma, where he leads his own detachment, gets a look in at Egypt and generally has a good time.* That sort of life I know down to its bootheels and I fancy 'twould interest boys between fifteen and eighteen. There would be any amount of blood in the pages but the slaughtering should be of a practical kind and a large amount of rough-cast morality could be worked in. No one seems to care to tell the youngsters what life on foreign service and the handling of men really means. I think I could interest 'em. That sort of work might with advantage be syndicated in America.

If you think anything of the notion would you kindly give me (a) your most preferred size and (b) your rates. The story could be compressed or pulled out to suit.

Yours sincerely
Rudyard Kipling.

Letter to W. E. Henley,* [?September] 1890

Dear Henley,

I am in trouble and furious. You know that I have written within the past few months some tales for MacM[illans]. *Mag[azine]*. and others. Harper and Co. bought the serial rights for America and paid me. The series in MacM. I intended to be one of twelve stories into which I purposed to put as good stuff as I could do, revise extensively and eventually republish with a preface. Today I receive a note from Harpers (leading publishers) announcing that they have reprinted in book form *The Courting of Dinah Shadd, The Incarnation of Krishna Mulvaney, The Man who Was* and all the others. They will give it their own title.* (They have given it their own title.) They have not had the decency to apprise me of their intention and to complete the insult they fling a £10 note (the wages of one New York road scavenger for one month) at my head. They call it an *honorarium*. Now I may turn out work too quickly. They are at perfect liberty to steal when I have done my work but the grotesque Yahoodom of nipping pieces off a half-presented foetus and slamming it into the market makes me jump. It isn't literature, it isn't honour. It is simply a piece of cowardly and huckstering sharp-practice to exploit a name that, for the time being, sells. Rather less than 12 months ago that firm in a letter one line and seven words long* told me that they would not republish *Soldiers Three, The Gadsbys*, and all the rest. What do you recommend me to do? I have of course returned the money and told them that I cannot authorise the thing which they call an 'Edition'. This month's Harpers magazine brings in an elaborate patronisation of me in the Editors Receiving Shop.* Look at it. It completes the circle. I don't know who the man is but the whole notion of the article is intensely funny. The American, he says, lives in a 'nimbler atmosphere' or something of the kind. When the man was writing that his blasted owners were stealing my work. The critic himself was criticising stolen work with adjectives stolen from England. I am much too wrath just now to write to the papers disclaiming the Edition, but I must blow off somehow so I go to you, who can see the insult of the burglary – the savage indecency and the utter disregard of anything except the dollars on the part of the leading publishing firm in America. Send me your notions on the matter. As a journalist, two years ago I should have lifted the scalp of Harpers and the amiable critic who 'deplores' for me, and my vulgarity. It isn't the critic's fault that he lives, as every man must live, under the laws of his own life and environment, when he calls my stuff lacking in apprecia-tion of the subtler values. The thing that makes it like a Gilbert-Sullivan operation is the raw, rank theft that runs through the 'business' of his firm. When a burglar sits down on the front door steps to quarrel with the pattern of the silver-ware that he hath stolen he may be an authority on silver but he is first of all a thief and secondly he lacks a sense of humour. I suppose I shall be able to laugh at the business in a little time but at present I'm too savage to do more than swear.

Ruddy.

'Some Notes on a Bill'*

Oh, peruse a Simple Story – read a parable detached
From the vice of vending pullets ere the little beasts are hatched;
A weird bilingual prophecy with flying foot-notes shored,
On the means of slipping sideways from the world's je-joggle board.[a]

'Twas the Broncho[b] among Nations – a severely cultured race –
Though their mode of spelling centre proved them clearly off their
base,[c]
Passed a Bill of three Dimensions – two of which concerned the trade –
And one, but this was fiction, books the British Author made.

Softly sang the British Author, for a dream was in his brain
Of Landaus from Longacre and of houses in Park Lane;
But ere he went to Tattersall's,* or changed his modest dwelling,
He explained, per Western Union, his objections to their spelling.

'Oh, my Largest Reading Public', thus the coded cable came,
'You drop one (h)ell in "travelling" and – get there just the same.[d]
If to Webster and to Worcester,* and your sauce at large, I grovel,
It will vulgarise our Fiction – taint the Holy British Novel.[e]

'Yet I'll vitiate the spelling of the children of my friends
If you pay me something extra for my labor.' *Message ends.*

And it filled that author's system with severe electric shocks
When his Largest Reading Public cabled back: 'You're on the box.'[f]

'The fact of being shouted for a dime along the cars*
Does not fix you for a planet among Literary Stars;
Nor is it a safe assumption you can teeter continents
When our high-toned Mister H-rp-r[g]* sews you up for fifty cents.

'British parsons make us tired; British Dukes, our daughters doubt 'em;
Cuss words of the British Army, we can mosey on without 'em;
Take a walk and get your hair cut;[h] sit on Mister Mudie's shelves;
If we've *got* to pay for reading guess we'll read about ourselves.'*

So they read by free selection on a principle their own –
'Twas the most exhaustive weeding that an ink-stained earth had
known
And the palpitating cable sizzled madly under-sea,
'*Honor* without "u" I'll stomach. What is *Honor* without *me*?'

No, the fame the newsboys give you when they board the C.B.Q.*
Does not predicate your kiting into honor without 'u'.
If you cannot bang the big drum, you must twang the harp of Tara,[i]*
With McGinty[j]* and O'Grady[k] and the man that struck O'Hara.[l]

It was good for Zenas Mather, Independence Psickafoos,
Ada Isaacs Menken Shuswap, Janet Thackeray Van Dewze –
They stood pat as home-grown produce, with some seven thousand
more;
They were paid at full face-value – *they* came in on the ground floor.[m]

For they wove their country's fiction, triple-ply, of many shades,
From the big blue bergs at Sitka to the rotting Everglades;
And never since the Pilgrims furled the *Mayflower*'s sea-worn sail
Had the Bounder among Nations seen herself done out to scale.

It was woolly – wild and woolly – it was more than three feet wide,
For it ran from Maine to Oregon and out the other side.

With one nasal Hallelujah, like a giant jews-harp drone,
The Bounder among Nations claimed a bookcase of her own.[n]

* * * * * * * * * * * * * * *

Now they're running ninety Shakespeares – all with Variegated
  dictions;
They have put the growth of Miltons under Inter-State restrictions;
They brake the C.P.* freight cars with the Laureates of the West,
And a vigilance committee is sub-editing the rest.

They are writing of Proportion and Reserve, and Racial Feeling,
Like an introspective sneak-thief who has just abandoned stealing;
And we can't attend to Baby, and we can't lie down at night,
For those queer self-conscious school-boys howl – 'Git up and see us
  write!'

But they're learning not to 'wiggle' when you photograph their
  manners;
They are guessing at a medium 'twixt 'you skunk!' and mad Hosannas;
And the men who knew 'em fancy – if the measure they have made
  lasts –
That some day they'll be a Public – not a girls' school swapping 'Trade-
  lasts'.[o]

Ends my lurid, lucid legend, halts my parable divorced
From the blame of hunting Navajos before your scouts are horsed.
Oh, the author's in the *purée*,[p] and the deuce is in the Bill,
But the Holy British Novel – yes – it's wholly British still.

a An elastic seat found in the verandas of Southern houses.
b An underbred animal with a swelled head, given to jumping nervously on inspection. *Anglice*, 'Bounder'.
c They are very like their babies – if you notice 'em they cry;
If you don't, they steal your candy, and their teachers call 'em 'Spry'.
Their father's name was Washington – mis-statements made him wince;

But his sons declare on 'honor' there's been no one like him since.

d V.l.* Suppressed by Western Union as a *casus belli.* 'Your views of spelling "honour" match your notions on the same.'

e Now the Holy British Novel – from this verdict none shall warp us –
Is the Maiden's Magna Carta and the Matron's Habeas Corpus;
For when Maid and Wife have finished with the volumes Father paid for,
You can read it to the Baby. This is what all books are made for.

f V.l. 'Come off the rocks.' *Anglice,* 'You labour under a misapprehension.'

g The leading Sporting bookmaker of the United States. He does not bet on outsiders.

h Mutilated in transmission. Supposed to indicate esteem and personal interest.

i This instrument is distinguished for its enduring silences.

j Famous for his exploration of the depths of the ocean.

k He was owed ten dollars – presumably on account of American royalties, for the money was never paid.

l The remains of this gentleman would not furnish a biography.

m *I.e.* There was no necessity in their case for abasement.

n They abandoned watered Herrick, and Elizabethan echoes;
They were not stuck on Browning like a horde of homeless geckoes;
'Twas a second Boston bust-up, but it cost us more than Tea,
For the alphabet of authors they discarded – a to zee.

o Saidie tells Maimie that Hattie's new frock is pretty. Maimie repeats the compliment to Hattie, who tells Maimie that Sadie is 'just too Sweet to live'. This is a trade-last. It is also called criticism.

p This is the position formerly occupied by the Oyster.

From a letter to Mary Mapes Dodge,* 15 October 1892

. . . I enclose herewith *The Potted Princess** for your most stern inspection. My rates are $100 per 1000 words seeing this goes no where but to Saint Nicholas. I don't think it will run much over 2000 words. If it does the extras don't count. If it doesn't let them deduct $10 per 100 words shortage.

From 'The Three-Decker'

I hold the book-rights of the tale. Perhaps we'll be able to do some more and make a little book some day; but it's a mighty difficult kind of composition; that public being particular to distraction. Therefore if it does not fit in your estimation, send him back and I'll do it again. There's only one man that could illustrate it and he's my father too far away for this present need. I'll return the proof within 48 hours of receipt, and I do most sincerely hope it will be an acceptable yarn. . .

From 'The Three-Decker'*

Full thirty foot she towered from waterline to rail,
It took a watch to steer her, and a week to shorten sail;
But, spite all modern notions, I found her first and best –
The only certain packet for the Islands of the Blest.

Fair held the breeze behind her – 'twas warm with lovers' prayers.
We'd stolen wills for ballast and a crew of missing heirs.
They shipped as Able Bastards till the Wicked Nurse confessed,
And they worked the old three-decker to the Islands of the Blest. . .

I left 'em all in couples akissing on the decks.
I left the lovers loving and the parents signing cheques.
In endless English comfort by county-folk caressed,
I left the old three-decker at the Islands of the Blest!

That route is barred to steamers: you'll never lift again
Our purple-painted headlands or the lordly keeps of Spain.
They're just beyond your skyline, howe'er so far you cruise
In a ram-you-damn-you liner with a brace of bucking screws. . .

Her crew are babes or madmen? Her port is all to make?
You're manned by Truth and Science, and you steam for steaming's sake?
Well, tinker up your engines – you know your business best –
She's taking tired people to the Islands of the Blest!

From a letter to Frank N. Doubleday,* 6 October 1896

Dear Doubleday –

Today's cable will have told you not to print the Plain Tales till you hear from me. The reason is this: *and it is very important.*

I have finally screwed myself up to re-grouping the whole kit and boodle of the books, i.e. am arranging the military; native; and fantastic tales in batches by themselves...

P.S. You will readily see how this re-arrangement (which has long been demanded by the public) gives the edition a pull of its own...

From a letter to Frank N. Doubleday,* 7 October 1896

Dear Doubleday –

We have now advanced another step on our weary path. The work of putting the stories into groups has not been easy; but you will see from the enclosed indexes that I have managed it. They come – all my short stories – now under three heads – *Soldiers Three* – *In Black and White* – and *The Phantom Rickshaw* – military – Asiatic and ghostly or ghastly...

As to *The Jungle Books* I have re-arranged them. The first contains all the stories of Mowgli concluding with 'In the Rukh': in one volume. The second has the scattered stories of beasts, seals, etc. by themselves – *The Light* and *Naulakha* are not changed at all but, under the new grouping, *Life's Handicap* and *Many Inventions* are wiped out of existence...

I am adding as you will see two new pieces – 'The Enlightenments of Pagett M.P.'* to *Black and White* and 'Mrs Hauksbee Sits Out'* to *Under the Deodars*. No other edition has these tales in 'em...

Introduction to the Outward Bound Edition,* 1897

To the *Nakhoda* or Skipper of this Venture
A Letter of Bill or Instruction from the Owner

In the Name of God, the Compassionate, the Merciful!

This, O *Nakhoda*, is a new voyage, nothing at all like those which you have already taken to Aden or Muscat, or even to Macassar and the islands where we can count upon the monsoons. Therefore consider the matter carefully. I have given you a new compass, with new rigging, masts, sails and other gear suitable to the *buggalow,** and these cannot be picked up for the asking at Sewree or on Sion Bunder.* The cargo is all in new mats, stowed like to like, to be reached more easily; and I have painted her before and behind, and I have put a new plank deck in place of the old bamboo one, and the tiller-ropes are new as well. This is at my risk, and the returns must be prepared with zeal and a single heart. Many men of the seas have told me lies, secretly selling anchors and cables and ascribing the loss to the waves, sharks and sea-fairies. That was long ago, O *Nakhoda,* and now I do not believe all the stories that come up from the beaches.

The road is West and by South from England, where she will not touch, for the cargo is all for the Western ports, and these, if Allah please, you will find upon the other side of the sea. It is cold water, heavy with fog, and ships go up and down in their hundreds bellowing. Avoid these, for they are of iron and suddenly divide wooden vessels. None the less I have carried many cargoes across, and in lighter craft than the *buggalow.*

The men of those ports – I have lived among them, and Allah, whose name be exalted, has augmented my understanding – come down to trade early in the day, and their hours are longer than we use in the East. Do not, then sleep in the forenoon or sling a hammock under the stern-awnings; neither unroll the sleeping-mats at sundown. On Bhao Malung* we pray before the voyage; at the Jakaria Musjid we give thanks when the voyage is over, but during the voyage we must trade.

In trading it is to be remembered that there be many who can immediately discern the bad from the good. Do not seek to overwhelm such men with market-talk, or else we two are shamed. Say nothing: let them choose; and throw a sail over certain bales of lesser worth.

Yet there be others who, stamping on the deck and talking loud, infallibly choose the worst. To these it is lawful to sell beads, brass rods and coarse cloths, since it is written: 'The blind pay for him who hath eyes.'

And there is a third muster, very cunning in the outside of things, and full of words as a foresail of wind. Take these to the lower hold and show them that I do not altogether sell toys or looking-glasses.

Remember, too, that many of the cloths are double- and treble-figured, giving a new pattern in a shift of light. Some are best seen in full sun, others under a lamp and a few are only good to be used in dark places where they were made. The women should know this.

When, however, the little children come down to the beaches hide away that which is uncomely; let down the gang-plank with the railing on either hand; and spare nothing of the painted clay figures, the talking apes, the dancing bears, the coloured lights or the sweetmeats to give them pleasure. Thus they will first plague their parents to buy, and later – for a child's memory is very long – will bring down their own babes when we return. But have a care that they do not wander unchecked through all the holds or sully themselves in the bilges.

But the chief part of our business lies with men who are wearied at the end of the day. It is for the sake of these men that I have laded the *buggalow*. Seek these, O *Nakhoda*, before all others – at the end of the day, as I have said, and in whatever dress (I have put many dresses aboard) may make them look up. Then, little by little, entice them away from their houses and their occupations till they come aboard the *buggalow*. And whether they descend into the run and read the private marks I have put upon the bales, or whether they lie upon the deck in the moonlight pricing the small-arms and *krises*; whether they stare a little and go overside again; or whether they take passage in the *buggalow* for a far voyage, you are the servant of these men, O *Nakhoda*, and the *buggalow* is theirs so long as they please. For though I am only a trader with no ware upon which there is not an open price, I do not forget how, when I was wearied at the end of the day, certain great captains sold me for a little silver that which I could not now find in any market. Pay, then, that debt to these men who are my brothers. (They will not bring their women-folk aboard, so the talk may be trimmed with a slack sheet.)

The chances of the sea are many and come on all. If ye spy any struggling in broken water or on hen-coops that roll over and over, do not consider the voyage, but go to him, and, with the tackle I have put aboard for such use, work as Allah allows to his comfort. I have myself been many times extricated from calamity by ships whose very names and *Nakhodas* were unknown to me.

Answer questions as to the sun, moon and stars openly, according to the custom of the sea; for we find our way thereon only by the Lights of God the refuge of terminations which are common to all. It is not needed to show strangers our charts, for these be of man's making, and each must prick his own for himself.

Do not press her overmuch in a following wind, nor think that one good slant will serve without change to land. And I have met long-lasting calms.

I know that all chance-found wreckage is the free gift of Allah to him who finds it, but still I say let not my *buggalow* be first in this work. It is not auspicious to use stray-gathered gear; and who knows but in the very next port may wait the lawful owner and an open shame?

For the rest, her place in port is sideways to the quay, with all hatches clear; and your place, O *Nakhoda*, is upon her after-deck by the gangway, to receive those coming aboard, to make my salaams to friends who remember me when I traded there, to open out the bales, to tempt new men to buy, to give no credit and to keep a strict account of all.

On the black water it must be as it is ordained, but in my estimation she is well found.

Get ready now, and take her out when the wind serves, remembering this one thing sure in all uncertainty; as it is written:–

O true believer, his destiny none can escape:* And safe are we against all that is not predestined!

'The Handicaps of Letters'*

Hades keeps not faith with us later singers, but releases the great ones full-tongued to overbear us when we would ply our art. Who can sing against Homer and Sappho, or the voices that have told all?

I am greatly honoured by being allowed to propose the toast of 'Prosperity to the Royal Literary Fund' – in other words, to appeal to you on behalf of certain men and women of letters who stand in need of your assistance. And since one speaks of the workmen, one must speak also a little of the craft to which they have given or are giving their lives. I shall be specially careful to guard against making extravagant claims for either. If you go no further back than the Book of Job you will find that letters, like the art of printing, were born perfect. Some professions, law and medicine, for example, are still in a state of evolution, inasmuch as no expert in them seems to be quite sure that he can win a case or cure a cold. On the other hand, the calling of letters carries with it the disabilities from which these professions are free. When an eminent lawyer or physician is once dead, he is always dead. His ghost does not continue to practise in the Law Courts or the operating theatre. Now it cannot have escaped your attention that a writer often does not begin to live till he has been dead for some time. In certain notorious cases the longer he has been dead the more alive he is, and the more acute is his competition against the living. I do not ask you to imagine the feelings of a barrister exposed to the competition of all the dead Lord Chancellors that ever sat on the woolsack, each delivering judgements on any conceivable case at 6d. per judgement, paper-bound. I only ask you to allow that what lawyers call the 'dead hand' – in this case with a pen in it – lies heavy on the calling of letters. In other callings of life there exists a convention that what a man has made shall be his own and his children's after him. With regard to letters, the world decides that, after a very short time, all that a writer may have created shall be taken from him and shall become the property of anybody and everybody except the original maker.* This may be right. It may be more important that men should be helped to think than that they should be helped to live. But those on whom this righteousness is executed find it difficult to establish a family on letters. Sometimes they find it difficult to feed one. That letters should be exempted from the law of continuous ownership seems to constitute another handicap to the calling. Most men are bound by oath, or organisation, or natural instinct not to work for nothing. When his demon urges a man of letters to work, he will do so without any regard to wages or the sentiments of his fellow-workers. This may be incontinence or inspiration. Whichever it is, we must face the fact and its consequences, that at any moment a man of letters may choose to pay, not only with his skin, but in cash and credit for leave to do his work, to say the thing he desires to say. This is perhaps not fair to himself or his fellows, but it is a law of his being, and as such constitutes yet another handicap.

And there is a legend in Philistia – a pharisaical legend – that those who follow letters are disorderly-minded, unstable of habit and thus peculiarly open to misfortune. Now, since the Pharisees originate very little that has not been put into their minds by the Scribes,* it is possible that men of letters, writing about men of letters, have themselves to thank in some measure for this unkind judgement. Every man in trouble naturally cries that there is no sorrow like his sorrow; but not all men, not all men's friends, nor all men's enemies, can draw the world's attention to that complaint. Writers have been their own interpreters in this respect – not always to their own advantage. It does not square with experience that any class of men has pre-eminence over any other class in the zeal and perseverance with which its members go about to compass their own ruin. Is it not more reasonable to hold that the triple handicap I have mentioned, and not so much individual folly, is responsible for the high percentage of casualties among men of letters? Men perpetually measured against the great works of the past; men debarred by law from full possession of their own works in the present; men driven from within to work whether their world desires that work or not – such men must always enjoy the privilege accorded to minorities. They must suffer. Much of this suffering is inevitable, but some of it the Fund, by your good help, can reach and alleviate as few other institutions can. It has had over a century's experience of all the chances and misfortunes that can overtake men and women. Its work is done, as we would desire it to be done in our own cases, in silence and discretion, and for that very reason it is difficult, as the report says, to bring home the value of the work to the public.

We cannot foretell in the multitude of words about us whose words are destined to survive, to rule, to delight, to persuade or accuse those that come after. We hope that some will so survive. All we are sure of now is that among the many men and women who have followed letters in this high hope a certain number have been overborne by evil chances, accidents and misfortunes, which, but for the mere whim of time and fortune, might have come to any one of us.

I give you, then, that you may give, 'Prosperity to the Royal Literary Fund'.

6

THE WRITER AND HIS CRITICS

*

'The Conundrum of the Workshops'*

When the flush of a new-born sun fell first on Eden's green and gold,
Our father Adam sat under the Tree and scratched with a stick in the mould;
And the first rude sketch that the world had seen was joy to his mighty heart,
Till the Devil whispered behind the leaves, 'It's pretty, but is it Art?'

Wherefore he called to his wife, and fled to fashion his work anew –
The first of his race who cared a fig for the first, most dread review;
And he left his lore to the use of his sons – and that was a glorious gain
When the Devil chuckled 'Is it Art?' in the ear of the branded Cain.

They builded a tower* to shiver the sky and wrench the stars apart,
Till the Devil grunted behind the bricks, 'It's striking, but is it Art?'
The stone was dropped at the quarry-side and the idle derrick swung,
While each man talked of the aims of Art, and each in an alien tongue.

They fought and they talked in the North and the South, they fought and they talked in the West,
Till the waters rose on the pitiful land, and the poor Red Clay had rest –
Had rest till the dank blank-canvas dawn when the dove was preened to start,
And the Devil bubbled below the keel: 'It's human, but is it Art?'

'In the Neolithic Age'

The tale is as old as the Eden Tree – and new as the new-cut tooth –
For each man knows ere his lip-thatch grows he is master of Art and
    Truth;
And each man hears as the twilight nears, to the beat of his dying heart,
The Devil drum on the darkened pane: 'You did it, but was it Art?'

We have learned to whittle the Eden Tree to the shape of a surplice-peg,
We have learned to bottle our parents twain in the yelk of an addled
    egg,
We have learned that the tail must wag the dog, for the horse must be
    drawn by the cart;
But the Devil whoops, as he whooped of old: 'It's clever, but is it Art?'

When the flicker of London sun falls faint on the Club-room's green
    and gold,
The sons of Adam sit them down and scratch with their pens in the
    mould –
They scratch with their pens in the mould of their graves, and the ink
    and the anguish start,
For the Devil mutters behind the leaves: 'It's pretty, but is it Art?'

Now, if we could win to the Eden Tree where the Four Great Rivers*
    flow,
And the Wreath of Eve* is red on the turf as she left it long ago,
And if we could come when the sentry slept and softly scurry through,
By the favour of God we might know as much – as our father Adam
    knew.

'In the Neolithic Age'*

In the Neolithic Age savage warfare did I wage
    For food and fame and two-toed horses' pelt;
I was singer to my clan in that dim, red Dawn of Man
    And I sang of all we fought and feared and felt.

Yes, I sang as now I sing, when the Prehistoric spring
    Made the piled Biscayan ice-pack split and shove;

And the troll and gnome and dwerg, and the Gods of Cliff and Berg
    Were about me and beneath me and above.

But a rival, of Solutré,* told the tribe my style was outré –
    'Neath a hammer, grooved of dolomite, he fell.
And I left my views on Art, barbed and tanged, below the heart
    Of a mammothistic etcher at Grenelle.*

Then I stripped them, scalp from skull, and my hunting dogs fed full
    And their teeth I threaded neatly on a thong;
And I wiped my mouth and said, 'It is well that they are dead,
    For I know my work is right and theirs was wrong.'

But my Totem saw the shame; from his ridgepole shrine he came,
    And he told me in a vision of the night: –
'There are nine and sixty ways of constructing tribal lays,
    And every single one of them is right!'

Then the silence closed upon me till They put new clothing on me
    Of whiter, weaker flesh and bone more frail;
And I stepped beneath Time's finger, once again a tribal singer
    [And a minor poet certified by Tr- -ll].*

Still they skirmish to and fro, men my messmates on the snow,
    When we headed off the aurochs turn for turn;
When the rich Allobrogenses* never kept amanuenses,
    And our only plots were piled in lakes at Berne.

Still a cultured Christian age sees us scuffle, squeak, and rage,
    Still we pinch and slap and jabber, scratch and dirk;
Still we let our business slide – as we dropped the half-dressed hide –
    To show a fellow-savage how to work.

Still the world is wondrous large, – seven seas from marge to marge, –
    And it holds a vast of various kinds of man;
And the wildest dreams of Kew are the facts of Khatmandu,
    And the crimes of Clapham chaste in Martaban.

From a letter to T. J. B. Needham

Here's my wisdom for your use, as I learned it when the moose
And the reindeer roared where Paris roars tonight: –
There are nine and sixty ways of constructing tribal lays,
And – every – single – one – of – them – is – right!

From a letter to Charles Eliot Norton,* 16 Dec. 1897

. . . my spirit is brought very low and Macmillans have sent me the Atlantic Monthly's review* of *Captains Courageous* which has made me lie down and cry salt tears. Do you happen to know who wrote it. It's amazing in its coincidences for behold the writer misses in C.C. precisely and identically those very qualities I missed in his land. Had I gone about with a lantern to describe America I could not have hit on a more splendid description than 'relief at the cost of life'. Relief from the material cares of the Elder Peoples at the cost of what the Elder Peoples mean by life! And again 'There is an almost incredible insignificance in parts of it, *as if it were a steamer underengined in its length.*' Why, hang it! that's his own very country and in half a dozen words he gets at the nub of the thing I was laboriously painting in C.C. Only he *will* apply it to the book and expects me to extract from a two hundred year old background all the tints of the gilded East. For this did I change my style; and allegorise and parable and metaphor; subduing my hand to the stuff I wrought in! I tried to get it thin, and tinny, and without passion . . . and I've done it only too well. Even down to 'every body being reasonably safe' does he parallel my concept of America. If you know him, I wish you'd breathe in his ear gently that he has paid me a gigantic compliment – the wrong way round. You see what I resent is a chap coming out of that *milieu* (he *must* because he accepts the note of the book as 'healthy', 'simple' and 'vigorous' whereas – c.f. Harvey Cheyne's talk with his father and his father's talk with him – it is flagrantly un-moral not to say heathen), belonging to that life and serenely accepting its grubby ideals talking to me as though he didn't so accept 'em. But I won't bother you any more about it . . .

From a letter to Mrs T. J. B. Needham,* 18 July 1907

My dear Mrs Needham.

Very many thanks for your letter with the cutting, and for what you say about my work. I'd like to think a little of it was true – in spots – some time.

But I'm very pleased. I'm sorry you don't approve of my remark about women but remember I only said that 'Blind Nature had made her for one End.'* I never said what the woman said about being made for that one end, and of course my own opinion is that it's the highest and holiest of all. It seems to me that a woman who *makes* one man – even though he mayn't be quite a success – does more than a million who say how men should be taught etc. Perhaps that's because I wasn't born in a white man's country: and the idea of a woman going out to work for her living among men doesn't ever please me. *She's too good for that job,* even when she says she isn't...

7
AFTERWORDS

*

Manuscript notes 'Buried Treasure',* for '"Teem":
A Treasure Hunter'
(The Romance of a Brave Young Dog)

[Note at top left hand corner]: Egotistist [sic] 1st personal always
[Note along side of page]: consumptive girl's name: *Jane*: She-dog's name:– Bessie" but L'Abbé calls her "*Ma tante*".

L'Abbé.* (truffle-dog) in the Perigord. His Master Dominic who owns his Father and Mother – Mother has to be worked on the cord: she always wants to eat the truffles she finds. Father – pure artist for whom finding the truffle sufficient. [Describe them through L'Abbé's eyes. Like Maltese terriers – a secret, silent long descended breed, with a Nose that is their Soul and conscience. L'Abbé's enormous pride in his Art. Imitates and improves on his Parents' art. Before he is 1 yr old he has invented his own code to tell Dominic* which kind of truffle (*there are 3*) he is scenting. If D tells him to confine himself to one sort of truffle for the day, he will
[*Mem: English truffle blacker and longer than Perigord. different smell*]
Perigord truffe carries scent like strawberries (several kinds in P.]
Not MOREL.
Mem. a low grade puff-ball found in Epping Forest by Italians *for use in cheap London Res'ts.*
The Mother's maxim:– "If it isn't something it's sure to be something else"
Father's maxim:– "You can not do wrong if you bite a pig walking by himself and wrinkling his nose. They know too much those dirty pigs do."
Monsieur le Vicomte Bouvier de Brie – big iron-gray cattle dog on next farm,

in charge of bulls – which he escorts at intervals "beyond the end of the world." "I am a Marshall of Bulls." A born aristo and in his line an eminent artist. L'Abbé in his puppy-hood attaches himself to the Vicomte whom he adores. Vicomte allows him all sorts of liberties and from beneath the Vicomte's belly L'Abbé hurls insults at the masterless dogs of the village when the Vicomte goes to the Railway Station to fetch up "his bulls". V's philosophy: gentleness: strength.

L'Abbé (at 6 mo's old) hears his Mother (at work) say to his Father:– "Our master would be nothing – could earn nothing without us. That is truth." L'A asks his F. if that is true. Father replies:– "My Son, the only truth which it is necessary for you to know is that no one criticises his Mother." L'A turns away but hears his Father say, half aloud:– "Have I then engendered a revolutionary?" Refers his mother's saying to his adored Vicomte. The great dog (L'A between his paws) says that there *is* truth in his mother's observation *but*, it is equally true that if there was no Dominic to set him to find truffles, he (L'Abbé) would be eaten up with all his family, by Wolves. "And I – even I, without whom my master [Antoine?] could not control a single bull, – were Antoine to disappear, would presently have to fight wolves in order to live, little one. It is by your Dominic and you: and my Antoine and me, *together* that all the world which is so big, continues to give us all bones, and warm places by the fire &c &c." But the V. puts it more tersely. That philosophy helps L'Abbé later on: as, indeed, does everything he learns from his parents.

Pluton & Dis, the big black [mated?] dogs who pull from the axle of the little wooden cart in which Dominic takes his truffles to the big *white chateau* outside the village where he bargains with the fat, red haired Norman *chef*, every week. Then, goes on to sell a few to the curé's housekeeper, a prominent shop-keeper or so: and so on. *Pluton* & *Dis* are simple, devout and *very* humble. L'Abbé rather patronizes them. They too have a peasant's philosophy.

When he is nearly a year old his Mother has a litter of three [[Mem. *L'Abbé is the sole* survivor *of his litter and is also a* dwarf. Dominic rears 'em carefully & when they are two months old sells L'Abbé to a friend at a very high price. The two peasants & D's wife bargain in L'Abbé's presence. He is peasant enough to know that there *is* a bargain on the tapis. D boasts of L'Abbé's attainments and offers to give a demonstration of L'Abbé working on only one kind of truffle. L'Abbé is taken out, with his parents, praised & petted. His Father cautions him *not to work too well unless he knows the reason why.* Carried away by an artistic pride in his *metier* L'Abbé excels himself and is sold "at *more than the price of a cow!*" (1000–1500 fr?) but under promise *not* to be used within 100 kms of Perigeux. "On no" says the purchaser "He'll be sold in England where a friend of mine wants a good truffle dog. They don't know much these English. L'Abbé will show 'em."

He is thrust into a pocket. Goes by car: steamer: car again (all interpreted in his own way) smells new smells [[*his nose is his mind and must be dealt* with wholly *from that angle*]] Smells sheep: hears crook. His car is upset and he is slung into a hedge. Working back sees his captor, the strange man, lying under car being "devotedly bitten" by a large blue and white she-dog. L'Abbé goes up his ditch and creeps into a brick culvert to rest himself. [He's had his shoulder wrenched] The She-dog's head appears at mouth of culvert *whoofs*. Her master calls her to her duty (sheep clicking over the culvert waked L'Abbé. He dozes till the sun is high. Then sets out to explore this new land (*all* smells different) into which he has been pitched [[[*Neither then nor later does he know what the land is called*]]]

Description of large-wooded Park, with "white chateau" in a valley &c &c [Wilts landscape something like Clouds]* as seen through L'Abbé's eyes. Presently his Nose which has been outraged by the automobiles and ship smells begins to function & brings him truffle scent. Not Perigord but allied to it. He walks up the scent and finds that this land also carries truffles [as in Wilts and may be all over the shop]:

Scent: scent: scent: all through here: very serious. *Scent of* burning charcoal: one after another all proper scents of his own lost Perigord. Scent of authentic peasant (*minus* garlic) He finds a charcoal burner, patting down earth on the cone of wood. Understands this. Watches man from cover and finds all the scents of him *delightfully comprehensible & comforting.*

Man comes to coat, takes out bread & cheese (good strong cheese) & eats. L'Abbé "produces himself". Man receives him affably: notices his loose shoulder: Eventually picks him up, carries him to small cottage in wood. [[[L'Abbé has never known anything like affection from humans. Dominic & his wife looked after the truffle-dogs as money-getters, but (naturally) waste no time on them, nor handle 'em. L'Abbé's head is caressed by charcoal burner. He licks man's hand. Emotion comes upon him bit by bit.

The Vicomte has told him once that the greatest thing (greater even than art) a dog can have is "to find his Man" – or, in *lingua canina* "to find his Bone." L'Abbé speculates on this as the man returns to his work, leaving L'Abbé in the cottage with a pan of water, shoulder bound up . . . .

GIRL. comes in about evening. Tuberculous & sleeping by Dr's orders in a cot outside the house protected from wind by hurdles but *not* roofed. Not pretty: coughs & spits. The smell of her, frightens and revolts L'Abbé. To him it is (tho' he knows not) the fear of Death. The big Black She pats his head and the chill of her bony fingers strikes through him. Fear, disgust, horror but intense desire to see Man again.

Man returns: Girl sets tea. They eat & talk – as peasants. The very tones soothe L'Abbé. They talk about money – the stuff Dominic put under the hearth-brick. In this case it is up the chimney. Man gets Girl money for next days purchases. L'Abbé delighted "They have admitted me to their inmost confidence." GIRL goes into inner room, changes into dressing gown and as dark comes, goes outside to the cot: saying Good night to her father. L'Abbé goes out too (as a good dog should) sees girl just getting on to her bed: is knocked over in dead silence by the large blue "She-Dog" – has just time to bolt into a bush before the girl calls her off him. Dead silence while girl goes to sleep. She-dog watching her and occasionally licking her hand.

TALK IN THE NIGHT. When G. properly asleep, She-dog systematically quarters ground till she gets L'Abbé's wind. Then says (not wanting to wake up G) GO. This is *my* Bone! Go: or I tear out your throat." Logical Abbé says: – I daresay you could not only kill but eat me but, who on earth should I a stranger concern myself with a person who fills me with – canine equivalent for – the fear of death. She-dog angrily says it is not "That Taint" but merely distemper. She herself when a pup had distemper through which the G. nursed her. Since which date, she (the she-dog) has worked with the sheep all day (the shepherd is the girls uncle) and at evening has come over to be with the girl When the girl took sick the she-dog took on night-duty so that no one would wake her. Here comes *night-piece*: in course of which: (moon: bats: smells: stars: noise of small things. The she-dog opens her old barren heart (L'Abbé calls her Ma Tante for the rest of the yarn) She has borne no pups: she is old: ugly: savage: half-blind but "her life in itself" says L'Abbé "was as rounded and as fragrant as the very best truffle. L'Abbé confesses to her that very little would make him the abject slave of the charcoal man. (the girl's father). *Ma Tante* proposes peace & alliance. He (L'Abbé to give her every night a full account of the girls' every action through the day where she went & what she did &c. Then if he liked he could help keep part of the night watch: [Mem. Ma Tante (Bessie) slept a lot when the sheep were quiet: L'Abbé like every dog could sleep at a second's notice) so it was all easy. [[Mem. Disquisition on sheep by L'Abbé]]

From '"Teem": A Treasure-Hunter'*

. . . Oh, wise and well-beloved guardian and playmate of my youth – it is true – it is true, as thou didst warn me – Outside his Art an Artist must never dream!

From *Something of Myself**

This is the doom of the Makers – their Daemon lives in their pen.
If he be absent or sleeping, they are even as other men.
But if he be utterly present, and they swerve not from his behest,
The word that he gives shall continue, whether in earnest or jest.

Explanatory notes

Notes to the introduction

1 Letter to Edmund Gosse, 19 April 1910 (British Library).
2 Angus Wilson, *The Strange Ride of Rudyard Kipling* (London, Secker & Warburg, 1977), p. 169.
3 Edward Burne-Jones was his uncle by marriage. Kipling rejected many of the Movement's ideas but absorbed their passion for craftsmanship.
4 There is not space here for a full study of nineteenth-century criticism. Readers are referred to George Watson, *The Literary Critics: A Study of English Descriptive Criticism* (London, Woburn Press, 1973); and Chris Baldrick, *The Social Mission of English Criticism 1848–1932* (Oxford, Clarendon Press, 1987).
5 John Bayley, *The Uses of Division: Unity and Disharmony in Literature* (London, Chatto & Windus, 1976), p. 56.
6 W. H. Auden, 'The Poet of the Encirclement', *New Republic* 29 (1943), p. 579.
7 Lord Birkenhead, *Rudyard Kipling* (London, Weidenfeld and Nicolson, 1978), pp. 384–5.
8 David Cecil (ed.), *Desmond McCarthy, The Man and his Writings* (London, Constable, 1984), p. 154.
9 *Something of Myself*, p. 123.
10 *Letters*, II, pp. 185–6.
11 *The Letters of George Gissing to Edward Bertz, 1887–1903*, ed. A. C. Young (1961), p. 140.
12 It must have been bitter for Gissing to watch a younger man succeed after his own long struggle with timid publishers and prudish librarians. The envy of fellow-writers ten years later is recorded by Ford Madox Ford in 'Mr James and Mr Kipling'. The Kiplings had visited Henry James in their new car. According to Ford, James later comments:

> . . . such are the rewards of an enviable popularity! – a popularity such as I – or indeed you my young friend if you have any ambitions which I sometimes doubt – could not dream of far less imagine to ourselves – such are the rewards of an enviable popularity that Mr Kipling is in the possession of a magnificent one thousand two hundred guinea motor car. . .

(*The Bodley Head Ford Madox Ford*, ed. Graham Greene, 5 vols. (London, The Bodley Head), I (1962), p. 289.)
The price of the car is much exaggerated.

13 David Christie Murray, *Guesses at Truth: Ethical, Social, Political and Literary* (London, Hurst & Blackett, 1908), pp. 277–8 (quoted from Robert H. MacDonald, *The Language of Empire* (Manchester University Press, 1994)).

14 Leonard Woolf, *Growing: An Autobiography of the Years 1904 to 1911* (London, Hogarth Press, 1977), p. 46.

15 H. Morse Stephens papers, University of California at Berkeley.

16 Kipling refused their invitation in the verses 'Mulvaney Regrets' (*RG*, verse 1, p. 5366).

17 C. E. Carrington, *Rudyard Kipling* (London, Macmillan, 1953), p. 254.

18 Jeffrey Meyer, *Ernest Hemingway* (London, Macmillan, 1986), pp. 110–12; James K. Lyon, *Bertolt Brecht and Rudyard Kipling* (The Hague, Mouton, 1975); Peter Keating, *Kipling the Poet* (London, Secker & Warburg, 1994), pp. 240–3.

19 Jorge Luis Borges, *Labyrinths* (London, Penguin, 1970), p. 216. For Borges on Kipling, see e.g. *The Aleph and other Stories 1933–1969*, ed. and trans. N. T. di Giovanni (London, Jonathan Cape, 1971), pp. 51, 239–40.

20 T. A. Shippey, *The Road to Middle Earth* (London, Allen & Unwin, 1982), p. 226.

21 Edmund Wilson, 'Kipling's *Debits and Credits*', *New Republic* 12 (1926), pp. 194–5.

22 S. P. Rosenbaum, *The Early Literary History of the Bloomsbury Group*, 2 vols. (London, Macmillan, 1987), vol. 1, *Victorian Bloomsbury*, p. 138. Kipling would be the subject of some discussion in Bloomsbury. When *Something of Myself* was published, after Kipling's death, Virginia Woolf wrote in her diary: 'I went back to old talks with Lytton – talking shop about Kipling's style' (*The Diary of Virginia Woolf*, ed. Anne Olivier Bell and Andrew McNeillie 5 vols. (London, Hogarth Press, 1984, London, Penguin, 1985), v, p. 62). Desmond McCarthy's 1920 review of *Letters of Travel* suggests what was said at that time:

> His style is loved by the unliterary and often irritates the literary because the aim of his virtuosity is a violent precision. That comes first; he is not indifferent to beauty, very far indeed from it, but it comes second; precision and vigour first. He will force you first to see, hear, touch, smell (above all, see and smell) what he describes as vividly as words can do it; if the greatest vividness is inconsistent with an aesthetic quality, well, beauty must suffer . . . *New Statesman*, October 16, 1926.

Virginia Woolf, who was working out her own future style at this time, condemns Kipling's methods of description in her review of the same book. ('Mr Kipling's Notebook': Review of *Letters of Travel 1892–1913*, in *The Athenaeum*, 16 July 1926. Later collected in *Books and Portraits*, ed. Mary Lyon (London, Hogarth Press, 1977; Triad Paperback, 1979), pp. 80–3).

23 Edgar Wallace, 'Tommy to his Laureate', *Writ in Barracks*: quoted, *Kipling Journal*, 21 (March 1932), pp. 21–2.

24 Lancelyn Green (ed.), *Kipling: The Critical Heritage* (London, Routledge & Kegan Paul, 1971), p. 289.

25 Card-index to the books in the study, Bateman's, Burwash, Sussex; inventory for probate on Kipling's death, Kipling Papers, Sussex University. Reading lists can be found in ch. 1 of *Something of Myself*, 'The Last Term' (*Stalky & Co.*), and 'An English School' (*Land and Sea Tales*).

26 T. S. Eliot, *Selected Essays* (London, Faber & Faber, 1932; 3rd edn (enlarged) 1951; repr. 1972), pp. 29–30.

Notes to the texts

1 **replies to a printed questionnaire**: (Dalhousie University Libraries) Unpubl. Not an official questionnaire but one devised for amusement. The words in bold type are those of the printed form.

1 **Whittier, Emerson, Browning, Tennyson, Poe**: John Greenleaf Whittier (1807–92), author of *Legends of New England in Prose and Verse* (Hartford, 1831); 'Skipper Ireson's Ride' is mentioned in *CC*.

Ralph Waldo Emerson (1803–82), philosopher and poet, is mentioned in *SOM*, pp. 14 and 75, and quoted p. 76. The last verse of 'Give all to love' (slightly misquoted) is the epigraph of 'Children of the Zodiac' (collected in Ralph Waldo Emerson, *Poems*, Boston, James Munroe, 1847).

Robert Browning (1812–89) was a friend of RK's aunt and uncle Sir Edward and Lady Burne-Jones. RK describes his first encounter with Browning's *Men and Women* (first published London, Chapman and Hall, 1855), at about the time this must have been written, in *SOM*, p. 22; many critics have noticed a resemblance between Browning's monologues and RK poems like 'McAndrew's Hymn' and 'The Mary Gloster'.

According to *SOM*, p. 7, Alfred Tennyson (1809–92; Poet Laureate 1850–92) was one of RK's earliest literary discoveries.

RK's self-acknowledged debt to the poet and short story writer Edgar Allan Poe (1809–49) was documented in Burton R. Pollin, 'Poe and Kipling: A Heavy Debt Acknowledged', *KJ*, March 1980, pp. 13–24.

Browning, Tennyson and Emerson are all parodied in *Echoes* (Lahore 1884; SB). There are books by all five poets in the study at Bateman's, RK's Sussex home (NTInv).

1 **Macaulay, Hume, Gibbons**: Thomas Babington Macaulay (1800–59), politician and historian, whose biographies of Clive and Warren Hastings are at Bateman's (NTInv).

David Hume (1711–76), philosopher and historian.

'Gibbons' is presumably Edward Gibbon (1737–94); there is a set of *The History of the Decline and Fall of the Roman Empire* (first published in 6 vols., London, Strahan and Cadell, 1776–80) in RK's study (NTInv). He would draw on ch. xxvii for the Roman stories in *PPH* (*KJ*, March 1993, p. 44).

1 **E. About, Zola, Ouida, Miss Braddon**: Edmond-François Valentin About (1828–85), French journalist, art critic and author of *nouvelles*. At least two About titles were available in English translation (*The King of the Mountains*, tr. L. Wraxall, London, Ward and Lock, 1862; *Colonel Fougas' Mistake*, tr. J. E. Maitland, 2 vols. London, Remington, 1878), but RK also read French. RK would help his father write an obituary of About (*SOM*, p. 202).

Emile Zola (1840–1902), leader of the naturalistic movement in French fiction and author of the Rougon-Macquart series of novels, which were still appearing at this time (see also p. 17).

Ouida (Marie-Louise de la Ramée, 1839–1908), writer of best-selling romances.

Mary Elizabeth Braddon (1837–1915), author of (amongst other novels) *Lady Audley's Secret* (3 vols., London, Tinsley Bros., 1862).

None of these writers is represented at Bateman's (NTInv).

1 **Bismark [sic], Gladstone**: 'Moltke' written first and then deleted: Field-Marshal Count Helmuth von Moltke (1800–91), German Chief of Staff and reformer of the German Army. Count Otto von Bismarck (1815–98), Imperial German Chancellor and architect of German unity. William Ewart Gladstone (1809–98), Liberal Prime Minister 1868–74, 1880–85, 1886, 1892–94.

The juxtaposition of Gladstone and Bismarck suggests that RK is writing in 1880. During the election campaign that May, Gladstone suggested that world peace could be ensured by a 'concert of Europe' in which Germany would play a stabilising part. RK's Headmaster Cormell Price and his English teacher W. C. Crofts were Gladstonian Liberals. In adult life RK would be hostile to Liberals, and from his 40's also to Germans.

1 **La Dame aux Caméllias, John Ridd**: The novel (later a play) *La Dame aux Caméllias* (Paris, 1848), by Alexandre Dumas, *fils* (1824–95). Important in the story is a copy of Prevost's *Manon Lescaut* (Paris, 1733), the influence of which on *The Light that Failed* is acknowledged in *SOM*, p. 132.

John Ridd is the hero of R. D. Blackmore's novel *Lorna Doone: A Romance of Exmoor* (3 vols., London, Sampson Low, 1869). Ridd is 'Herculean' in size, strength and fighting prowess (though loth to kill even an enemy); he effortlessly attracts women. RK was short and myopic.

Neither of these texts is at Bateman's (NTInv).

1 **Rossini, Meyerbeer, Wagner**: Gioachino Rossini (1792–1868), Giacomo Meyerbeer (1791–1864) and Richard Wagner (1813–83). All three wrote operas. RK had no ear for music, but his mother sang, played and composed (*SOM*, p. 4).

2 **Flaxman, H. Thorneycroft [sic], Leighton**: John F. Flaxman, 1755–1826, sculptor; Hamo (later Sir William) Thornycroft, 1850–1925, sculptor; Frederic (later Lord) Leighton, 1830–96, painter and sculptor.

2 **Lorna Doone, Yeast, Moths, L'amant d'Amanda**: *Lorna Doone* by R. D. Blackmore (see note, p. 1 above).

Yeast (London, Collection of British Authors, 1850) was the first novel by Charles Kingsley. The resort where RK was at school had been named Westward Ho! after another Kingsley novel.

In Ouida's *Moths: A Novel* (3 vols., London, Chatto and Windus, 1880), a young girl is trapped by her worldly mother into marriage with a 'brutal' rake.

L'amant d'Amanda has not been identified.

2 **before reaching maturity**: This suggests a date for the questionnaire later than August 1880, when RK went to Southsea and met Florence Garrard, his calf-love. He would be 15 in December 1880.

2 **their vices**: Not identified.

2 **that he would hear**: Not identified. Perhaps by RK's mother?

2 **Introduction to Schoolboy Lyrics**: RK's juvenile poems, privately printed (Lahore 1881) by his parents without his knowledge. *EV*, OB17, SB; not in *DV*.

3 **Letter to E. K. Robinson**: (KP) Robinson (1857–1928), then assistant editor of *The Pioneer*, had been staying with the Kiplings at Simla. The following year Robinson would be transferred to Lahore as editor of *The Civil and Military Gazette*, where he allowed RK a column of his own and encouraged him to write and publish both verse and prose.

3 **In the House of Suddhoo**: Collected under this title in *PT*: first published as 'Section 420 I.P.C.' in *C&MG*, 30 April 1886.

3 **Mother Maturin**: Title of an unpublished novel (now lost), parts of which were later absorbed into *Kim*. At the end of 'To be Filed for Reference' (*PT*) there is a fictional account of it as written by a drop-out from British Indian society.

3 **Fleet Street**: Robinson had previously been employed by *The Globe*, a London newspaper.

3 **Letter to Unidentified Recipient**: (KP) *Letters*, II, p. 11n. quotes a suggestion from C. E. Carrington that this was Wolcott Balestier, RK's new American friend, who was London agent for the New York publishing house John W. Lovell Company. This company became the authorised American publishers of RK's work. The two men would collaborate in writing *The Naulahka* (1892; serialised in *Century Magazine*, Nov. 1891–July 1892).

4 **walketh in the noon-day . . . destroyeth in the study**: See Psalms XCI:6: '. . . for the pestilence that walketh in the darkness; nor for the destruction that wasteth at noonday'.

4 **shot at**: RK had visited the Khyber Pass in March 1885. He later claimed to have been shot at by an Afghan there (*SOM*, p. 28).

4 **bossed a hundred and seventy men**: In the *C&MG* printing shop. Accounts of it can be found in 'My First Book' (*SOM*, pp. 173–7) and in 'The Man who would be King'.

4 **in the Himalayas**: RK visited the Himalayas in May 1885 and wrote about it in his diary (see *SOM*, pp. 36–7, also pp. 208–9). Some of the atmosphere of this expedition found its way into *Kim*, ch. xiii. The quotation is from Tennyson's *The Princess: A Medley* (London, E. Moxon, 1847), part vii, line 189.

4 **been through once already**: RK had been suffering from flu and depression; his sister visited him on 11 February and was shocked at the state in which she found him.

4 **If the success comes**: It did: with the first *Barrack-Room Ballads* (see note, p. 138 below). At about this time RK telegraphed his parents 'Genesis 45:9' (Alice Macdonald Fleming, *KJ*, April 1948, p. 7). The verse reads in part: '. . . God hath made me lord of all Egypt, come down unto me, tarry not'.

6 **those commission verses**: 'Cleared'.

6 **'Cold Iron'**: First published *Delineator*, September 1909. Collected *RF*. The Boy is the orphan son of a slave under the Anglo-Saxons, stolen by Puck (who narrates and is speaking in this extract) and raised by fairies. Many critics identify the boy as a young writer resembling RK himself.

7 **'The Story of Mohammad Din'**: First published *C&MG*, 8 Sept. 1886; collected *PT*. The little boy, son of an Indian servant in a British house, begs for and is given an old polo-ball to play with. A *bhistie* is a water-carrier.

AW suggests (p. 185) that RK's imagination works best when 'like Muhammed Din's as he plays in the bungalow garden, [his] fancy can find a small place to make the universe'. See *SOM*, p. 8 for RK's magic 'ring or fence' in childhood games at Southsea.

7 **False Dawn**: First published in *PT*. A man, confused by an Indian dust-storm, proposes to the wrong sister. This passage suggests one reason why 'truth' is impossible in fiction.

7 **'Under the Deodars'**: This preface is only in the Indian Railway Library editions (no. 4). Preceded by a note, '[Reprinted in chief from "*The Week's News*"]'. 'At the Pit's Mouth' had not previously been published.

9 **Seventh Commandment**: See Exodus xx:14. Of the six stories, there are adulterous love affairs in four: 'The Education of Otis Yeere', 'At the Pit's Mouth', 'A Wayside Comedy' and 'The Hill of Illusion'. The eponymous character in 'A Second-Rate Woman' shows up the moral standards of the Simla belles who despise her. All these are in *WWW*. See also two drawings from a notebook (pls. 2a and 2b).

9 **Robert Hanna Wick**: 'Only a Subaltern' (*WWW*). Many critics have complained that Wick is too perfect and inspires too much hero-worship in the soldiers.

9 **The Phantom Rickshaw and other Eerie Tales**: The stories are collected

in *WWW* without this preface from the Indian Railway Library editions (no. 5). Preceded by note '[Reprinted in chief from "The Week's News"]', but of the four only 'My Own True Ghost Story' is so reprinted. 'The Phantom Rickshaw' and 'The Strange Ride of Morrowbie Jukes' were originally in *Quartette*. 'The Man who would be King' had not been previously published.

In the English edition of the Railway Library this text has been altered.

11 **'The Last of the Stories'**: First published *The Week's News*, 15 Sept. 1889; collected only in *AF* and SB.

11 **kench**: From *khenchna*, to pull.

13 **'Dante once prepared to paint a picture'**: See Robert Browning, 'One Word More', *Men and Women*, v, 32: 'Dante once prepared to paint an angel.' The *Inferno* of Dante Alighieri (1265–1321) inspired an early RK parody, written at school and now lost (see *SOM*, p. 22).

13 **three columns**: The story took exactly three columns in *The Week's News*.

13 **Sainted Leopardi**: The Italian poet Giacomo Leopardi (1798–1837). James Thomson's poem *The City of Dreadful Night* (London, Reeves and Turner, 1880) has epigraphs from Dante and Leopardi. Thomson's poem influenced RK: see *SOM*, p. 22.

13 **feuilletons**: RK's series 'Turnovers' in the *C&MG*, 1888–90, could be so described.

14 **floor-cloth**: 'Jail-durrie' in *AF* – a form of cheap matting made by prisoners in Indian jails.

15 **Man of Us**: Job I:1: 'There was a man in the land of Uz, whose name was Job . . .' Yorkshire people like RK's father's family would pronounce 'us' as 'uz'. The quotation in the previous paragraph is from Job XXXI:35: 'Oh that one would hear me! behold, my desire is, that the Almighty would desire me, and that mine adversary had written a book.'

15 **Balzac and Théophile Gautier**: French writers Honoré de Balzac (1799–1850) and Théophile Gautier (1811–72). Balzac wrote of the supernatural in *Etudes philosophiques*; his novel series *La Comédie Humaine* partly inspired the Realist movement. Gautier's *Madame de Maupin* was seen as origin of the Decadent writers: but *RG* suggests that RK refers here to 'La morte amoureuse'.

15 **three-volume novels that never reach the six-shilling stage**: For most of the nineteenth century, largely due to the influence of lending libraries like Mudie's, English novels were published at three guineas in three-volume, limited editions. The more popular of them would then appear in cheaper, one-volume form. (See also RK's poem 'The Three-Decker', p. 143).

16 **Mr Maliphant and the Bormalacks**: Characters from the novel *All Sorts and Conditions of Men* (3 vols., London, Chatto and Windus, 1882), by Walter Besant (1836–1901).

16 **Mr John Oakhurst, gambler**: Character from Bret Harte (1836–1902) 'The

Outcasts of Poker Flat' (*The Luck of Roaring Camp and other Sketches* (Boston, MA, 1870)). Brown of Calaveras, eponymous character from another story by Harte; Yuba Bill is the stage-coach driver in this and 'Miggles'. All are set in the American West. As editor of *The Week's News*, RK published at least one story by Harte (see *SOM*, p. 43).

16 **Caliban**: See Browning's 'Caliban upon Setebos, or Natural Theology in the Island', in *Dramatis Personae* (London, Chapman and Hall, 1864). The poem is quoted in *S&Co.*, 'Slaves of the Lamp Pt. I'; 'Natural Theology' is the title of a poem in *YB*.

16 **Bishop Blougram**: From Robert Browning, 'Bishop Blougram's Apology: A Bishop addresses his Critic' (*Men and Women*). See *SOM*, p. 22.

17 **Robert Elsmere**: Eponymous character in the novel *Robert Elsmere* (3 vols. London, Smith and Elder, 1888) by M. A. (Mrs Humphry) Ward. In an uncollected passage in 'An Interview with Mark Twain' (*FSS*, II), RK was astonished that Twain should admire the book 'for the workmanship' and 'the grace and beauty of the style', since to RK it was: 'the laboured truck of the schools where men act in obedience to the book they read, and keep their consciences in spirits of home-made wine' (*KJ*, Sept. 1992, p. 21).

17 **Marie Pigeonnier**: Not the Frenchwoman who tempts Robert Elsmere. Perhaps a character from the Opéra Comique.

17 **The Tyneside Tail-Twisters**: Bobby Wick's regiment in 'Only a Subaltern' (see note to p. 9 above). See also 'What it comes to' in 'The Smith Administration' (*C&MG*, 5 Nov. 1888; *FSS*, II).

17 **Black Tyrone . . . Old Regiment**: Mulvaney's regiments in 'With the Main Guard' (*S3*).

17 **Coupeau**: Vol. VII of Zola's Rougon-Macquart series is *L'Assommoir* (Paris, 1877), in which the Parisian artisan Coupeau becomes a drunk.

18 **Tom Sawyer**: Eponymous character in the novel by Mark Twain (*Tom Sawyer*, Hertford, CT., The American Publishing Co., 1876).

18 **Mr John Wellington Wells**: Character in Gilbert and Sullivan's comic opera *The Sorcerer* (1877). Dagonet was King Arthur's jester in Tennyson's *Idylls of the King* (extended edition, London, Strachan and Co., 1869).

18 **Allan Quatermain**: Eponymous character in the novel by H. Rider Haggard (1856–1925), who would later become a friend of RK's (*Allan Quatermain*, London, Longmans, 1887).

18 **Little Lord Fauntleroy**: Eponymous character in the children's novel by Frances Hodgson Burnett (*Little Lord Fauntleroy*, New York, Charles Scribner's Sons, 1886).

18 **Good's passing with a maiden of the Zu-Vendi**: Good is another character from *Alan Quatermain*, the Zu-Vendi a Zulu tribe.

19 **'She began to weep . . . none of I'**: From the nursery rhyme 'The Little Woman and the Pedlar'.

19 **Mrs Hauksbee**: Character in *PT* and 'Under the Deodars' (*WWW*); introduced in 'Three and an Extra' (*PT*).

19 **the Devil and all his works**: See Church of England Catechism.

20 **Mrs Mallowe**: Mrs Hauksbee's best friend in 'The Education of Otis Yeere' and 'A Second-Rate Woman' (see note, p. 19 above).

20 ***Litera scripta manet***: The quotation continues: 'verbum impelle perit': 'What is written is permanent, the spoken word dies powerless.'

20 **Delectus**: *Delectus* (1828), a book of Latin and Greek extracts for use in schools.

20 **Peterhof**: The Viceroy's summer residence at Simla, 1862–88.

20 **Gilead P. Beck**: Character from *The Golden Butterfly* (3 vols., London, Tinsley Bros., 1876), by Walter Besant and James Rice.

21 **Wayside Comedy**: 'A Wayside Comedy' (*WN*, 21 Jan. 1888; *WWW*).

21 **Gunner Barnabas and Private Shacklock**: See 'The Opinions of Gunner Barnabas' (*C&MG* 7 Oct. 1887; *FSS*, II) and 'The Likes o' Us' (*WN*, 4 Feb. 1888; *AF*; *UP*).

21 **Captain Gadsby and Minnie**: Characters in this paragraph are from 'The Story of the Gadsbys'. One section was published in *C&MG*, May 1888; six more in *WN*, May–June 1888. The remaining part, 'Fatima', first appeared in A. Wheeler's Railway Library edn, no. 2 (Allahabad, 1888), which also includes an introductory letter (not reprinted in subsequent editions) to Jack Mafflin, Gadsby's friend and best man. Collected in *S3*. 'The Brigadier-General' is a nickname for the Gadsbys' baby son.

21 **Trewinnard . . . Otis Yeere**: Mrs Mallow tells in 'The Education of Otis Yeere' how she has forwarded a man's career. In 'A Supplementary Chapter' (*WN*, 19 May 1888; *AF*; *UP*) his name is given as Trewinnard.

21 **Crook O'Neil**: 'With the Main Guard' (*S3*); 'The Ballad of Boh Da Thone' (*WN*, 1 Sept. 1888; *BRB*).

21 **Bobby Wick**: 'Only a Subaltern'.

21 **Janki Meah**: 'At Twenty-Two' (*S3*).

21 **Afzul Khan**: Elsewhere spelt Afzal Khan. 'At Howli Thana' (*S3*).

21 **the murderous Pathan horsedealer**: Anonymous narrator of 'Dray Wara Yow Dee' (*S3*). In *AF* and SB the next semicolon and comma are interchanged, confusing this character with Durga Dass (see next note).

21 **Durga Dass**: 'Gemini' (*S3*).

21 **Dana Da**: 'The Sending of Dana Da' (*S3*).

21 **Leander of the Barwhi ford**: 'In Flood Time' (*S3*).

21 **Peg Barney**: 'The Big Drunk Draf' (*S3*).

21 **Mrs Delville**: 'A Second-Rate Woman' (*WWW*).

21 **Dinah Shadd**: 'The Big Drunk Draf' (see note, p. 21 above). She would also appear in 'The Courting of Dinah Shadd' (*LH*).

21 **Simmons, Slane and Losson**: 'In the Matter of a Private' (*S3*).

21 **Georgie Porgie**: 'Georgie Porgie' (*LH*).

21 **the Hawley Boy**: Mrs Hauksbee's most devoted admirer, especially in 'A Second-Rate Woman'.

21 **Hill of Illusion**: 'The Hill of Illusion' (*WWW*).

21 **Tents of Kedar**: 'The Tents of Kedar', one of the parts in 'The Story of The Gadsbys'.

21 **His Majesty the King**: Eponymous character in the story in *WWW*.
22 **Jackanapes and Lollo**: The child and his pony in *Jackanapes* (1879) by Juliana Horatia Ewing (1841–85). See also *WWW*.
22 **babes and sucklings**: Psalms VIII:2.
23 ***In saecula saeculorum***: 'For ages of ages'; another quotation from the *Delectus*.
23 **a sign**: This and other references in the sentence are Masonic. An Entered Apprentice is a new initiate.
23 **Trajan is a fisher of frogs**: See Bk II, ch. XXX of *Gargantua and Pantagruel* by François Rabelais (tr. Sir Thomas Urquhart, London, 1653–1708).
24 **What leisure to grow wise?**: Matthew Arnold (1822–88), 'Stanzas in Memory of the Author of Obermann', in *Empedocles on Etna and other Poems* (London, B. Fellowes, 1852), 18th verse. This verse was inscribed by RK in the copy of *Plain Tales from the Hills* presented to his parents, January 1888. It is also quoted in 'Aunt Ellen' (*LR*).
25 **Unpublished prefaces to Departmental Ditties**: From an unissued copy of the first English edition in the British Library. A letter to Thacker Spink, Jan. 1890 (Yale, Tyler Collection) gives the reason for their cancellation:

> I've taken Eminent Advice about those prefaces. No. They won't do, so I've cut 'em out and I think I'm on the safe side. No use telling the public you think 'em a damned ass.

26 **Watson's Hotel**: Watson's Esplanade Hotel, Bombay.
26 **brandy-panee**: brandy and water.
26 **kuga**: The context suggests a misprint for 'huqa' (also spelt huqqa or hookah).
27 **Letter to William Canton**: (Berg Collection, New York Public Library) Unpubl. Canton (1845–1926), poet, sub-editor and leader writer on the *Glasgow Herald*.
27 **the Thibetan story**: The *Englishman* of Calcutta had published (9 July 1889) the story of one Namgay Doolah, wounded and taken prisoner during a battle with the Tibetans in Sikkim, who was then discovered to be the son of Tim Doolan, an army deserter of Irish birth, and of a Lepcha mother. It was reprinted in *The Globe*, 8 August 1889. RK would adapt this story, using the real names of the two men, for his 'Namgay Doolah' (first published in *Mine Own People*, John W. Lovell Co., New York 1891; *LH*). Two aspects of the newspaper report were not included: that the man tried to attach himself to the British Army, and that a Tibetan Lama was instrumental in revealing his identity. Both can be found – transmogrified – in *Kim*.
27 **'Home'**: Published in *C&MG*, 25 Dec. 1891; reprinted in the *C&MG Annual*, 1935. RK sailed from Australia in the Peninsular and Orient Line ship *Valetta* on 24 November 1891. Landing at the extreme south of India (an area he had never before visited), he made a long zigzag northwards

by train to join his parents in Lahore, almost touching the east and west coasts on the way.

27 **Anglo-Indians**: Used by RK and his contemporaries of British nationals living in India.

27 **B.I.**: British India Steamship Co.

27 **Tuticorin**: Port near the southern tip of India; terminus of the South Indian Railway.

27 **khitmatgars**: Butlers or waiters.

27 **Vizagapatam**: Vishakhpatnam, a port in Andhra Pradesh, on the east coast.

28 **Little Henry and his Bearer**: Children's novel by Mrs Mary Martha Sherwood (*The History of Little Henry and his Bearer*, Wellington, Houlston, 1815). It is not set nearly so far south.

28 **kutcha**: Kachcha – literarily 'raw' or 'unripe'; widely used to mean temporary or badly finished. Here perhaps built of unbaked earth.

28 **Dawson No. 1**: A cheroot of dark leaf from Trichinopoly.

28 **before this life**: Not identified.

29 **telegraph forms**: Lionel Johnson, reviewing *LH* in *The Academy*, XL, pp. 327–8, 17 Oct. 1891 queried the reality of Kipling's Anglo-Indian officials 'making cynical epigrams about life and death . . . men who seem to talk like telegrams . . .'

29 **S.I.R.**: South Indian Railway Co.

29 **Arconum**: Arkonam, junction west of Madras where the Madras railway and the S.I.R. joined.

29 **Khundwa**: Khandwa junction, Madhya Pradesh, on the Bombay, Baroda and Central Indian Railway. The transfer to another company's line meant extra paper-work for the clerk, besides writing out the ticket by hand and calculating its cost. Indian clerks were often over-educated for such menial positions; they were expected to enforce British-imposed regulations that annoyed them as well as their customers.

29 **Raichur and Wadi**: Both in Mysore. Raichur was the junction of the Madras Railway with the Great Indian Peninsula Railway. Wadi was the junction with the Nizam's State Railway into Hyderabad.

29 **shikar**: Hunting or shooting.

29 **tonga**: Light two-wheeled, horse-drawn vehicle, in which the passenger faced backwards.

30 **Dhond-Manmar**: The Dhond-Manmar State railway in Maharashtra ran north from Dhond, just outside Poona, connecting the north-east and south-east branches of the Great Indian Peninsula Railway.

30 **the Guides, the Goorkhas or Bengal Cavalry**: Indian regiments with British officers. The Indian Staff Corps was a list of officers who would serve in India with one or another such regiment.

30 **dugabashi**: Military training. RK uses this word in 'The Maltese Cat' (*DW*), where he translates it 'horse-trick-work'.

30 **sowars**: Indian cavalry troopers.

31 **Asseerghur jungle**: Asigarh (Madhya Pradesh), a fort stormed by Wellington in 1815, stood in 'wild country, full of game' (Murray's *Handbook to India, Ceylon and Burma*, London, Murray, 1894 edn). This is believed to be the nearest RK ever came to the country where he set *The Jungle Book*.

31 **'Stunt**: Assistant Collector – a title uneducated Indians found hard to pronounce. It was shortened to 'Estunt': hence 'Stunt. See also poem 'Estunt the Griff' (*EV*).

31 **Neemuch**: Nimach on the Rajputana and Malwar Railway, at the border of Central India and Udaipur. RK was there in 1887 (*FSS*, I, ch. vi).

31 **Bhopal**: Junction in Madhya Pradesh.

31 **huqqa**: Hookah, the Indian pipe for smoking through water.

31 **Lord of the Iron Horses**: Since RK addresses him later as 'S – ', H. A. Scott, Traffic Superintendent of the North-Western Railway, is probably meant.

31 **Ghaziabad**: A junction in Uttar Pradesh, east of Delhi, where the train made a halt so that European passengers could eat 'tiffin' (lunch).

31 **six months**: British officers in the Indian Army were entitled (conditions permitting) to six months' leave on reduced pay for every third year of active service. Such leave, which could be accumulated, was long enough to go to England. But 'D' and his bride were lucky to get it: it was often cancelled.

32 **Manipur business**: In the summer of 1891 there was unrest in this princely state, lying between Assam and the Burmese border. The Government intervened and deposed its Maharajah. Several British officials were killed.

32 **no camp for me**: Such a camp is described in 'The Courting of Dinah Shadd' (*LH*).

32 **khaki undress**: Working rig as opposed to 'dress' uniform. Khaki was first worn at the siege of Delhi during the Sepoy Rising.

32 **Kalka by rail**: The first section of the Delhi–Kalka railway had been opened earlier in 1891. The characters in 'William the Conqueror' (*DW*) travel back from South India to Lahore for Christmas, with some of the same reactions as RK's, but on a different line. See also *Kim*, ch. ii.

32 **Ataree**: Now the frontier station between India and Pakistan.

32 **chota hazri**: Literally 'small breakfast', consisting of tea and fruit.

33 **Jats**: Punjabi farming caste. See *Kim*, ch. xi, for a Jat character.

33 **hathis**: Elephants.

33 **Plot and Passion**: The large railway complex at Lahore (with junction and repair yards) had its own staff theatre. Here on 20 and 22 Dec. 1883 the Lahore Amateurs staged a performance of the play *Plot and Passion* by Tom Taylor and John Lang (1853), in which RK played Desmarets, a principal part. A prologue written by RK for the occasion is reprinted in *EV*.

33 **Mozung**: A village south of the walled city of Lahore; in between them lay the 'Civil Station' where the non-military British lived.

33 **Kadir Buksh**: RK's personal servant, who accompanied him in his travels in India, was the son of his father's servant (*SOM*, p. 25). Kadir Buksh is a character in 'My Own True Ghost Story' (*WWW*), and 'The Collar-Wallah and the Poison Stick' (*St Nicholas Magazine*, Feb. 1893; *UP*). The preface to the Railway Library edn (1888) of *In Black and White* is put into his mouth. In 'The New Dispensation' (*C&MG*, 16 Dec. 1889; *AF*; *UP*), RK in London marvels at the lack of mutual respect in British master-servant relationships, and seeks vainly to replace him.

33 **Hussaini kabab for hazri**: Lamb curry cooked on skewers for breakfast.

33 **Kafir**: Non-Muslim.

33 **jail dhurries . . . choukuts**: The *dhurries* were rugs made by prisoners in Lahore jail. Ruggled *chitai* – tattered rush matting. *Almirahs* – free-standing cupboards (originally a Portuguese word). *Chaukut* – door-frame or threshold.

33 **Vixen**: She appears in the stories 'Her Majesty's Servants' (*JB*); 'My Lord the Elephant' (*MI*); 'Garm – a Hostage' (*AR*).

33 **thermantidote**: A device combining a fan and wetted grass screens, to create a cool draught.

34 **chaprassi**: Messenger.

34 **duftar**: Office or records.

34 **ferashes**: Tamarisk trees.

34 **surki**: Pounded brick mixed with lime to form a mortar.

34 **thunda suruk**: Paved road with shade trees: *thanda*, cold or dead or frozen; *sarak*, a road or street.

34 **chappar kargaz**: Printed newspaper.

34 **columbiad**: Sic. Probably 'Columbia', a well-known type of printing-press.

34 **chick**: Bamboo screen over an open door or window, for shade and privacy.

34 **comps.**: Compositors.

35 **'Kitna in hand hai, kul se?'**: 'How much is there in hand, altogether?'

35 **dak**: Mail.

35 **'Kingdom of Bombay'**: An article in *The Pioneer*, 10 Apr. 1888, satirised political rivalry between the administrations of Bengal, Bombay, Madras and the Punjab.

35 **Capua and the Exodus**: Capua was an Etruscan hill town, famed in Roman times for its luxury – hence a nickname for Simla. RK's poem 'The Faithful Soul' in *C&MG*, 13 Dec. 1886 (*EV*) lampooned a press campaign against the 'Exodus' of government from Calcutta to Simla during the hot weather. 'A Tale of Two Cities' (*C&MG*, 2 June 1887; called 'Love among the Ruins' in the 3rd edn of *DD*) describes the resentment of the Calcutta merchants, who had to stay behind for business reasons.

35 **ask Madras whether it had an army**: During the summer of 1886 *The Pioneer* had run a series on administrative scandals in Madras.

35 **charpoy**: Bedstead.

36 **Thomas of the K.O.S.B.'s**: Thomas Atkins, generic name for a private soldier. It was used for samples of official Army documents from 1815.
K.O.S.B.'s: the King's Own Scottish Borderers (25th Foot), RK's brother-in-law's regiment.

36 **guardroom in the wall**: See 'With the Main Guard' (*S3*).

36 **Akbar**: Mogul Emperor of India, 1542–1605.

36 **Jahangir**: Son of Akbar. His tomb at Shadera lies on the bank of the Ravi, one of the Five Rivers from which the Punjab takes its name. 'Minars' are towers (more usually 'minarets').

36 **chilumchee**: A metal washing-bowl.

36 **Naulakha pavilion**: Built in the grounds of the fort, of marble inlaid with precious stones in the manner of the Taj Mahal, it is so-called because it was supposed to have cost nine lakhs (hundred thousands) of rupees. RK called his house in Vermont after it, also the novel that he wrote with Wolcott Balestier, *The Naulahka* [sic]. The novel was appearing in serial form when 'Home' was written. A telegram announcing the mortal illness of Balestier would cut short RK's holiday.

37 **Mohurrum riots**: Mohurrum is the first month of the Islamic year. The Mohurrum festival, in honour of the prophet Mohammed's grandsons who were killed in battle, is celebrated by processions carrying papier-mache towers on bamboo frames. Philip Mason in *The Men who Ruled India* (1985; abridged edition, London, Pan Books, 1987, p. 289) relates how these processions would try to cut low-hanging branches from wayside trees in which the towers might catch; the Hindus, to whom these trees were sacred, would defend them violently. A fictional account of such a riot can be found in 'On the City Wall' (*S3*). Mohurrum processions were reported in two articles entitled 'The City of the Two Creeds' (19 and 22 Oct., 1885, reprinted in *RG*, I; and 1 Oct. 1887, reprinted in *KI*, pp. 266–9).

37 **'Captain, Colonel or knight at arms'**: John Milton, sonnet no. viii.

37 **Roshnai Gate**: Of Fort Lahore, at the north-east corner of the Fort grounds.

37 **tazia**: Tower commemorating Mohammed's grandsons (see note, p. 37).

37 **Soneri Musjid**: The Golden Mosque in the old walled town of Lahore.

37 **Jews of Shushan**: Eponymous characters in the story in *LH*.

37 **Lalun's naughty little house**: Lalun is a courtesan of education and culture in 'On the City Wall' (*S3*).

37 **Azizan of the Douri Bagh**: Character in 'The Vision of Hamid Ali' (*EV*, SB). A prostitute in the story 'In the House of Suddhoo' (*PT*) has the same name. The Douri Bagh (gardens) are either fictitious, or too small (or too disreputable) to be named on the city plan in Murray's *Handbook* (1894).

37 **cricket**: A cricket-mad boy is described in 'The Finances of the Gods' (*LH*).

37 **bunnia**: Merchant or moneylender.

37 **kullam**: Qalam – pen.

38 **Delhi Gate**: At the east of the old walled city.

38 **pagal**: Fool, madman. RK probably means a clipping in a KP press cuttings-book, mistakenly ascribed to *The Spectator* of 9 Aug. 1890 (there was no such issue, and 9 Aug. 1891 does not contain a review of any RK work):

> As much as is shown is shown with almost exaggerated clearness – everything in the foreground, no gradations of mist or distance. But dabs of bright light revealing a scene here or a scene there, in which everything is so vivid that it almost hurts the startled eyes, do not make a landscape . . .

Henry James would later complain that RK's work lacked 'shades'.

38 **Badami Bagh**: Gardens where Ranjit Singh, Sikh ruler of the Punjab in the first half of the nineteenth century, used to hold reviews.

38 **'A Matter of Fact'**: First published *The People*, 24 Jan. 1892; collected *MI*. In the first part of the story three journalists on a steamboat see a dying sea-monster thrown up from the depths. The rest of the story tells how they try to report it and are disbelieved.

39 **Letter to Edward Lucas White**: (Syracuse University Library) White (1866–1934), was a classicist and schoolteacher in Baltimore, Maryland, author of poems and historical romances.

39 **Euterpe**: Muse of music and lyric poetry. According to CK he was working on verses for *The Jungle Book* that month. The first edition would be published on 22 May. The poems in it were: 'Hunting-Song of the Seonee Pack'; 'Road-Song of the Bandar-Log'; 'Mowgli's Song'; 'Lukannon'; 'Darzee's Chaunt'; 'Shiv and the Grasshopper'; 'Parade-Song of the Camp Animals'. Each story also has a verse epigraph.

39 **Donne**: John Donne (1572–1631), metaphysical poet, politician and Anglican priest. The epigraphs to 'William the Conqueror', Parts I and II (*DW*) are from Donne's 'The Undertaking' and 'A Valediction, Forbidding Mourning'.

39 **Fletcher**: Phineas Fletcher (1582–1650), author of the allegorical poem *The Purple Island, or the Isle of Man*, in which a man's anatomy is described in topographical terms. RK seems to have met it at school (see 'The Last Term', *S&Co.*).

39 **Drayton – or Drummond**: Michael Drayton (1563–1631), poet; RK would borrow the metre of his 'The Battaile of Agincourt' for the pastiche Elizabethan poem 'The Two Cousins' in *Rewards and Fairies*.

William Drummond of Hawthornden (1585–1649), poet and author of *Ben Jonson's Conversations with William Drummond of Hawthornden* (Edinburgh, Watson, 1711; reprinted in C. H. Herford, Percy Simpson and Evelyn Simpson (eds.), *Ben Jonson*, 11 vols., Oxford, Clarendon Press, 1925–52, vol. I (1925), pp. 128–78). RK drew on it for the character of Ben Jonson in 'Proofs of Holy Writ' (see pp. 99–110 and notes, pp. 185–8).

There is a copy of 'Conversations' (ed. Philip Sydney, 1900) in RK's study (NTInv).

39 **Doughty cracking his very courteous jests**: In 1578 Sir Francis Drake went to South America with his friend, the courtier Thomas Doughty. They quarrelled over command of the party; Doughty was supposed to have incited the sailors to mutiny. At Port St Julian, near the Straits of Magellan, Doughty was put on trial and condemned to be either marooned, executed or taken home in chains. He chose execution and was beheaded.

39 **block and the headsman**: RK did not write the poem. Some part of this story is alluded to in 'Simple Simon' (in *RF*); and 'With Drake in the Tropics' (C. R. L. Fletcher and Rudyard Kipling, *A History of England*, 1911).

40 **a man I know pretty well**: RK himself. 'You *are* so dam' inaccurate!' complains Stalky to Beetle in 'The Propagation of Knowledge' (D&C).

40 **Wale**: Mrs Gamp's pronunciation of 'vale [of tears]' in Charles Dickens's *The Life and Adventures of Martin Chuzzlewit* (London, Chapman and Hall, 1843).

40 **The Last Rhyme of True Thomas**: First published *To-day*, 17 March 1894; collected *SS*. RK had not yet been offered a knighthood. A note from his daughter (Lord Birkenhead, *Rudyard Kipling*, London, Weidenfeld and Nicolson, 1978, Appendix B, p. 384) says that at some time between 1892 and 1896 he was 'thought of' as Poet Laureate in succession to Tennyson, but refused to let his name go forward. (No official offer could be made without the prior consent of the recipient.)

45 **Letter to Robert Barr**: (KP) A Glasgow-born Scots Canadian journalist, Barr (1850–1912) was proprietor of *The Idler* monthly magazine (1892–1911). He edited it jointly with Jerome K. Jerome from 1892–5. He also wrote a number of novels (see p. 93), but is better known for his detective stories in e.g. *The Triumphs of Eugene Valmont.*

45 **a Mulvaney tale**: The last stories narrated by Mulvaney had been published in *MI*, 'My Lord the Elephant' and 'Love o' Women'. He would make a brief final appearance in 'Garm, a Hostage' (*Saturday Evening Post*, 23 Dec. 1899; *AR*).

46 **'Leaves from a Winter Notebook'**: Barr did not buy this. It was first published in *Harper's Magazine*, May 1900; collected in *Letters of Travel (1892–1913)* (London, Macmillan, 1920).

46 **Edward Everett Hale**: (Cornell University) Hale (1822–1909) was a Unitarian minister in Boston and author of the short story 'The Man without a Country' (quoted by RK in 'The Prophet and the Country' (*D&C*)).

46 **companion collection**: *The Second Jungle Book* (Oct. 1895) contains 'How Fear Came', 'The Miracle of Purun Bhagat', 'Letting in the Jungle', 'The Undertakers', 'The King's Ankus', 'Quiquern', 'Red Dog', 'The Spring Running'.

46 **tales . . . the Bodhisat tells**: The Jatakas, traditional tales of the previous lives of the Buddha. In *Kim*, ch. ix the Lama tells one to the boy (see also *SOM*, p. 83).

46 **'cribbed' freely**: For instance in 'Rikki-Tikki-Tavi' (*JB*), where he has used situations from two stories in the *Panchatantra* series: 'A Remedy Worse than the Disease', and 'The Brahman and the Mongoose'.

46 **Letter to Mrs Mapes Dodge**: (Princeton University Libraries). Mrs Dodge (1831–1905) was editor of *St Nicholas*, a monthly magazine for children.

46 **a child's tale**: RK was writing a dog story, 'Garm – a Hostage' (*AR*), in October 1895. All through November he was writing verse (CK).

46 **tale in several parts**: In January 1896 he wrote 'The Tomb of his Ancestors' (*DW*), but then began again on *Kim*. Many critics have noticed that the novel falls into three parts (see note, p. 27 for its beginnings as a short story).

46 **Letter to Miss Welman**: (*KP*). Unpubl. She is not identified.

47 **not about the Jungle**: *Just So Stories for Little Children* (1902). The first three stories would be published December 1897–February 1898 (see note below).

47 **'Just So Stories'**: Sic. This preface (not reprinted in the book) introduced the first story, 'How the Whale got his Throat', as first published in *St. Nicholas*, xxv, part I, Dec. 1897, pp. 89ff. 'How the Camel got his Hump' and 'How the Rhinoceros got his Skin' were published in xxv, part I, Jan. and Feb. 1898, respectively.

47 **Blue Skalallatoot stories**: All that survives of these is a letter and a map ('The Blue Skallatoot Stories', *KJ*, Mar. 1968, pp. 6–8; see also p. 1).

47 **Orvin Sylvester Woodsey**: Not traced. Perhaps never written down.

47 **A Fleet in Being**: *A Fleet in Being: Notes of Two Trips with the Channel Squadron* (1898). First published in *The Times* and *Morning Post*, 5, 7, 8 and 9 Nov. 1898; not in OB. On his trips RK found material for some sea stories, especially 'Their Lawful Occasions' (*TD*). See also the poem 'The Liner She's a Lady' (*DV*).

48 **ch. viii of *Kim***: Expanded as 'The Two-Sided Man' in *Songs from Books*. In *Kim* these verses refer both to the boy's dual heritage, Indian and British, and to the spiritual and worldly paths offered by his different role models. The poem has also been read as a personal statement by RK, both as sharer of Kim's dual heritage, and as a man split between conscious writer and 'Daemon'. It is this split, many think, that allows him to express so many contradictions (see Introduction, p. 22).

49 **Literature**: Speech given at the Anniversary Banquet of the Royal Academy, 5 May 1906. Collected *BW*. The President, RK's uncle by marriage Sir Edward Poynter, proposed the toast 'Literature', to which RK responded.

49 **makers**: This and other epigraphs in *BW* are by RK in imitation of *Anthologica Graeca*, vols. I and II (tr. W. R. Paton, 5 vols., Loeb Classical Library, London, Heinemann, 1916–18; only the first two vols. are in RK's study (NTInv)).

49 **'walked up and down in the hearts of his hearers'**: Not identified.

51 **a tinker in Bedford gaol**: John Bunyan (1628–88) was the son of a brazier (sometimes called a tinker). He was arrested for preaching without a licence. See also RK's poem 'The Holy War' (*DV*).

51 **a pamphleteering shopkeeper**: Daniel Defoe (1660–1731) was a butcher and author of many political pamphlets. See *SOM*, p. 8 for RK's early devotion to *Robinson Crusoe*.

51 **a muzzy Scot**: James Boswell (1740–95), biographer of the lexicographer Samuel Johnson (1709–84).

51 **a despised German Jew**: Heinrich Heine (1797–1856) emigrated from Germany to Paris, where he learned to write in French as well as German.

51 **a condemned French thief**: François Villon (1431– ?) narrowly escaped hanging in 1463 for stealing and other crimes.

51 **an Admiralty official**: Samuel Pepys (1633–1703) became Secretary to the Admiralty. See also p. 124 and poem 'Samuel Pepys'.

52 **The Claims of Art**: Speech delivered at the Artists' General Benevolent Institution anniversary dinner, 9 May 1907. Collected *BW*. RK presided. His uncle-by-marriage Sir Edward Poynter was President of the Institution.

52 **the swift**: Ecclesiastes IX:11.

54 **Cruikshank**: George Cruikshank (1792–1878), illustrator of Dickens, Thackeray, etc.

54 **Speech at Trinity College**: Unpubl. From a manuscript in KP press-cutting album, 'Speeches', p. 11. At a dinner in the hall of Trinity College, Cambridge, following the award of Honorary Degrees, RK replied to a toast to the recipients.

54 **those who have been honoured today**: Listed in *The Times* as: the Prime Minister Herbert Asquith, the Duke of Northumberland, Lord Halsbury, Admiral Sir John Fisher, Sir Hubert von Herkomer RA, the Hon. C. A. Parsons, Sir George Trevelyan, Sir James Ramsay, Sir Andrew Noble, Sir William Crookes, RK, Professor Horace Lamb, Professor G. D. Liveing and Professor Arthur Marshall.

54 **so fortunate as**: amended from 'have not been fortunate enough'.

54 **or against**: 'men' deleted.

54 **the atmosphere**: 'atmosphere' substituted for 'influences'.

54 **profited through**: 'through' substituted for 'by', apparently in another hand.

55 **conversation**: substituted for 'speech'.

55 **all the things**: 'things' substituted for 'those', apparently in another hand.

55 **thrusts his**: substituted for 'puts his'.

55 **sword**: the alternative 'knife' has not been deleted.

55 **loneliest**: 'or least respectable' deleted.

55 **come**: 'are' has been substituted but 'to' four words on has not been deleted.

55 **diverse**: substituted for 'widely differing'.

55 **Miss M. Hooper**: (Syracuse University Library) Unpubl. Miss Winnard, eldest of the Three Ladies of Kensington (*SOM*, p. 15), had a married sister called Hooper who gave them a home when their house at Warwick Gardens was given up. RK had met the Hoopers while staying at Warwick Gardens in his teens. Margaret L. Hooper, who was probably a daughter, stayed at Bateman's 15–18 June 1906. She was a portrait painter, exhibiting 1881–1911.

55 **The Knife and the Naked Chalk**: *RF.*

55 **Thor and Fenris**: Thor was the Norse God of smiths and thunder. Fenris Wolf was his enemy, a sinister demon that tried to eat the moon.

55 **impelled that steal**: Byron, *English Bards and Scotch Reviewers: A Satire* (London, James Cawthorn, 1809), lines 844–5: 'He nursed the pinion which impelled the steel.'

56 **great God Tyr**: From 'Song of the Men's Side', following 'The Knife and the Naked Chalk' in *RF.*

56 **The Uses of Reading**: Speech given in May 1912 at Wellington College, to a meeting of some fifty boys, members of Pearson's House (including RK's son) and of the College Literary Society, with their friends and guests. Collected *BW.*

Wellington College, a boarding school, was founded 1859. Originally for army officers' sons, it later admitted other boys. Attended by John Kipling 1911–13.

57 **position in life**: Henry Dircks, *Perpetuum Mobile, or Search for Self-Motive Power*, London, Spon, 1861 (slightly misquoted and RK has cut one sentence). The book is not now at Bateman's (NTInv).

58 **early Anglo-Saxon writer**: Unknown author of 'The Ruin', in the eleventh-century manuscript *The Exeter Book*. The exact wording given here has not been traced and may be RK's own translation.

59 **Chaucer wrote a poem**: 'Balade de Bon Consaile' ('If it befalle'), collected in John Stow (ed.), *The Works of Geffrey Chaucer*, London, 1561. The attribution to Chaucer is now seen as dubious.

59 **Sir Walter Raleigh**: In *The History of the World*, Bk. v, ch. i, section x (*The Works of Sir Walter Ralegh, Kt*, 8 vols., Oxford University Press, 1829, vi, pp. 108–9). Raleigh compares a naval campaign between Romans and Carthaginians with recent English history. RK has cut the passage quoted in three places, omitting fifteen lines after 'tear him in pieces'; eight lines after 'trouble and charge'; and a six-word phrase after 'is so set'. The missing material contains names and references that would have meant little to his hearers.

60 **out of it decently**: A digression about the military career of Lord Roberts has been omitted here.

61 **what splendid fellows we were**: This resembles the account of George Cottar's waking life in 'The Brushwood Boy'.

61 **Sanna's Post**: A British defeat near Bloemfontein in March 1900.

62 **ballad of 'Chevy Chase'**: Collected in Thomas Percy, *Reliques of Ancient*

English Poetry (1765), of which there is a set in RK's study (NTInv). Originally a fifteenth-century ballad; the quotation is from the 'modern' version, 100 years or more later.

62 **Bohn's cribs**: Translations of Greek and Latin authors published by Henry George Bohn (1790–1884).

64 **Ranji**: Kumar Shri Ranjitsinhji, an Indian Prince who played cricket for Cambridge, Sussex and England.

64 **to govern India**: The Viceroy of India whom RK knew personally was Lord Dufferin, 1884–8.

65 **Mr Pecksniff did not say about the Sirens**: See Dickens, *Martin Chuzzlewit* (1843) ch. xxxiii: '. . . those fabulous animals (pagan, I regret to say) who used to sing in the water . . . Dear me, sirens, of course.'

66 **The Green Curve**: Major-General Dunlop Swinton, *The Green Curve and other Stories*, Edinburgh, Blackwood, 1909; published under the pseudonym 'Ole-luk-oie'. 'The Second Degree' concerns the importance of knowing one's enemy.

67 **Some Aspects of Travel**: Lecture given to the Royal Geographical Society of London, 17 February 1914. Collected *BW*.

AW, p. 280 suggests that RK's remarks here contain 'more revealing insights into his approach to his writings' than any of his overt statements on the subject, since they imply 'how his own vision worked under creative stress and illuminate the sense of place and particularity that are his most powerful artistic strengths'. Also implied is RK's theory of travel-writing.

69 **Stanley**: Henry Morton Stanley (1841–1904), British-born journalist commissioned by the *New York Herald* to find the explorer and missionary Dr Livingstone, reported missing in Central Africa. His book *How I found Livingstone* (1872) was widely read.

74 **champak**: A fragrant shrub.

74 **West Coast**: Of Africa.

74 **Falstaff's sack**: See *Henry IV*, Part II: Act IV, scene iii.

75 **Melville, of the *Jeanette***: George Wallace Melville (1841–1912), ex-USN and Chief Engineer of the *Jeanette*. On an expedition to explore the Arctic, the ship was caught in the ice. Melville led a party of survivors to safety; later he went back to find and bury his dead comrades.

75 **rimpje on a Dutch farm**: Riempje (Dutch) – a leather thong.

75 **Selkirks**: The Selkirk Mountains are a range running across the American–Canadian border between British Columbia and Montana.

76 **'three blind 'uns and a bolter'**: A team of four inferior and ill-matched horses.

77 **'ignominiously reported or exceedingly condemned'**: Not traced.

78 **unplumbed, salt, and estranging**: Matthew Arnold (1822–88), 'To Marguerite' (*Empedocles on Etna and other Poems*, London, 1852): 'The unplumbed, salt, estranging sea'.

79 **Drake clinched by Magellan**: See note, p. 175.

79 **Oates a little farther south**: Captain Lawrence Oates, a member of Scott's 1912 expedition to the South Pole, had bad feet and could not continue marching. Not wishing to be a burden on the others, Oates left the tent and disappeared into a blizzard.

79 **The Edge of the Evening**: These two verses introduce the story (about an early spy-plane) in *DOC*. They were extended into the poem 'The Benefactors' in *YB*. (Cf. Walter Savage Landor's 'Rose Aylmer', *Simonidea*, Bath, W. Meyler, 1806.)

79 **A Thesis**: From a speech given at a banquet following RK's award of an honorary doctorate by the Sorbonne, Paris, November 1921. Collected *BW*. The rest of the speech is a diatribe against the Germans.

80 **Fiction**: Speech delivered at the Royal Society of Literature's centenary banquet on 7 July 1926. Collected *BW*. In the chair was the Society's Vice-President, Lord Balfour, who presented RK with the Society's Gold Medal.

80 **Lord Balfour**: A. J. Balfour, Conservative Prime Minister 1902–5. Created earl 1922. See Ann Parry, *KJ*, Dec. 1988, pp. 18–19 for parallels between Balfour and the effete mill cat in 'Below the Mill Dam' (*TD*).

80 **to brigade me**: Previous recipients were Walter Scott, George Meredith and Thomas Hardy.

80 **dogmatic (or doubtful, Lord Balfour)**: Books written by Balfour include *A Defence of Philosophic Doubt* (1879) and *Theism and Thought* (1923).

83 **The Irish Guards in the Great War**: (1923), 2 vols. This extract is from the introduction to vol. I. RK's son John was commissioned in the Irish Guards in 1915 and killed in his first battle.

In January 1917 RK was asked to write the regiment's official war history (CK). He worked on it over the next five years, read diaries and letters and interviewed many survivors. During this period he wrote almost nothing else, but had some ideas for stories (CK) which would later be written for *D&C* – in which see also poem 'A Legend of Truth'. In the last line, Truth cables Fiction from the battlefields, 'Facts out of hand . . . / They need us both, but you far more than me!'

83 **Chartres Windows**: Published *Daily Telegraph*, 15 Apr. 1925, with an article, describing a visit to Chartres and other French churches, by RK's friend Perceval Landon.

85 **Letter to Edmonia Hill**: (Typed copy, KP. The originals of RK's letters to Mrs Hill were bought by his widow and destroyed; the copies were later acquired by his daughter.) The recipient, born Edmonia Taylor of Beaver, Pennsylvania, married Alec Hill, Professor of Physical Science at Muir College, Allahabad. After RK's transfer to *The Pioneer* of Allahabad in 1887, he got to know the Hills and became their lodger. It has been suggested that she and RK were lovers. She is not mentioned in *SOM*.

85 **The man was a fiction**: Captain Gadsby in 'The Story of the Gadsbys', which became a cycle of eight stories. The only part in print when this letter was written was the second, 'The World Without', in which men at the club discuss Gadsby's engagement and the general problems of

marriage in India; also revealing his earlier affair with a married woman. The first part of the story, in which Gadsby meets his future wife, appeared in *WN* on 26th May. The series was collected in *S3*.

85 **David Beames**: Lt David Beames of the South Yorks Regiment, but currently serving with an Indian regiment. He was the son of a civil servant who had been demoted for taking bribes. He would still be a Lieutenant in 1891.

85 **Mian Mir**: Military complex outside Lahore.

87 ***chukker***: Polo matches are divided into four or more *chukkars*, with intervals between, to allow the riders to change ponies.

87 **a silver thread**: In *SOM* (p. 43) RK says the work was inspired by the French novel *Autour du Mariage* (1883), by Gyp (pseudonym of Sibylle-Gabrielle-Marie-Antoinette de Riquetti de Mirabeau, Comtesse de Martel de Janville (1849–1932)). RK's tale has the same form (dramatic dialogue), but lacks both Gyp's satirical edge and her outspokenness on sexual matters. Like her hero, Gadsby is a wealthy aristocrat ('The Swelling of Jordan'). His army rank is higher and his career more promising than Beames's. His is a fashionable cavalry regiment: 'the Duke of Derry's Pink Hussars' (preface to Indian Railway Library edn).

87 **Letter to Augusta Tweddell**: (KP). Daughter of Lt-Col. Francis Tweddell, a British officer in the 31st Bengal Infantry (Sikhs), and of a German mother. RK's letter to Edmonia Hill of 9–10 July (*Letters*, vol. 1, p. 244) describes how he met Miss Tweddell at a Simla party and how he and his sister laughed over her 'poor little versifications'.

88 **Shape from that thy art**: Henry Wadsworth Longfellow (1807–82), 'Gasper Becerra', *The Seaside and the Fireside*, Boston, Tickner, Reed and Fields, 1850, last verse: it should be 'Shape from that thy work of art'.

88 **Besant's novels**: Sir Walter Besant (1836–1901). In *SOM*, pp. 39–40, RK tells how much Besant's *All in a Garden Fair* (1882) had meant to him during a period of depression.

89 **Letter to Mary Mapes Dodge**: (Princeton University Libraries).

89 **Kim o' the Rishti**: Title on the manuscript of *Kim* (British Library).

89 **Her Pottedness**: 'The Potted Princess', published in *St Nicholas*, xx, January 1893; collected only in *UP*.

89 **Letter to Mary Mapes Dodge**: (Princeton University Libraries).

89 **monkeys and the poison stick**: 'The Collar-Wallah and the Poison Stick', published in *St Nicholas*, xx, February 1893; collected only in *UP*.

90 **a tale about an elephants' ball**: 'Toomai of the Elephants', first published *St Nicholas*, Dec. 1893. Collected in *JB*.

90 **Assam Terai**: A belt of marsh and jungle leading to the Garo Hills in Assam, south of the Brahmaputra river.

90 ***Keddah***: A stockade into which wild elephants were driven; this operation is described in the story.

90 **mucknas**: Male elephants without, or with very small, tusks.

90 **a camel tale**: Though this is mentioned again in correspondence with

Mrs Dodge, no camel tale appeared either in *St Nicholas* or *JB*. Possibly the Just So story 'How the Camel got his Hump'.

90 **Letter to Mary Mapes Dodge**: (Princeton University Libraries).

90 **Keddah camp**: see note, p. 181 above. Particulars of elephant-catching in the story come from G. P. Sanderson, *Thirteen Years among the Wild Beasts of India*, London, Allen, 1878.

90 **little verse**: 'Shiv and the Grasshopper'.

90 **little boy herd**: 'Tiger! Tiger!' was published in *St Nicholas*, Feb. 1894. Mowgli is the herd.

91 **a wolf tale**: First mention of Mowgli by name. 'Mowgli's Brothers' came out in *St Nicholas*, Jan. 1894. According to CK it was finished four days after this letter was written. Much of the plot summary given in this letter was never used in the series. *SOM* (p. 67) says that 'In the Rukh', in which an adult Mowgli uses his wolf brothers to win a job with the Indian Forestry Commission, was the first wolf-boy story to be written; CK has him revising it in February 1893. It is not in *JB* or *JB2*, but was collected in *MI* (1893). In OB7 and SB it is included with the other Mowgli stories.

91 **Oudh**: The old Kingdom of Oudh is in Uttar Pradesh. 'In the Rukh' is thought to take place in the forests of the Doon there. But 'Mowgli's Brothers' as published is located in the Seonee Hills, Madhya Pradesh, though the panther Bagheera was imprisoned in Udaipur in Rajasthan, and Cold Lairs in 'Kaa's Hunting' derives from the ruined cities of Amber and Chitor, also in Rajasthan. See R. Lancelyn Green's *Kipling and the Children* (London, Elek Books, 1965) for a full discussion of the settings.

91 **Letter to Edward Lucas White**: (Pierpont Morgan Library).

91 **Paeonic lilt**: Cf. RK's previous letter to White (*Letters*, II, p. 78); White may have suggested there was a 'Paeonic lilt' in 'The Galley-Slave'. Paeonic verse, in English, uses a foot of one stressed and three unstressed syllables; the stressed syllable may be in any position.

91 **vapour over shrines**: Elizabeth Barrett Browning, 'Wine of Cyprus', *Poems*, 2 vols., London, Chapman and Hall, 1850, verse 10.

92 **nine-storied pagoda of a song**: CK notes 'The Song of the Banjo' on 1 March 1893. It varies the iambic pentameter with more lightly stressed syllables; perhaps this was the 'paeonic lilt' RK had been shouting at bullocks.

92 **the beat of engines**: *KJ*, Sept. 1971, pp. 2–3 quotes academic and nautical correspondents on the onomatopoeic rhythms in 'McAndrew's Hymn', written November 1893 (CK).

92 **Letter to Howard Pyle**: (Cornell University Library) Pyle (1853–1911) was a famous American illustrator and writer.

92 **verses of mine**: 'McAndrew's Hymn' was first published in *Scribner's Magazine*, with two full-page plates and four other illustrations by Howard Pyle, December 1894.

92 **the old Doric**: The *Doric* (1885) was one of the White Star Line's first

steel ships. RK had sailed in her from South Africa to Australia in the autumn of 1891 (*SOM*, p. 58).

92 **Germanic or the Brittanic** [sic]: The *Germanic* (1875) and *Britannic* (1874) were White Star mail steamers, built by Harland and Wolff of Belfast, running between London, Liverpool and New York.

93 **Letter to Robert Barr**: (Lewis Collection, Sussex University Library) Unpubl.

93 **seriatim**: RK is reading Barr's first novel, the farcical *In the Midst of Alarms*, London, Methuen, 1894.

93 **Yates**: A brash young American, one of two heroes who are on a walking tour of the Canadian borderlands when an army of Irish-Americans arrives (the Fenian raids, 1866–70).

93 **in quick time**: After hesitating between the two heroines, confident that either would have him, Yates proposes to one and is refused; whereupon he asks the second and is accepted.

93 **Bartlett**: Canadian farmer in Barr's novel.

94 **Letter to Richard W. Gilder**: (Dalhousie University Libraries) Gilder (1844–1909) was editor of *Century Magazine*.

94 **The Brushwood Boy**: First published *Century Magazine*, Dec. 1895; collected *DW*.

94 **the boil**: In an episode of the hero's boyhood, he meets a little girl who sympathises on his recently cut finger.

94 **unflinching realism**: The hero's waking life is all effortless success and popularity. His dream life has been seen by at least two critics as authentically Freudian (D. M . E. Roskies, 'Telling the Truth in Kipling and Freud', *English* (Spring 1982), pp. 7–11; Zohreh T. Sullivan, 'Kipling the Night-Walker', *Modern Fiction Studies*, 30 (Summer 1984), pp. 217–28.) It has been suggested that the two levels represent different kinds of dream (see also p. 61).

95 **Letter to Louisa Baldwin**: (Dalhousie University Libraries) Louisa (née Macdonald, 1845–1925) was RK's mother's third sister, wife of Sir Alfred Baldwin.

95 **The tales**: Louisa Baldwin, *The Shadow on the Blind and other Ghost Stories*, London, J. M. Dent, 1895.

95 **Letter to Robert Barr**: (Syracuse University Library) Unpubl.

95 **American story**: *CC* was first published in *McClure's Magazine*, Nov. 1896–May 1897, and *Pearson's Magazine*, Dec. 1896–Apr. 1897.

95 **Mary Wilkins**: Mary E. Wilkins (Mrs Freeman) (1853–1930), author of *A Humble Romance, and other Stories* (1887), etc. RK met her in Vermont.

95 **Sarah Orne Jewett**: (1849–1909). Author of *Deephaven* (1877), *The Country of the Pointed Firs* (1896), etc.

96 **The Runes on the Sword**: (by special permission of the National Trust and the Keeper of Western Manuscripts, Bodleian Library) Unpubl. According to CK, the verses for the book were written in May 1906. The rest of the note lays out in the manner described a version of the poem

'The Runes on Weland's Sword'; since this differs from the published text, which follows the story 'Old Men at Pevensey' (*PPH*), it cannot be included because of the terms of the Kiplings' gift of the manuscript to the Bodleian (MS Eng. misc. 127, f. 42).

No source has been traced for this verse-form in a runic inscription. RK was familiar with the runic alphabet (see illustration with 'How the First Letter was Written' (*JSS*)). The published poem imitates the stresses and alliterations of Old English metre; its theme may have been inspired by lines 455 and 1693–7 of *Beowulf*, and by the 'Riddles' in *The Exeter Book*. It is one of the poems (inspired in whole or in part by Anglo-Saxon originals) in which T. S. Eliot finds 'some very remarkable innovations indeed' (Introduction to *A Choice of Kipling's Verse*, London, Faber and Faber, 1941).

96 **Letter to Ian Colvin**: (Syracuse University Libraries) Unpubl. RK met Colvin (1877–1938) in South Africa. Later he would become a leader-writer on the *Morning Post*.

96 **City of Brass**: 'The City of Brass', poem, was first published in the *Morning Post*, 18 June 1909; collected *YB*.

96 **Arabian Nights**: 'The Story of the City of Brass' is ch. xxi of E. W. Lane's *Arabian Nights*. (*The Thousand and One Nights, commonly called in England, the Arabian Nights' Entertainment*, first edition London, Murray, 1859; new edition ed. Edward Stanley Poole, 3 vols., London, Chatto and Windus, 1883, III.) RK's epigram to the poem quotes two lines of verse from p. 115.

96 **Letter to Louisa Baldwin**: (Dalhousie University Libraries).

96 **gone over them unkindly**: She had sent him four typed sonnets on which he made numerous alterations and detailed comments (*KJ*, Mar. 1968, p. 10).

97 **before it**: The first ten lines open 'The Pro-Consuls', first published in *The Times*, 5 Aug. 1905, collected in *YB* with one alteration: 'The strength and glory of our reputations' in line 7. The last four lines given here end the published poem.

97 **Letter to Lucas White**: (University of Texas at Austin).

97 **to the skirts of his clothing**: Psalm CXXXIII: 2 (Church of England Prayer Book version).

97 **other folks' heifers**: Judges XIV: 18. The previous three sentences elaborate a passage in *SOM*, p. 111.

98 **Philadelphia sings**: in 'Marklake Witches' (*RF*; no prior publication).

98 **Shenstone . . . ode**: William Shenstone (1714–63), poet and landscape gardener: 'A Pastoral Ballad in Four Parts' (1733), pt IV: 'Disappointment', verse 4, lines 4–8. Collected in vol. IV of *Collection of Poems*, ed. Robert Dodsley, 6 vols., London, R. Dodsley, 1745–58. The girl in RK's song is dying, Shenstone's is merely faithless.

98 **Alexander Selkirk**: 'Verses supposed to be written by Alexander Selkirk', by William Cowper (1731–1800), first published 1782; H. S. Milford (ed.),

Cowper's Poetical Works, London, Oxford University Press, 1905, revised edition 1967, p. 311, lines 1–2.

98 **Schoolboy**: Letter from a private collection whose owner has asked to be anonymous, and that the recipient not be named. The recipient, who was 18, went on to have a highly successful career and wrote several books, but never became a professional writer.

98 **How I Taught a Youngster to Write Verse**: Not identified under this title. RK had a copy of Tom Hood (1835–74), *The Rules of Rhyme*, London, 1869; revised edition 1877 (NTInv dates RK's copy 1896).

98 **Saintsbury**: The critic George Saintsbury (1845–1933) was a friend of RK's (see also note, p. 99); his book *The Peace of the Augustans* (London, G. Bell, 1916) is referred to obliquely in 'The Propagation of Knowledge' (*D&C*). His *Notes from a Cellar-Book* (London, Macmillan, 1920) were dedicated to RK.

99 **'The Bull that Thought'**: First published *Cosmopolitan*, Dec. 1924; collected *D&C*. The narrator meets a Frenchman who tells the story of a bull that defeats matadors in a Spanish bull-ring. Its life is saved by an elderly matador who understands bulls. There are frequent comparisons to writers and writing in the description of the fight.

99 **'Proofs of Holy Writ'**: Title from *Othello*, Act III, scene iii. Written February 1932–August 1933 (CK). First published in *Strand Magazine*, April 1934. Collected only in SB. John Buchan claimed to have given RK the idea; George Saintsbury helped with details (see *SOM*, p. 86; *KJ*, Mar. 1988, p. 33, and Dec. 1989, pp. 18–27). RK had also, while visiting Cardinal Gasquet at Rome in 1917, seen the room where a team of Catholic priests worked on biblical texts (letter to Mrs Kipling and Elsie, 7 May 1917, KP).

The story takes place in approximately 1611, at Shakespeare's home near Stratford-on-Avon. The two characters and their relationship resemble the account in 'Ben Jonson's Conversations with William Drummond of Hawthornden' (see p. 39 and note, pp. 174–5).

100 **Dekker**: 'The War of the Theatres' (1599–1601), in which John Marston, Thomas Dekker and Ben Jonson lampooned each other in their plays.

100 **my trade as they called it**: See Dekker, *Satiromastix* (1601), Act IV, scene iii. Jonson's stepfather was a master-bricklayer who had tried unsuccessfully to make the boy follow his trade.

100 **mocked my face**: See *Satiromastix*, Act IV, iii and Act V, scene vii.

100 **humour**: Jonson's first success was *Every Man in his Humour* (1597). Shakespeare is listed in the cast in the 1616 Folio, and may have helped get the play staged. *Every Man Out of his Humour* (1599) included satirical portraits of both Dekker and Marston. Dekker's *Satiromastix* had for subtitle, 'The Untrussing of the Humorous Poet'.

Medicine in those days divided humanity into four 'humours': the Melancholic, the Choleric, the Sanguine and the Phlegmatic, each with its characteristic temperament and liable to different diseases.

100 **Gabriel**: Jonson killed fellow-actor Gabriel Spencer in a duel in 1598. Condemned to hang for the killing, he pled benefit of clergy and was branded instead.

100 **my Poetaster**: According to Drummond's *Conversations* (see p. 39 and note, pp. 174–5), Jonson claimed to have disarmed Marston of a pistol, beaten him up and 'wrote his *Poetaster* on him' because in *Histiromastix* Marston had 'represented him jn the stage jn his youth given to Venerie [womanising]'. The play gave offence to so many that Jonson had to write 'Apologetical Dialogue' as its epitaph. Dekker had been described in it as 'thick and verminous'; he retorted by writing *Satiromastix*.

101 **sea-beaches**: See *The Winter's Tale*, Act III, scene iii, 'the sea-coast of Bohemia'. Drummond quotes Jonson as mocking this error.

101 **teres atque rotundus**: (Latin) smooth and round: see Horace, *Satires*, II, 7.86.

101 **that place was not my sphere**: *The Fall of Sejanus* (1603), Act I, line 3: '**Silius**: Indeed, this place is not our sphere.' Shakespeare is said to have acted in it, but his part has not been identified. The first production was booed.

101 **common as Moorditch**: Moorditch was a London drain. For Jonson's denunciation of second-hand plots, see 'Ode to Himself' (1629), *Ben Jonson*, in *Underwoods*, ed. Herford, Simpson and Simpson, VIII, pp. 74–5.

102 **how I came to write that**: See 'Shakespeare and the Tempest' (pp. 115–18).

102 **Dick Burbage**: Richard Burbage (?1567–1619), famous for his tragic roles, played the leading part in plays by Shakespeare and Jonson. He inherited an interest in both the Blackfriars and Globe Theatres from his father, who was also an actor.

102 **How fortune . . . To practise 'em**: *The Fall of Sejanus*, Act V, scene X, lines 878–9.

103 **Miles Smith**: Smith was appointed, with Thomas Bilson, to make the final revisions of the text of the Old Testament for the King James Bible, first published in 1611. He would later become Bishop of Gloucester.

103 **most noble and most equal**: See Jonson's 'Dedication' of *Volpone* to Oxford and Cambridge (*Ben Jonson*, ed. Herford, Simpson and Simpson, V, pp. 17–21).

103 **Geneva . . ., Douai, Rheims, Coverdale, Matthews, the Bishops', the Great**: Earlier versions of the Bible in English. Coverdale's (1535) was translated from the German of Martin Luther. Matthews's (1537) was the first official Bible of the Church of England. The Great Bible (1539–41), commonly known as Cranmer's, revised the earlier translations. The Genevan (1560) conflated the Great Bible with Hebrew and Latin texts. The Bishops' (1568) revised the Great Bible for Church of England use. The Rheims (1582) was translated from the Latin Vulgate by seminarians of the English College at Douai (then at Rheims): the first English version to be authorised by the Catholic Church, its use was proscribed in

England under Elizabeth I. The Douai (1609–10) is the name given to the official Bible of the Latin Church in England.

103 **text against text**: RK may be thinking of Fulke's *Confutation* of 1589, which printed the Rheims text side by side with the Bishops' text and added critical comments; it was said to have influenced the King James' version, but it did not include Isaiah.

103 **Condell**: An actor and shareholder in Shakespeare's company who (with Heminge) edited the First Folio of the plays for publication in 1623.

103 **armiger**: Shakespeare's father received a grant of Arms in 1596, later borne by Shakespeare himself.

104 **Holofernes**: A comic schoolmaster in *Love's Labour's Lost*, fond of using Latin tags.

105 **Ovid, Quintilian, Terence, Columella, Seneca**: Ovid (Publius Ovidus Naso, 43 BC–AD 18), Roman poet, was considered improper by the Christian Church, but was popular with Renaissance readers and the Pre-Raphaelites. Quintilian (Marcus Fabius Quintilianus), 1st century Roman writer and critic, quoted by Jonson in *Timber* (1640). Terence (Publius Terentius Afer), 2nd century Roman comic poet and playwright. Columella, a native of Gades in Spain, author of a work on agriculture (*c.* AD 65). Lucius Annaeus Seneca (?4 BC–AD 65), Roman Stoic philosopher and playwright, tutor to the young Emperor Nero. His plays had been translated into English some thirty years before the date of this story.

Drummond wrote of Jonson (in *Conversations* (see p. 39 and note, pp. 174–5): 'He was better versed and knew more jn Greek and Latin, than all the Poets jn England and quintessence[th] their braines.'

105 **Demon**: Kipling credits Shakespeare with a Socratic Daemon or Demon of inspiration, similar to that he claimed for himself (*SOM*, pp. 121–3).

105 **Pliny**: There were two Roman writers called Pliny: Gaius Plinius Secundus (AD 23–79; Pliny the Elder), and Gaius Plinius Caecilius Secundus (AD 62–*c.* 112, Pliny the Younger). *RG* suggests that the reference here is to Pliny the Younger's description of Vesuvius in eruption.

106 **rams'-horns**: See Joshua, VI: 4.

107 **David before Saul**: See I Samuel XVI: 23.

107 **Greek word**: It is not clear what is meant here. The word might be '*amphibrachys*' ('both ends short'), which according to Saintsbury is the metre of 'shall be thy' in this passage. 'Both hands' may suggest to Jonson that Shakespeare has confused the last two syllables with Greek *brachion* (arm). Or it might be that RK thought Jonson would read 'Non erit tibi amplius Sol ad lucendum per diem' as a dactylic pentameter, from the Greek *dactyl*, finger and *penta*, five. In classical Latin this scansion is not correct, but the mediaeval rules were slightly different.

In 'To the Memory of My Beloved, the Author, Mr William

Shakespeare' (1623) Jonson wrote 'thou hadst small Latin, and less Greek' (*Ben Jonson*, ed. Herford, Simpson and Simpson, IV, p. 391).

108 **horses of the dawn**: From the Greek myth of the sun as Helius' chariot driving through the heavens.

109 **Boanerges**: Loud-voiced preacher (see Mark, III: 17). See also RK's poem 'The Craftsman'.

109 **other seven devils**: See Matthew, XII: 45.

109 **upsee-dejee**: This seems to be a coinage combining 'upsee-Dutch', a drinking term used by Jonson in *The Alchemist*, with 'ajee' (askew).

109 **burned**: The Globe theatre would burn down in 1613.

109 **did sing of thee in thy markets?**: Ezekiel, XXVII: 3 and 25 (slightly misquoted).

109 **Kit**: Christopher Marlowe, killed in a tavern brawl in 1593.

110 **I have felt the hurt, and paid home**: Drummond describes Jonson as jealous and 'Vindicative'. In the two 'Odes to Himselfe' he seeks consolation for the success of lesser writers (in *Underwoods* (see note, p. 186), and with his play *The New Inn*, *Ben Jonson*, ed. Herford, Simpson and Simpson, VI, pp. 492–4).

110 **virtue had gone out of him**: See Mark, V: 30.

110 **'Mine earnest vehement botcher ... with you.'** See *The Alchemist*, V, V, lines 104–5.

111 **Review**: Authenticated as RK's by KP press-cutting album, 'Articles and Verses 1884–1886', p. 57.

111 **From Recruit to Staff Sergeant**: Calcutta, Thos. S. Smith, 1885.

111 **Rev. G. Gregson**: Author of *Through the Khyber Pass to Sherpore Camp, an Account of Temperance Work*, London 1883.

111 **campaign of the Army of the Sutlej**: The second Sikh War 1845–6, after which the Punjab was annexed by the British.

111 **brutality**: See reprint by Ian Henry Publications, Hornchurch, Essex, 1979, pp. 50–1. RK would use details from this account in his poem 'Snarleyow', first published *National Observer*, 29 Nov. 1890. The battle of Ferozeshah took place on 22 Dec. 1845.

112 **Letter to W. C. Crofts**: (Dalhousie University Libraries). Crofts was RK's English teacher, part-original of King in *S&Co.* and especially in 'Regulus' (*DOC*).

112 **P. M. Gazette**: A *Pall Mall Gazette* supplement, *The Best Hundred Books*, contains articles or letters from Gladstone, Carlyle, Ruskin and other celebrities. Morris contributed a letter. See *SOM*, pp. 9 and 224n. for his friendship with RK's uncle and aunt the Burne-Joneses.

112 **Mahabarat**: Morris's list opens with a section he calls 'Bibles', among which 'Kalevala, Shahnameh, Mahabharata' are placed jointly at number six.

The Sanskrit epic *The Mahabharata* is over 100,000 verses long. An English translation by Protap Chandra Roy was published in monthly parts 1884–96: *The Mahabharata of Krishna-Dwaipayana Vyasa*, Calcutta,

Bharata Press. RK would review the latest volume in the *C&MG* on 24 Aug. 1886, in similar terms (reprinted in *KI*, pp. 175ff.). Young British officials were encouraged to read such translations, which were literal and lacked a critical apparatus to connect them with the beliefs of the local population; RK's reaction is not untypical.

112 **the Shah-nameh**: Epic by the tenth-century Persian poet Abdul Kasim Firdausi. In RK's study there is a copy of a verse translation by Joseph Champion (NTInv).

112 **the Ramayana of Tulsi Dass**: The Ramayana of Valimki is the other great Sanskrit epic. A Hindi version of it, *Ram-charit-manas* ('The Lake of the Deeds of Rama') was written by the sixteenth-century poet Tulsidas. This was translated into English by F. S. Growse: *The Ramayana of Tulsi Dass*, 1877–80. The 1883 edition is in RK's study (NTInv).

112 **the Rig-Veda**: A collection of over 1000 Sanskrit hymns to the Gods, preserved by oral tradition until it was written down as the earliest known Indo-European document. It was translated into English by H. H. Wilson, *Rig-Veda-Sanhita: A Collection of Ancient Hindu Hymns*, London, Allen 1850. The version in RK's study is *Athar-Veda Samhita*, translated into English by William Dwight Whitney (Cambridge, Mass., 1905: second part only) (NTInv).

112 **Monier-Williams**: Sir Monier Monier-Williams, K.C.I.E. (1819–99), Professor of Sanskrit at Oxford from 1860, founded the Indian Institute there. He translated a number of Sanskrit classics.

113 **navel of the illustrious Guru**: F. S. Growse, *Ramayana*, I (2nd edn, Allahabad, North-West Provinces and Oudh Government Press, 1880), p. 3:

> . . . I reverence the pollen-like dust of the lotus feet of my master. Applied to the forehead as a *tilak* [caste-mark] it cleanses from defilement the fair mirror of the human mind and gives it the mastery of all good. By recalling the lustre of the nails of the reverend guru's feet, a divine splendour illumines the soul, dispersing the shades of error with its sun-like glory . . .

113 **Obituary**: Authenticated by KP press-cutting album, 'Articles and Verses, 1884–1886'. Ellen Wood (née Price) (1814–86).

113 **The Mill on the Floss and the Woman in White**: *The Mill on the Floss* (1860), by George Eliot (1819–80). *The Woman in White* (1860), by Wilkie Collins (1824–89).

113 **Letter to Edmonia Hill**: (Typed copy, KP).

113 **English version of Madame Bovary**: By Gustave Flaubert (1821–80). The novel, first published 1857, was translated by Eleanor Marx-Aveling (1855–98) (daughter of Karl Marx) as *Madame Bovary: Provincial Manners*, London, Vizetelly, 1886. Her translation made no attempt to reproduce the subtleties of Flaubert's style.

113 **Woodbury or autotype**: Photographic printing processes, the former named 'woodburytype' after its inventor.

114 **Letter to Edmonia Hill**: (typed copy, KP) On 30th April 1888 RK had written to Mrs Hill to tell her that he was ordered up to Lahore again to stand in for E. Kay Robinson, editor of the *C&MG*, while the latter went on holiday (*Letters*, I, p. 163).

114 **Cape Cod Folk**: Sarah Pratt Greene (1856–1935), *Cape Cod Folks* (Boston 1881).

114 **blue books**: Official Government reports.

114 **an Aka and a Madan Kheyl**: Afghan tribesmen.

114 **The Descent of Man**: Charles Darwin, *The Descent of Man, and Selection in Relation to Sex*, 2 vols., London, John Murray, 1871. There was a second edition, revised and augmented, London, John Murray, 1874. For RK's further comments, see 'The Question of Givens', Jan. 1889 (*EV*, pp. 448–9).

114 **Athalie**: Play by Jean Racine (1639–99), after II Kings XI; RK is probably thinking of the incidental music composed for it by Mendelssohn, 1845.

114 **The Children of the Zodiac**: First published *Harper's Weekly*, 5 Dec. 1891; collected *MI*. A tale of gods who find they are mortal. Leo becomes an itinerant singer, marries Virgo and is killed by Cancer. Carrington, who had read family papers now destroyed, suggests that the story is 'personal – something between himself and the woman he was about to marry'. This passage suggests what RK may have intended to do in writing, e.g. 'Only a Subaltern'. See also letter to St Loe Strachey, 2 Jan. 1899 (p. 118).

114 **Letter to Robert Underwood Johnson**: (Dalhousie University Libraries) Johnson (1853–1937) was associate editor of *Century Magazine*.

114 **exceeding big job**: To write about the Indian Sepoy Rebellion of 1857.

114 **John Lawrence**: (1811–79), Chief Commissioner of the Punjab at the time of the rising; later Viceroy of India.

115 **Mrs Flora Annie Steel**: (1847–1929) lived in the Punjab for twenty years and knew the Kiplings there. Her 'Mutiny' novel was published as *On the Face of the Waters* (1896).

115 **S. Levett Yeats**: A Deputy Examiner in the Public Works Department at Lahore, known to the Kiplings.

115 **Shakespeare and the Tempest**: First published in *The Spectator*, 2 July 1898; collected only in SB. See also the poems 'The Craftsman' (*YB*) and 'The Coiner' (*LR*). RK had gathered material for *CC* at 'queer meals in sailors' eating-houses' (*SOM*, p. 76). Two months after writing this letter RK would go cruising with the Royal Navy (see note, p. 176); he would afterwards put a farcical sea story into the mouth of an increasingly drunken sailor in 'The Bonds of Discipline' (*TD*).

115 **Your article on 'Landscape and Literature'**: *The Spectator*, 18 June 1898. Reviews Sir Archibald Geikie's Romance Lecture at Oxford, in which it was suggested that topography had an effect on literature. The article argues that the island in *The Tempest* had no part in Shakespeare's experience.

115 **Malone**: Edmond Malone (1741–1812), Shakespearean editor and critic; author of *An Account of the Incidents, from which the Title and Part of the*

Story of Shakespeare's The Tempest were Derived, and its True Date Ascertained, London, privately printed, 1808.

115 **Sir George Somers**: In 1609 Sir George Somers and Sir Thomas Gates commanded a fleet bound for the English colony in Virginia. A pamphlet was issued by the Virginia Company in their names, denying exaggerated accounts of their shipwreck on Bermuda. Malone suggests that the word 'Tempest' came from this, while the details of the wreck and landing in Act I, scene i came from a later pamphlet by a survivor: S. Jourdan, *A Discovery of the Bermudas, Otherwise Called the Isle of Divels, by Sir Thomas Gates, Sir George Sommers, and Captain Newport, with Divers Others*, 1610.

115 **for the name of king**: The Tempest, Act I, scene i, lines 17–18: 'Boatswain: What cares these roarers for the name of king?' In *The Spectator* the phrase is misquoted 'these brawlers'.

116 **dead Indian**: Act II, scene ii, line 33. For 'Strange fish' see line 28.

116 **for an apple**: Act II, scene i, lines 90–4. There is an echo of this passage in 'Simple Simon' (*RF*), where Simon's mother sees an apple she has given Sir Francis Drake as 'the great world lying in his hand'.

116 **a tawny coloured country**: Act II, scene i, line 53: 'Antonio: The ground, indeed, is tawny.'

116 **full of noises**: Act III, scene ii, line 142: 'Caliban: Be not afeard, the isle is full of noises.'

116 **blistered one all over**: Act I, scene ii, lines 323–4: 'Caliban: a south-west blow on ye / And blister you all o'er!'

117 **Hamilton**: A town on an inlet off the Great Sound, on the north coast of Bermuda.

117 **these eyes have seen it**: The Kiplings had spent three weeks in Bermuda in 1894.

117 **my cellar is in a rock**: Act II, scene ii, lines 137–8.

117 **officers' clothes**: Act IV, scene i, lines 229–30.

117 **a swamp**: Act IV, scene i, lines 181–2: 'Ariel: . . . at last I left them / I' the filthy-mantled pool beyond your cell . . .'

118 **Aurelio and Isabella**: Juan de Flores, *Histoire de Aurelio et Isabelle*, tr. into English 1556.

118 **Letter to St Loe Strachey**: (Records Office, House of Lords) Strachey (1860–1927) was editor and proprietor of *The Spectator*, 1899–1925.

118 **'poet as interpreter'**: 'The Poet's Function as Interpreter' is the second essay in Strachey's book *From Grave to Gay, being Essays and Studies*, London, Smith, Elder, 1897: partly reprinted from *The Spectator*. RK is taken as example of a poet who tells his middle-class countrymen facts about other people in a way they can accept.

119 **born already**: There are parallels between the career of T. S. Eliot (born 1888 and descendant of colonial New England stock) and that which RK projects for his 'real poet'. RK was an admitted, if not a major, influence on Eliot's poetry (T. S. Eliot, 'The Unfading Genius of Rudyard Kipling',

KJ, March 1959; Lyndall Gordon, *Eliot's New Life*, Oxford University Press, 1988, paperback edition 1989, p. 292n.).

While writing *Four Quartets*, Eliot anthologised RK's verse (*A Choice of Kipling's Verse*, London, Faber & Faber, 1941) and wrote an approving preface. *Four Quartets* links Eliot's roots in England and the United States, but it is also the spiritual pilgrimage of a 'contemplative master' (see RK's postscript to this letter).

119 **Ferguson did for Burns**: Robert Fergusson (1750–74) was a poet whose Scottish dialect poems influenced Robert Burns (1759–96).

119 **drew from the '40s and '50s**: Edward Burne-Jones, William Morris and RK's headmaster Cormell Price were at Oxford together during the 1850s.

By 'people who drew from the '40s' RK may mean the Three Ladies of Warwick Gardens, with whom he had stayed during school holidays (see *SOM*, p. 15); the father of two of them was George Lillie Craik (1798–1866), a personal friend of Carlyle (1795–1881).

119 **Letter to St Loe Strachey**: (Records Office, House of Lords).

119 **Sherman**: Francis Joseph Sherman (1871–1926), author of *Matins*, of which there is a copy at Bateman's (NTInv).

119 **ferashes**: Servants.

120 **'The Flowers'**: First published in the *Daily Chronicle*, 10 Jun. 1896. In *DV* the poem is introduced by a quotation from *The Athenaeum*, questioning the value of poems by the overseas British.

120 **Theodore Roberts**: (1877–1953). Journalist on the New York *Independent*. He published a collection of poems, *Northland Lyrics*, in 1899.

120 **Letter to Brimley Johnson**: Quoted in Maisie Ward, *Gilbert Keith Chesterton*, London, Sheed and Ward, 1944. Johnson published G. K. Chesterton's early works, including *The Wild Knight and other Poems* (1900), which Johnson had sent to RK. He had been engaged to RK's secretary Gertrude Bloggs, recently killed in a traffic accident. The tragedy delayed Chesterton's courtship of Gertrude's sister. The rest of the letter speaks of grief.

121 **'Wireless'**: First published in *Scribner's*, Aug. 1902. Collected *TD*. The five lines are: 'Charm'd magic casements, opening on the foam / Of perilous seas, in faery lands forlorn' (John Keats, 'Ode to a Nightingale'); and 'A savage place! as holy and enchanted / As e'er beneath a waning moon was haunted / By woman wailing for her demon lover!' (Samuel Taylor Coleridge, 'Kubla Khan').

121 **Letter to Sir Alfred Milner**: (Bodleian Library) Later Viscount Milner (1854–1925). RK met him through Cecil Rhodes, and they would become neighbours in Sussex. RK had written many stories and poems in support of the South African War, 1899–1902, and of welfare for British troops.

121 **[Chamberlain's]**: Sir Joseph Chamberlain, Conservative politician, had been visiting Capetown. CK noted in her diary that he addressed a meeting on 23 February but that RK did not attend it.

121 **reconciliatory poem**: 'The Settler' (*FN*) was published in *The Times*, 27

Feb. 1903, with an extract from Chamberlain's farewell speech of 24 February:

I leave this shore more convinced than ever that the forces – the national forces – that are drawing you together are more potent than those evil influences which would tend to separate you . . . Above all, South Africa needs the best capacities of all its children.

121 **Letter to H. A. Gwynne**: (Dalhousie University Libraries) Unpubl. Gwynne (1865–1950) was a Reuter's correspondent; he and RK had worked together on *The Friend* newspaper at Bloemsfontein. Gwynne would become editor of the *Standard* from 1904–11 and the *Morning Post* from 1911–37; and was one of a number of RK's friends who reinforced his Toryism and encouraged him to write in favour of rearmament and conscription.

121 **'The Dream of Belligerontius'**: Title on the manuscript of 'The Army of a Dream', published in the *Morning Post*, 15–18 June 1904; collected *TD*. A pun on Cardinal Newman's religious poem, 'The Dream of Gerontius' (1865).

122 **Letter to Edmonia Hill**: (typed copy, KP) Unpubl.

122 **Sahib's War**: Story 'A Sahib's War', first published in the *Windsor Magazine*, Dec. 1901 and *Collier's Weekly*, 7 Dec. 1901; collected *TD*. The story is narrated by a Sikh officer.

122 **gali**: abuse.

122 **Letter to Edward Bok**: (Syracuse University Library) Unpubl. Bok was editor of the *Ladies' Home Journal* from 1889–1919.

122 **my child-stories**: 'Weland's Sword' (Jan. 1906), 'Young Men at the Manor' (Feb. 1906), 'The Knights of the Joyous Venture' (Mar. 1906) and 'Old Men at Pevensey' (Apr. 1906) all had their first US publication in the *Ladies' Home Journal* (collected in *PPH*).

122 **Letter to H. S. Canby**: (Beinecke Library, Yale University) Unpubl. Henry Seidel Canby, Assistant Professor of English, Scientific School of Yale University. Author of *The Short Story in English*, Henry Holt, New York 1909.

122 **Aphra Behn**: Mrs Aphra Behn (1640–89), playwright and poetess.

122 **Oroonoko**: Her anti-slavery novella (1688) is given four pages in Canby's book.

122 **about Henry James**: Canby devoted seven pages to James but a whole chapter to RK, suggesting them as the two most important writers of the contemporary short story.

123 **Letter to Henry James**: (KP) Unpubl. James (1843–1916) became a friend when RK first arrived in London and gave away the bride at the Kiplings' wedding. Later he (famously) had misgivings about the way in which RK's art had 'come down' from describing humans to animals to machines.

123 **The Out Cry**: Written as a three-act play in 1909. It was not performed in James' lifetime, but he converted it into a novel.

123 **Letter to C. R. L. Fletcher**: (KP) Unpubl. Fletcher (1857–1934), a historian, was Fellow of All Souls and Magdalen Colleges, Oxford; co-author with RK of *A School History of England.*

For RK's view of Austen, see also 'The Janeites' and its poems, *D&C.*

123 **Charles**: RK perhaps means Dickens, who was five in 1817 when Jane Austen died.

123 **Walter**: Sir Walter Scott (1771–1832).

123 **South African millionaire**: Not identified.

123 **Verses in the margin of a copy of Horace's *Odes***: Selected from a number of holograph verses in RK's copy of Quinto Horatius Flaccus, *Opera Omnia* (cura E. C. Wickham, London, the Medici Society, 1910), now in KP. Two of them were published in *Selections from the Freer Verse Horace,* New York, Doubleday Doran, 1932. The rest are in C. E. Carrington (ed.), *Kipling's Horace,* London, Methuen 1978 (also paperback edition privately printed for the Kipling Society). Undated; possibly contemporary with 'Regulus' (*DOC*).

123 **'Ille et nefasto te posuit die'**: Horace has had a fright when a tree fell almost on top of him. In the first three verses he abuses the man who planted it; then goes on to compare his fear to sailors' in the Bosphorus and soldiers' in the Parthian wars.

124 **'Bacchum in remotis carmina rupibus'**: A song in praise of Bacchus by a poet who is 'pleno[que] Bacchi' (drunk).

124 **'Festo quod potius die'**: Horace calls on his mistress Lyde to celebrate Neptune's day with wine and song.

124 **strenuous Caecuban**: Horace has 'strenua Caecubum'. 'Strenua' can mean 'firm', or 'restless, turbulent', or 'nimble, busy'. Carrington suggests that this adjective applies to wine and girl both. Caecubum in southern Latium produced some of the finest wine the Romans had.

124 **Pepys**: Samuel Pepys (1633–1703), diarist and civil servant; his famous *Diary,* written from 1 January 1660 to 31 May 1669, *The Diary of Samuel Pepys* records both drinking bouts and sexual adventures. 'Deb' and 'Mercer' (Deborah Willett and Mary Mercer) were at different times maids in the Pepys household. Both were subject to his advances; his wife was jealous and insisted on sacking them.

124 **'Exegi monumentum aere perennius'**: The poet claims that his works will be a monument more lasting than bronze. The first five lines are not in Carrington but can be found in *The Freer Verse Horace.*

124 **'Donarem pateras grataque commodus'**: This ode is addressed to C. Marcius Censorinus, consul in 8 BC. The poet would like to give his friends ornamental chinaware (*pateras*) and other expensive gifts, but all he has is rhymes. The Muses, however, have immortality in their gift.

125 **'Audivere, Lyce, di mea vota, di'**: Horace's ex-mistress has grown old: attempts to preserve her beauty only make her ridiculous. Where has it gone, the charm that once enchanted him? (in *The Freer Verse Horace*).

125 **Letter to Ian Colvin**: (Syracuse University Library) Unpubl. RK's poem 'The Holy War' (*YB*) would be published in the *New York Times* and *Boston Evening Transcript*, 6 Dec. 1917. It is introduced by the quotation:

> For here lay the excellent wisdom of him that built Mansoul, that the walls could never be broken down nor hurt by the most mighty adverse potentate unless the townsmen gave consent thereto. – BUNYAN'S *Holy War* [1682].

125 **The Fabulists**: First published in *DOC*, preceding the story 'The Vortex', a political farce involving colonial relations and a swarm of bees.

126 **A Recantation**: First published in *YB*. The original of 'Lyde' (Horace's mistress in his Odes) has not been identified: Marie Lloyd, Yvette Guilbert and Harry Lauder (who had a son who was killed on the Western Front) have all been suggested. RK's daughter maintained that Lyde 'does *not* refer to any particular person and is quite imaginary' (*KJ*, July 1952, p. 17).

128 **Letter to C. R. L. Fletcher**: (KP) Unpubl.

128 **Lytton Strachey**: Strachey (1880–1932), biographer and essayist, published *Eminent Victorians* in the spring of 1918.

128 **Letter to Stanley Baldwin**: (KP) Unpubl. Baldwin (1867–1947), was the son of Louisa Baldwin (see pp. 95–6 and note, p. 183). Financial Secretary to the Treasury, 1917–21; later Prime Minister and Earl.

128 **Walton**: Sydney Walton (1882–1964), journalist, Director of Publicity for the Victory Loan (authorised by Parliament to pay off the budget deficit caused by the war). The campaign was launched on 6 June 1919.

128 **Mr David**: David Lloyd George, Prime Minister and First Lord of the Treasury.

128 **French**: Not identified.

128 **J. N. Shoesmith**: This seems to be an invented name.

128 **Dr Brigdes**: Robert Bridges (1844–1930), Poet Laureate from 1913. He had trained as a doctor.

129 **Letter to James Rennell Rodd**: (Syracuse University Library) Unpubl. Rodd, later Lord Rennell (1858–1941), had been British Ambassador in Rome when RK visited there in 1917, and had arranged the visit to the Italian front described in *The War in the Mountains* (SB).

129 **Byron**: 1924 was the centenary of Byron's death. He is now commemorated in Poet's Corner, Westminster Abbey.

129 **Letter to E. V. Lucas**: (Lewis Collection, Sussex University) Lucas (1868–1938), journalist and essayist, was a fellow-member of the Beefsteak Club. An extract from this letter was published in Lucas's preface to Tusser's *Good Husbandry*, London, Raven Press 1931; the rest is unpubl.

129 **Tusser Redivivus**: Thomas Tusser (?1524–80) was the author of *A Hundreth Good Points of Husbandrie* (1557), later expanded to *Five Hundreth Points of Good Husbandry* (1573). The bibliography in William Mavor's edition (London, Lackington, Allen, 1812) includes:

1710. Tusser Redivivus . . . published by Daniel Hilman, a Surveyor of Epsom in Surry, 8vo. pp. 150.
1744. The same, with a new Title-page only. Printed for M. Cooper in Paternoster Row [London] . . .

129 **Markham's Farriery**: Gervase Markham (1568–1637). His writings on the horse were collected as *Markham's Faithful Farrier*, 1635.

129 **'Worn threadbare by the thumbs of men'**: Epigram by Sir William Watson (1858–1935), 'On a People's Poet':

> Threadbare his songs seem now, to lettered ken:
> They were worn threadbare next the hearts of men.

129 **Hartlib and Tusser**: Samuel Hartlib (d. 1662), author of *The Reformed Husbandman* (1651) and *The Reformed Commonwealth of Bees* (1655). Mavor does not list this edition of Tusser, unless it is '1692. Bibliotheca Farmeriana, No. 7349', bound with another volume in the same series.

130 **that loseth the purse**: The first two lines of 'Baking', in *The Points of Huswifery*, included with *Five Hundred Points of Good Husbandry* in most editions since 1562. In Mavor's edn (p. 254): 'What that way dog catcheth, that loseth the purse . . .'

130 **his own profession of faith**: 'The Author's Belief', Mavor, pp. 295–301.

130 **Sit down Robin and rest thee**: Last line of Tusser's poem 'An Habitation Enforced: Better late than Never', Mavor p. xxxv. RK had borrowed the title for the first story in *AR*, to which Tusser's lines 1–4 and last 2 lines are given as epigraph.

130 **Cur mundus militat translations**: 'St Barnard's Verses, out of St Augustine: Eight of St Barnard's Verses, both in Latin and English' (Mavor, pp. 307–10). They are taken from the *De Contemptu Mundi* of St Bernard of Morlaix; this is quoted in 'The Eye of Allah' (*D&C*).

130 **Canadian Authors**: Speech delivered at a dinner given by the Royal Society of Literature for visiting members of the Canadian Authors' Association, 12 July 1933. Collected in *A Book of Words* (SB only). Lord Crewe, President of the RSL, was in the chair; RK proposed the health of the Canadian Authors' Association. G. K. Chesterton also spoke. RK's speech on this occasion was broadcast live on the BBC National Programme; there is a recording of it in the National Sound Archive.

130 **Jean Pigeon**: See account of the building of RK's Vermont house, *SOM*, p. 68. After 'house for me', the NSA recording adds, 'one not very far from your border'.

131 **first adventurers**: C. W. Gordon (1860–1937), who was present on this occasion, wrote novels of pioneer life under the pseudonym of 'Ralph Connor'. But RK may have been thinking of R. M. Ballantyne, *The Young Fur Traders* (1856).

131 **United Empire Loyalists**: Immigrants from the United States who had

taken the losing side in the American War of Revolution. They would become a powerful pro-British and pro-Empire group in nineteenth-century Canada. William Kirby (1817–1906) wrote a verse epic about them: *The U.E.: A Tale of Upper Canada* (1859). A copy of A. J. Bradley's *The United Empire Loyalists: Founders of British Canada* (1932) is at Bateman's (NTInv).

131 **great famine year**: William Kirby, 'The Hungry Year' (1878), a verse epic in which a family of Empire Loyalists starve during a drought in (approximately) 1790. Collected in *Canadian Idylls*, Welland, Ontario, A. P. Watts & Co. 1894.

131 **Fenian raids**: In 1866–70 Irish-Americans raided across the Canadian border with the United States as part of their campaign for Irish freedom. James McCarroll (1815–96) told their story from the Irish point of view in *Ridgeway* (1868); but RK is probably thinking of *In the Midst of Alarms* (1894) by Robert Barr (see p. 93 and note, p. 183).

131 **Riel's rebellion**: Louis David Riel (1844–85), leader of the French-Canadian Métis, was a central figure in the Red River Rebellion of 1869–70 and the later North-West Rebellion of 1885, after which he was captured and hanged for treason. Novels on this theme include *Dot it Down: A Story of Life in the North-West* (1871), by Alexander Begg (1839–1917); and *Annette, the Métis Spy: A Heroine of the North-West Rebellion* (1886), by Joseph Edmund Collins (1855–98).

131 **men to the War**: C. W. Gordon (see note, p. 196 above) had been chaplain to the Canadian Forces in World War I.

132 **Canada en bloc**: During his tour in 1907 (see *Letters of Travel*, London, Macmillan, 1920).

132 **Letter to Sir Herbert Baker**: (typed copy, KP) Unpubl. Baker (1862–1946) was the architect who designed the Bank of England, Rhodes House, etc., also The Woolsack, the house on Rhodes's South African estate which was put at the Kiplings' disposal and where they stayed in the winters of 1901–8. Baker became a lifelong friend.

132 **'Home-keepers'**: The Pre-Raphaelites; RK had met them during holidays spent with his aunt Lady Burne-Jones and her husband (*SOM*, pp. 9–10). He expressed some of these feelings in his poem 'The Sons of Martha' (1918).

133 **Letter to Nicholas Murray Butler**: (quoted, Howard G. Baetzhold, *Mark Twain and the British Connection*, Bloomington, Indiana Univ. Press, 1970) Butler was Chairman of the Mark Twain Centennial Committee in the US, while Kipling was chairman of the UK committee.

134 **Letter to Thacker Spink & Co.**: (Beinecke Rare Book and Manuscript Library, Yale University: Tyler Collection) Unpubl. Publishers of Thacker's *Directory*, an invaluable record of the British in India. They had refused *Echoes*, but accepted *DD* after RK had published and sold the first edition himself.

134 **Plain Tales from the Hills**: Thacker Spink had now agreed to take this

second book, containing stories reprinted from *WN* and *C&MG*, with eleven others previously unpublished.

134 **to do this in**: The book was not ready until the following January (letter to Thacker Spink & Co., 9 January 1888, Tyler collection). Unpubl.

135 **Letter to Thacker Spink & Co.**: (Yale University, Tyler Collection).

135 **25% commission**: This sentence follows a diatribe about their various deductions from his profits: as printers (20%), as booksellers (25% commission) and as publishers (50%).

135 **one of five books**: Nos. 2–6 in the Indian Railway Library series, *The Story of the Gadsbys, In Black and White, Under the Deodars, The Phantom Rickshaw, Wee Willie Winkie*, were published 1888 by A. H. Wheeler & Co. of Allahabad. No. 1, *Soldiers Three*, 1888, was published by the Pioneer Press.

135 **the Home market**: They were published in England in 1890 by Sampson Low Marston Searle and Rivington.

135 **Letter to Thacker Spink & Co.**: (Yale University, Tyler Collection) Unpubl.

135 **the book**: *Plain Tales from the Hills.*

136 **Letter to Thacker Spink & Co.**: (Yale University, Tyler Collection) Unpubl.

136 **a volume of verse**: Later *Barrack-Room Ballads and other Verses.*

136 **Edwin Arnold has said**: Not located. Possibly in private conversation.

136 **Letter to Caroline Taylor**: (typed copy, KP; see note, p. 180 on Mrs Edmonia Hill) Unmarried younger sister of Edmonia Hill. Her semi-engagement to RK would be broken off in January or February 1890.

136 **Literary Supply Association**: See letter to S. S. McClure of January 1890 (p. 137). McClure's Fiction Supply Syndicate had been founded in 1884; it sold stories and articles in many countries. R. L. Stevenson, Rider Haggard and Conan Doyle all wrote for it. McClure would make RK a similar offer two or three years later (see *SOM*, p. 74) and again be turned down.

136 **complet**: (French) entire or full.

136 **no originality in the present writers**: An unsigned story about a young author, of which this is the plot, would appear in *St James's Gazette*, 21 Nov. 1889: 'The Comet of a Season' (reprinted in *RG*, v, pp. 2395–401); James Low, editor of the *Gazette*, had asked for 'a Plain Tale'. RK did not include it in any of his collections, nor does it seem worth resurrecting here. A longer letter with the same theme can be found in *Letters*, II, pp. 14–15 and plate 7.

137 **poem of five stanzas**: *EV* records one stanza only:

> There is gold in the News they call Daily,
> There is pence in the sheets of Pall Mall,
> But I whistle in front of them gaily
> And softly consign them to – well,

If *you*, Sir, had suffered my anguish
    Alone, 'neath a tropical sun,
You'd let every newspaper languish,
    Ere making a contract with one.

137 **Letter to S. S. McClure**: Text from American Art Association catalogue, 20 April 1925, item 163 (extract and manuscript facsimile). Samuel Sidney McClure was a Scots-Irish, first generation American. Founder of *McClure's Magazine*, June 1893, which would publish several stories from the *Jungle Books* and the novel *Captains Courageous*. He would also be one of the founding partners of Doubleday McClure, RK's American publishers from 1898. RK described McClure as 'a cyclone in a frock-coat' (*Letters*, II, p. 290) and 'as clean and straight as spring water' (*SOM*, p. 74). See also note, p. 136.

137 **war experiences**: No such book was ever published. Part of the letter is missing at this point, between the end of the printed extract and the beginning of the facsimile.

137 **has a good time**: Some of the material mentioned would be used in writings of that year and later. 'A Conference of the Powers' (the *Pioneer*, May 23 and 24 1890; collected *MI* and OB3) describes an officer's adventures in Burma, as does 'The Ballad of Boh Da Thone' (*BRB*). *LF* (1891), written in the spring and summer of 1890, includes scenes in Egypt and war scenes in the Sudan. There is fighting on the Northern frontier in 'The Lost Legion' (*Strand Magazine*, May 1893; collected *MI*) and 'Slaves of the Lamp Pt. 2' (*Cosmopolitan*, May 1897; *S&Co*). 'The Brushwood Boy' (*Century Magazine*, December 1895; collected *DW*) is also a version of the story outlined in this letter.

138 **Letter to W. E. Henley**: (Pierpont Morgan Library) Henley (1849–1903) was poet and editor of, amongst other periodicals, the *Scots* (later the *National*) *Observer*. Henley was a good friend to RK at this time (see *SOM*, p. 50). The first thirteen Barrack-Room Ballads were published in the *National Observer* 22nd February–26 July 1890. The chapter-heading to '"The Finest Story in the World"' (*Contemporary Review*, July 1891; *MI*) is from Henley's 'To W.A.' The same poem is imitated in 'The Sack of the Gods', a chapter-heading in *The Naulahka* (later expanded in *Songs from Books*). It is parodied in 'The Changelings' (*D&C*).

See also letter from RK in *The Athenaeum*, 8 Nov. 1890 (*Letters*, II, p. 25), and his poem 'The Rhyme of the Three Captains', in *The Athenaeum*, 6 Dec. 1890 (collected *BRB*). His near-paranoia about unauthorised editions began in Yokohama in 1889, when he found that his first book to be published outside India was an American pirated version of *PT* for which he could not get a single cent.

138 **their own title**: *The Courting of Dinah Shadd and other Stories*, by Rudyard Kipling, author of 'Plain Tales from the Hills', etc., with a biographical and critical sketch by Andrew Lang, New York, Harper

and Brothers, September 1890. In March 1891 Kipling would authorise John W. Lovell Co. to publish the contents of the first edition in *Mine Own People*, with six new stories and a preface by Henry James. The stories were later collected in *LH* and *MI*.

138 **one line and seven words long**: When RK visited Harpers in 1889, he was told: 'Young man, this house is devoted to the production of literature.'

138 **Editors Receiving Shop**: 'Editor's Study' column by William Dean Howells, September 1890. Other regular columns were 'Editor's Easy Chair' and 'Editor's Drawer'.

139 **Some Notes on a Bill**: First published in *The Author*, 1 July 1891. Reprinted (including RK's footnotes) in *Harper's Weekly*, xxxv, no. 1802, 4 July 1891, p. 504. Uncollected. The Revised Acts of Congress, including the Provisions for Foreign Copyright, by Act of 3 March 1891, provided that from July of that year non-American authors' copyright in their original texts would be protected, once copies had been deposited with the Library of Congress and a fee paid.

RK had been annoyed by the Americanisation of his spelling in Lovell's editions of his work (*Letters*, II, p. 96).

139 **Longacre . . . Tattersall's**: Long Acre is a London street running between Leicester Square and Covent Garden. Tattersall's was a famous horse and vehicle dealer there.

139 **Worcester**: *Worcester's Dictionary of the English Language*, 1860.

140 **along the cars**: '. . . The news-boy came along the train with all the latest books' (*Letters*, II, p. 222).

140 **Mister H-rp-r**: See p. 138 and notes, pp. 199–200.

140 **we'll read about ourselves**: See *Letters*, II, p. 197: '. . . I hate to say "I told you so" but there's a ribald bit of verse in the *Author* written when the act was passed that prophesied as much . . .' RK suggests that only the most popular British authors will now find a market in the US.

140 **C.B.Q.**: Chicago, Burlington and Quincy Railroad.

140 **harp of Tara**: Popular drawing-room song with words by Thomas Moore:

> The harp that once through Tara's Halls
> The soul of music shed,
> Now hangs as mute on Tara's walls
> As if that soul were dead . . .

The Poetical Works of Thomas Moore, ed. Charles Kent, London, Routledge, 1876, p. 131.

140 **McGinty**: 'Down went McGinty', by Joseph Flynn, 1889. The other songs in this line have not been traced but may also have been part of Flynn's show.

141 **C.P.**: Central Pacific Railroad.

142 **v.l.**: printed as 'v.1' in *The Author*, bur presumably intended to stand for *varia lecto* (variant reading).

142 **Letter to Mary Mapes Dodge**: (Princeton University Libraries).

142 **The Potted Princess**: First published in *St Nicholas*, Jan. 1893; collected only in SB. The rest of this letter suggests three more short stories: 'The Collar-wallah and the Poison Stick', first published *St Nicholas*, Feb. 1893, collected only in SB; a tale about a small boy playing Noah's ark on an Indian tank, which, so far as is known, was never written; and an early version of *Kim*.

143 **The Three-Decker**: First published *Saturday Review*, 14 July 1894; collected *SS*, with the heading 'The three-volume novel is extinct.' In *SOM* (p. 133) RK says that he dreamed of writing one, an 'East Indiaman' that was presumably *Mother Maturin*.

144 **Frank N. Doubleday**: (Princeton University Libraries) Doubleday (1862–1934) worked for Charles Scribner's Sons, who were planning to publish by subscription the Outward Bound edition of RK's complete works. The author was still only thirty years old. Scribner's would add further volumes to the set as they appeared.

Not long after this, Doubleday would set up in business on his own. He became both RK's principal American publisher and his lifelong friend.

144 **Letter to F. N. Doubleday**: (Princeton University Libraries).

144 **The Enlightenments of Pagett M.P.**: First published in the *Contemporary Review*, Sep. 1890; written with the help of RK's father. Pagett was assumed by several reviewers to have been Charles Bradlaugh, the controversial Liberal freethinker. In the UK the story was only collected in the De Luxe and Sussex editions, but its place as finale to OB4 has made it important in American studies of RK's imperialism.

144 **Mrs Hauksbee Sits Out**: Published in *Illustrated London News*, Dec. 1890; *AF*; OB6; and with *MI* in SB.

144 **Introduction to the Outward Bound Edition**: Vol. I, New York, Charles Scribner's Sons, 1897. 'In the Name of God', etc., is the introduction to the Koran.

145 **buggalow**: Traditional Arab sailing-ship.

145 **at Sewree or on Sion Bunder**: Dock areas of Bombay.

145 **Bhao Malung**: A hill above Bombay; Jakaria Musjid is a mosque.

147 **O true believer, his destiny none can escape**: RK may be translating an Urdu saying. S. W. Fallon, *A Dictionary of Hindustani Proverbs*, Banares 1886 (of which there is a copy at Bateman's) includes: 'Qismat ke likhe ko koi nahin met sakta', and gives the meaning 'No one can erase what destiny has written' (p. 189). The language of RK's version echoes Lane's *Arabian Nights*, but the phrase is not to be found there. The doctrine derives from a passage in the Koran, Surah 74.

147 **The Handicaps of Letters**: Speech delivered at the Royal Literary Fund's anniversary dinner on 20 May 1908, when RK presided. Collected *BW*.

148 **original maker**: The subject was topical because the Berlin Convention of 1908 proposed new rights for authors. These would become British law under the Copyright Act of 1911.

148 **Pharisees . . . Scribes**: See Matthew, v: 20; John: viii: 3.

150 **The Conundrum of the Workshops**: First published in the *Scots Observer*, 13 Sep. 1890; collected in *Departmental Ditties, Barrack-Room Ballads and other Verses*, New York 1890.

150 **builded a tower**: the Tower of Babel, Genesis xi: 4.

151 **Four Great Rivers**: Genesis ii: 11–14.

151 **Wreath of Eve**: Cf. John Milton, *Paradise Lost*, in *The Poems of John Milton*, ed. John Carey and Alastair Fowler, London, Longman, 1968, p. 905: '[she] . . . had wove / Of choicest flowers a garden to adorn / Her tresses . . .' (Bk ix, lines 838–42).

151 **In the Neolithic Age**: First published in *The Idler*, Dec. 1892, with the title 'Primum Tempus' (*SS*).

152 **Solutré**: Palaeolithic site in Burgundy, famous for its elegant stone-work.

152 **Grenelle**: Area in the xvth arrondissement of Paris: a military base in the French Revolution, used for military executions under Napoleon.

152 **Tr—ll**: H. D. Traill (1842–1900), poet and journalist, listed sixty-five names in 'Our Minor Poets', *Nineteenth Century*, Jan. 1892. In a follow-up in the March issue Traill added six more names, especially reproaching himself for having forgotten RK.

152 **Allobrogenses**: The Allobroges were a Celtic tribe living in eastern France who supported Hannibal against the Romans; their chief towns were Vienne, Geneva and Grenoble.

153 **Letter to Charles Eliot Norton**: (Houghton Library, Harvard University) Norton (1827–1908) was Professor of Fine Arts at Harvard 1873–98 and a personal friend of Lockwood Kipling.

153 **Atlantic Monthly's review**: Unsigned, lxxx, no. 482, Dec. 1897, pp. 855–7. The review praises the book for 'the most vivid and picturesque treatment of New England fishermen that has yet been made', but finds the characters 'disappointing' and complains that 'after the first twenty pages there is no plot, no development, no surprise'.

153 **Mrs Needham**: (Syracuse University Library) Unpubl. Not identified: she apparently lived in Portland, Oregon.

154 **one End**: See *S&Co.*, 'The Flag of their Country'.

155 **Buried Treasure**: By special permission of the National Trust and University of Durham Library. From University of Durham Library, MS Add. 860, a bound volume of manuscripts including stories from *D&C*, *LR*, and SB, *The War* and *Uncollected Prose*. It is a somewhat random compilation, put together after RK's death and presented to the University by his widow. This is the only set of RK's working notes that is known to survive – probably in mistake for the manuscript of the story written from these notes, '"Teem" – a Treasure-Hunter' (see note, p. 159 below).

155 **L'Abbé**: In the note on RK's delirium, dictated by him in March 1899 during his illness in a hotel in New York (Birkenhead, *Rudyard Kipling*, p. 373), he remembers seeing himself dressed 'in the clothes of an abbé without any undergarments'.

155 **Dominic**: Perrounet in the published story.

157 **Clouds**: Near Tisbury, home of the Wyndham family, who were friends of RK's parents. Lockwood Kipling died in 1911 while visiting there.

159 '**"Teem": a Treasure-Hunter**': Begun January 1935 (CK). First published in the *Strand Magazine*, Jan. 1936 (the month of RK's death). Collected in *Thy Servant a Dog and other Dog Stories* and SB, *Uncollected Prose*; also available in *Mrs Bathurst and other Stories* (Oxford University Press, World Classics, 1992).

It has been suggested (*KJ*, Sep. 1937, pp. 75ff.; C. A. Bodelsen, *Aspects of Kipling's Art*, Manchester University Press, 1964, pp. 77–86) that the story is concealed autobiography (RK's daughter denied this). Michael Brock (Address to the Royal Society of Literature, 1986; *KJ*, Mar. 1988, pp. 9ff.) argued that the phrase 'outside his art' refers to RK's political writings. These can be found mainly in his verse; his political views are given in detail in his letters to H. A. Gwynne (KP).

AW (p. 341) read this passage as RK's self-prohibition on examining his own deeper feelings and motives.

159 *Something of Myself*: RK's posthumously published (1937) autobiography (pp. 121–2).

Index